SUDDEN DEATH, OVERTIME

1030-ZIEM

SUDDEN DEATH, OVERTIME

Dennis Courneya

To order additional copies of this book, contact:
Xlibris Corporation
1-888-7-XLIBRIS
www.Xlibris.com
Orders@Xlibris.com

CONTENTS

*This book is dedicated to my parents,
my son—Jerid, my brothers and sisters,
and those family members and friends
who continue to believe . . .
to search for the truth.*

*I am especially grateful to my sister, Julie.
It is because of her commitment
in helping me with this book
that I found the strength and courage
to persevere.*

PROLOGUE

To see a world in a grain of sand
and a heaven in a wildflower;
Hold infinity in the palm of your hand,
And eternity in an hour.

-William Blake

"Infinity"—perfection. There were few places as still and silent as the shores of Rose Lake at dawn. As usual, I had witnessed the sunrise in all of its majesty—welcoming the birth of a new day. The sky was going to be flawlessly blue, nary a cloud to be seen. A warm and caressing breeze appeared to have awakened all of nature—giving rise to the melancholy sounds that could only be found on a summer morning in July.

I walked across the dew-kissed grass to make my way to the waters that appeared to shimmer in spirited bliss. Venturing along the shore's edge, I marveled at how the velvet granules of sand would encase my feet and leave momentary imprints of my existence. I sank to my knees and dipped my hands into the warmth of the shallow water. As I raised my hands to my face, a few droplets escaped my fingers and fell back to their origin like pearls released from a strand. I walked to the edge of the dock, sat down, and dangled my feet in the water. I closed my eyes so that I could relish the mesmerizing solitude. I could hear the waves gently caressing the shore; I could sense the tempo of the elms as they waltzed with the breeze; I could envision the creatures that hid in anonymity amidst the swaggering reeds.

As with most mornings, I was greeted by the solitary cry of the loon. Its call would pierce the silence as if challenging all of nature to arise and take note. I listened intently to its woeful sound. Slowly, I raised my hands to my mouth, cupped them gently, and echoed the call of the loon. Silence. I tried once more—producing a sound that drew the attention of the evasive bird. With its velvet head held erect, it swam ever near, gazing defiantly upon the one who dared to enter its domain. For one brief moment, we were hypnotized with one another's presence. But just as quickly, the loon elusively disappeared beneath the water and emerged far beyond my immediate gaze. I gave my call of the loon once more. Silence.

I caught sight of my reflection in the mirrored water. I saw the face of a young boy who lived each moment with zest and with respect for hard work and family . . . I saw the face of a young adult who fought with pride for the principles and values of his country . . . I saw the face of an educator and coach who dedicated his life to the vocation that he loved . . . I saw the face of a man who must face the reality of the day . . . July 1, 1998.

We had stayed up fairly late that last night of freedom, Mom, Dad, and I. I think we all tried valiantly to maintain our composure. I was concerned that at any moment one of us would break down. I know the fear of the unknown pervaded my thoughts and theirs. Would it be more than two days? Would it be the full sentence? Where would they take me? Who would I see at the County Courthouse? What do I bring along? All unanswered questions. We had never understood the verdict and certainly did not accept it. I ate the customary dish of ice cream, noticing that Dad had given me an extraordinary large serving of Rocky Road. I ate it but did not taste it.

As I lay in my bed, I knew it would be a night of restlessness. I kept looking at the clock and, yes, thought about how blessed I had been to have grown up in midwestern Minnesota—land of beauty and perfection. I thought how fortunate I was to have been given the opportunity to be a part of such a loving family who placed a high value on loyalty, honesty, and the integrity of others. I also kept asking, "Is this all a dream?" It was incomprehensible that I could ever do what I had been convicted of that fateful day in April: Criminal Sexual Conduct P-2-3. The past year had been a virtual nightmare—something that only happens to other people . . . in the news, on television, or in the movies. I kept believing that one of the girls would show courage and character and come forward to say, "This has gone far enough . . . "I was wrong.

July 1, 5:45 am: As I awoke, I felt absolutely terrible—anxiety, stomach pains, headache. I cleaned up, went into the kitchen for the ritualistic cup of coffee and greeted my father, "Good morning." There really wasn't much else to say. Dad inquired, "Are you sure you don't want us to come with you?" I replied that I did not, but deep inside I wanted them to be with me; yet, I knew it would be easier this way. Mom came out of the bedroom. I tousled her hair a bit and gave her a big morning hug. I told her not to worry; I would be home soon . . . I knew better.

Following a brief sojourn down at the lake, I took a leisurely walk up the gravel road that led to the barn. I wanted to say goodbye to my dog, but that proved to be more difficult than thought. When I looked at him, I remembered all of our hunting escapades, our walks in the woods, and the quiet moments just sitting in the yard. You know what they say about "Man's Best Friend" . . . believe it. People may come and go through you life, but a good dog will stick by you through thick and thin,unconditionally. I knew that, no matter what, this dog would wait for my return. I seemed to notice things that I had never taken note of before: the beauty of the trees, the perfectly manicured yard and garden, and the melodious songs of the birds. I climbed into my pickup with heaviness of heart. I took a brief glance up the hill to where my younger brother, Tim, lived hoping to catch a glance of him or his family. All was quiet. As I drove by the picture window of my parents house, there they were standing in the window . . . waving farewell. I am glad that I could not really distinguish their faces. I am certain that their tears would have been a reflection of my own heartache.

The trip to the Stevens County Courthouse was one that I had taken many times the past year during the trial, but this trip hurt the most. I drove the same roads, the same streets, but it all looked differently now. Ironically, I discovered that I was following my older brother, Steve, in his pickup on his way to work. He turned off the road and went one way; I went another. In my mind, I kept saying, "This has to be a dream . . . let me awaken now from this nightmare . . . let me get on with my life—a life that I loved!"

Morris, Minnesota: I parked in the front parking lot of the County Courthouse and there waiting for me was my good friend, Don Bolluyt. I should have known. This friend of mine was present every morning when I would arrive for the trial. Today would be no different. Don was a quiet sort of man whose goodness of character is unquestionable. His presence was a reassurance of friendship and support. We talked for a bit, but the weight of silence dominated my remaining thirty minutes. Finally, I took my duffle bag, said goodbye to Don, and walked into the courthouse. There to meet me were two officers. They were definitely rookies because they acted very uncertain as how to proceed; they didn't even know what personal articles I was allowed to take with me. They made a telephone call to find out the particulars of the departure. Finally, they informed me that I could not wear a belt nor take my billfold. I was allowed to select one photo from my belongings; I took the picture of my son, Jerid. Before we walked out the door of the office, the officers put handcuffs on me and led me away. As we were departing from the courthouse, we met Dave Burns (a resident from the town in which I taught school, coached, and lived—Hancock). He looked me in the eyes and shook his head in disbelief.

We got into a squad car and departed. I did not know where we were going; the silence was deafening. As we drove through the neighboring town of Cyrus, I remembered the fans who had greeted my girls basketball team after we had won the state basketball championship. I could still hear their applause and see their jubilation. Before I realized it, we had taken the St. Cloud exit. I now knew where I was going—St. Cloud Correctional Facility. As the prison came into full view, I was confronted with its menacing presence. It reminded me of a Gothic fortress straight out of a medieval nightmare: dark grey stones, walls that appeared to be at least twenty feet high, and guard towers positioned at peak points around the enclosed courtyard. The severe pointed architecture indicative of Gothicism gave the dwelling a sinister quality as if to define the inhabitants within. Even though it was built in the late 1800's, it successfully imitated the fifteenth century's emphasis upon the supernatural and grotesque. It was to be my home.

I looked at my handcuffs. A year ago, I was Dennis Courneya, "Teacher of the Year". For many previous years, I was Dennis Courneya, "Coach of the Year". Within moments, I would be given my new identification; I would become "#198180"—Inmate, Minnesota Correctional Facility.

This is my journey.

CHAPTER ONE

How dear to this heart are the scenes of my childhood,
When fond recollection recalls them to view;
The orchard, the meadow, the deep-tangled wildwood,
And every loved spot which my infancy knew.
-Samuel Woodworth, *The Old Oaken Bucket*

A young boy could not have asked for a more wondrous place in which to grow up than in northwestern Minnesota. There were lakes, woods, and neighbors who had kids our own age. Additionally, we lived in the midst of "resort heaven." We were surrounded by family-owned lake resorts and, thus, we became acquainted with tourists from all over the United States—giving us what we considered a touch of "worldly" culture. Actually, most of the tourists were from the South; their strongest influence consisted of introducing us to grits, fried bullheads, and southern slang! However, what impacted my life the most was having a father and a mother who loved their six children very much and who taught us values and morals by their example.

We were a family of six children: three girls and three boys. In 1948, I was born— We all lived in a small white house approximately fifty feet from the shores of Rose Lake. This lake provided us with endless hours of recreation, fish to eat, and it certainly gave us an appreciation for the beauty and bounty of nature. I know that Minnesota has been nicknamed "The Land of 10,000 Lakes"; however, whomever was counting the lakes that day must have given up midway. Within one mile of our home, we could visit seven lakes: Big Rose, Little Rose, Lakes Five, Six, and Seven, Mud Lake, and Fairy Lake. The town of

Frazee was approximately five miles away and the town of Vergas was nearly four miles from home. Both towns never have been and never will be considered glamour spots; however, the hearts of the people living there outshine any described utopia. The prosperity of Frazee depended upon two factors: turkey farming and a family truckline. Vergas, in comparison, was inhabited by hard working German dairy farmers who knew the value of a dollar. What did the towns have in common? Both had a main drag running from one end of town to the other with just a few side streets branching off, and both became "World Capitals". Frazee came to be known as the "Turkey Capital of the World" and Vergas was referred to as the "Loon Capital". Today, if you were to drive into either town, you would be greeted by a gigantic turkey statue overlooking Frazee's Town Lake, and a majestic loon sitting on the shores of Long Lake would welcome you to Vergas. Regardless of your preference, both towns would leave you feeling enriched for having been a visitor or resident.

There is a passage in the *New Testament* which states: *If any would not work, neither should he eat (II Thessalonians, III, 10).* Yes, by today's standards our family worked very hard, but most people during the era of my youth did the same. Children were not only a source of pride and love, they were also an economic asset. Our mom was laced with a great deal of responsibility. Dad worked road construction six days a week, twelve hours a day. Therefore, it was Mom's job to make sure the farm work was finished, and anyone who grows up on a farm knows that there is always plenty of work! We did not awake in the morning wondering what we were going to do that day; we awoke wondering what work we would do *first*. Most of the tasks were accomplished by hand labor; we did not have a great abundance of machinery in those early days. One of our neighbors, Adolph Ratz, whom Dad considered to be the finest neighbor anyone could have, would bale our hay and staw. It was up to us to bring it in. Many hours, dawn to dusk, were spent in the fields hauling those bales. We were taught at a young age to run when we worked, and run we did! My older brother, Steve (and later, my younger brother, Tim), and I would load the wagon, pull it up to the barn, and then throw the bales in the hayloft. We had no elevators. This provided an incentive for creativity! We would build pyramids on the wagons (step-ups) so that we could get them up into the hayloft. We then went into the loft and carried them back into the barn to be stacked. Many times after Dad returned from work late at night, we would take the truck into the field and use its lights to pick hay bales off the fields.

Dad always had a way of making fun out of work. On hot summer nights after baling hay until dusk, Dad would say, "Let's go swimming!" In the dark of night, we'd all run down to the lake and jump in! Besides cooling us off, it was a ready-made bathtub. I can still feel the brisk lake winds, the lukewarm water and, most importantly, the pride in having been an integral part of a family endeavor. Now, don't think that the girls in the family (Judy, Cathy, and Julie) lived on "easy street". They, too, were required to contribute to the daily chores. They would assist with all of the household duties, garden, yard work, and with the haying and more! We boys were taught to always respect our sisters and to treat them as ladies; however, we knew that gender was not a determinant of value. Females and males were equally capable of obtaining success and equally expected to earn it.

Our original farm was 180 acres with the vast majority of it being woods—**dense woods!** It is quite difficult to farm woods, so we cut and we cut and we cut!! Each year, we would take a large strip of wooded land and cut it off; everything was used. The wood that could be used for firewood was used for that purpose; the wood that could be utilized for lumber was also distinguished. This work was done from the fall to the spring. It seems that the final portion of the job always had to be accomplished over Easter vacation. Dad, the boys and the girls, all went to the woods to cut the long poles into blocks. Many of the poles were actually log-type; in other words, we needed all the muscle we could muster. I do recall that this was one job my sisters did not exactly appreciate. One of my sisters, Cathy, would get "sick" quite often on the mornings she discovered we were to cut wood. Once completed, the wood would be hauled in, stacked, and come late fall or early spring, Dad would bring in the 'cat' and grub the stumps. This created another job for the summer—picking stumps, roots, etc. It was a never-ending challenge because, once cleared, Dad would bring in the field cultivator and guess what happens the following spring . . . the frost pushes up more roots, rocks, etc. Therefore, you start all over again. In all honesty, clearing land was not one of our favorite jobs. However, it did serve to enlarge our agricultural fields and our comraderie sp .

Yes, we learned to work and we learned not to complain about it. Frequently, we were given the opportunity to turn our deeds into money. I particularly remember one of the times that Dad provided an incentive for a little pocket money. We had been cutting woods for days . . . weeks, when he said, "There are some nice basswood logs. You boys mark them off, and we'll haul them to town and sell them at Franklin Fence Company." We would be cutting the wood and we'd run into a big stand of white oak, six-to-eight inches in diameter. We would measure six-feet, six-inches and then cut them for fence post. The larger ones we would split with the maul and wedges. This was typically done in the winter when splitting was the best. We hauled them out and sold them for 15 cents a post. I know we had over 1000 posts that winter.

The neighbors also seemed to appreciate our work ethic. They would hire us whenever we were available. They couldn't believe how we would "run when we worked"—whether it was baling hay, picking rock, or mowing the grass. They often expressed concern about our energized demeanor, "You're going to hurt yourselves running like that!" They didn't seem to understand that time and efficiency were of the utmost. Tomorrow did not yet exist. Today was the gift; therefore, accomplish all you must at the given moment. This was our work ethic.

An old Jewish proverb states, *God could not be everywhere and therefore He created mothers.* Mom was definitely the *heart* of our home. To us, our home was a castle, and after hearing the story of how the original house was built, we appreciated it all the more. Prior to Dad entering the U.S. Navy (World War II), he went to the bank to obtain a loan in which to build a house. He was told that he did not have enough collateral. Therefore, he went to a gentleman by the name of Petersen who lent him the materials in which to build the initial structure. Once the house was built, Dad went back to the bank and again asked for a loan. The banker inquired, "Do you have any collateral?" Dad's reply was, "Yes, I have a house." The loan was granted and everyone was paid off.

The original house was 22x24 with a small front porch accented by lattice work. Mom transfomed the house with beautiful flower gardens and immaculate care. The house had two main rooms—a kitchen and a living room. In the kitchen, there was a green and yellow wood stove that was used for cooking. A tea kettle always sat on top of the stove. There was no indoor plumbing; the hot water came from a reservoir on the stove. Water came from an outside hand pump. For drinking water, a pail and a dipper were located in the kitchen. As the family grew, Dad built on a small addition. The three boys shared a bedroom with one bed, and the three girls shared bunk beds in one room. For some strange reason, we boys handled it better than the sisters. To us, closet space was not an issue worthy of an argument!

Mom was a magnificent cook and meal time was not only a time for nourishment, but also a time to demonstrate our manners and our respect for the efforts Mom had put forth. Mealtimes were precisely at 7:00 am, 12:00 pm, and 6:00 pm. If you were late, you did not eat. Whenever I could, I would try to arrive before the others so that I could inspect the size of the dishes of sauce and rearrange them to my benefit, if necessary! We were required to arrive at the table with clean clothes, hair combed, face and hands washed, and never wearing a hat. We had designated seats in which to sit. The younger siblings had to sit by Dad so that they could learn good eating habits. At the table, we were expected to sit up straight and never were we allowed to put our elbows on the table. We learned at an early age how to hold and use our silverware properly. I can still recall one of us being told (only once) that the fork was not an oar and should not be held as such. You never reached for a dish of food because it was to be passed around the table, and you ate everything. You could not ask, "What kind is it?", nor did anyone ever dare say, "I don't want any" or "I don't like it." We learned to appreciate what we had.

We had fantastic meals and always plenty of food. We were fortunate in that we grew our own vegetables in the garden plus we had bountiful fruit trees and berries. Besides having fresh fish from the lake, we also butchered our own meat (beef, pork, and chicken). Additionally, we were avid hunters; therefore, we had an abundance of wild game: deer, ducks, pheasant, and partridge. Despite all of the above mentioned delicacies, we were always willing to try the unusual like squirrel or frog legs. Mom would not allow us to cook this type of varmint in the house; therefore, the woods became the boys' kitchen for frying up the wonders of the wilderness: rabbit, squirrel, chipmunk, frog legs, and other lesser known creatures. Our cattle provided the milk. Usually, Steve, Dad, and I had gotten up early in the morning (4:00 am) to milk the cows and feed. My early job was to keep the beef cattle out of the main barn while they milked the dairy cows. Often I would ride our dog, Jigs, back and forth to keep the cows out. Following the milking, we would crank the old separator in the basement, and then bring the skim milk back to the barn for the calves to drink. If we had any excess cream, Mom would bring it to the Creamery in town to trade for cheese and butter. We did not go hungry.

We learned the necessity of being conservative and being clean! During the early years, we had an outdoor toilet; it was as clean as any indoor bathroom—just a little colder at times! During the months of May through September, our bathtub was Rose Lake. I don't know what was in that lake water, but I will say we had the shiniest hair in the county. During the winter, we took baths in the kitchen in a big tub of water that had been heated on the wood stove. The boys used the same bath water and the girls shared their water.

I mentioned earlier that we would run as we worked; our demeanor in the house was a different story. We could not run in the house nor produce noise. Bedtime was at 9:00 pm, no later. Even though we may have been "dog tired" from the day's work, we always seemed to have enough energy to engage in brotherly frolic or to talk about all the money we were going to make selling those logs or gopher feet. Dreams die hard and for the most part, we envisioned a life full of promise and opportunity. Anything was possible. We knew how to work, we knew how to appreciate, and we learned the meaning of respect.

Respect. We were expected to treat everyone as an equal, regardless of ethnicity, color, gender, religion, social or economic standing. How did we acquire this just regard? We witnessed our parents' appreciation of worth, honor, and esteem. We were instructed to always remember that there was as much dignity in digging a ditch as any other noble endeavor. Yet, advice on the dignity of work went a little farther, "If you are going to be a ditch digger, then be the best ditch digger you can be." Respect for others was also indicated by how we spoke to individuals. "When speaking to people, look them in the eyes and reciprocate the same when spoken to." We knew that we were no better nor no less than anyone else. Bragging was not allowed. "Your deeds will speak for themselves; therefore, why interrupt?" We could not pick a fight, nor run from one. Most importantly, we knew we were always expected to tell the truth. Lies were intolerable.

Contrary to beliefs, kids are not always right; they do not always do what they are told to do and, at times, will alter the truth. No one is perfect and we kids, once in a while, did "stray" from what we had been taught was right. I particularly recall one incidence when I discovered the consequences of using poor judgement . Steve and I had received bows and arrows as a Christmas gift. The following summer, it was time to test them out! Rabbits and chipmunks were nearly impossible to hit; we felt we needed something larger and slower . . . like chickens!! We "accidently" sent some arrows in the direction of a chicken's rear end. In its fright, it disappeared into the woods. We looked but could not find that chicken. As the days went by, I feared that the chicken would somehow "reappear" with arrows stuck in its behind—evidence of our escapades. How would we talk our way out of that one? It was that chicken, and our conscience, that reminded us that bow and arrows were not intended for "hunting" the neighbor's chickens!

Our parents were never ashamed of the behavior of the six children, and we considered ourselves to be so fortunate to have parents who took the time to teach us right from wrong. They taught us the meaning of purpose, self-determination, and responsibility. The journey of becoming a responsible adult begins in childhood and the lessons learned along the way aren't always easy. However, because of the "lessons of life", we entrusted ourselves to have the ability and responsibility to impart upon this world a fraction of what was given to us unconditionally. Did we ever feel deprived or poor? Being poor is just a state of mind. We had a home, land, food, family, values, and abundant love. We were the richest people in the world.

CHAPTER TWO

Between the dark and the daylight,
When the night is beginning to lower,
Comes a pause in the day's occupations,
That is known as the Children's Hour.

-Longfellow, *The Children's Hour*

Fun *noun:* That which excites merriment; frolic; sport; amusement; also, the mirth and enjoyment derived therefrom (*Funk and Wagnalls New Practical Dictionary*).

People might ask, "Did you have time for fun?" My response would be,"We had more fun than you could possibly imagine, and we appreciated the opportunity for amusement, sport, and merriment!" There were two extra special days that occurred each year that, no matter how much work was left to be done, it would wait for another day—work came to a halt! These days of frolic and fun were because of Frazee's Turkey Days Celebration. This was an event sponsored by the turkey growers and the Frazee Fire Department.

What a grand two days we had! We would enter all of the contests and, for the most part, hang around with our friends. We were given two dollars and told not to spend it all in one place. That piece of advice may sound trivial, but it was directed at me. I had one major problem: the carnival was always in town, and the workers there could see me coming a mile away! There were so many games that I *knew* I could win . . . I was certain that I would win money, prizes, momentary fame, you name it! However, there was one small problem . . . I never did win and, in most cases, all my money was gone in a few short minutes. I knew I had been told to stay away from this temptation, but I truly believed that each year my luck would change.

Saturday night of the festivities was one of *royal* emphasis; it was the crowning of the Turkey Day Queen. Girls from all social and economic standing vied for the coveted title. All three of my sisters, starting with Judy, then sister Cathy, and finally Julie were recipients of the crown. We could not have been more proud. We always thought they were the most beautiful girls in the county; apparently, the judges agreed!

Sunday was the climax of the celebration. There were flea markets and contests in the morning followed by a free turkey dinner. People came from far and wide for the free meal—from all walks of life . . . "right out of the woods". Following the dinner, a parade was held and, by small town standards, this parade was something to witness! My sisters were baton twirlers, and they led the marching band. By my estimation, they twirled that baton the fastest and threw it the highest!

As exciting as the parade was, nothing could compare to the grand finale: The Turkey Throw. A group of the turkey growers would be up on top of the bank building (the tallest building in town) and they would throw live turkeys from the roof top to the street below. Hundreds of people were packed in a one block area trying to catch the birds. If you caught the turkey, it was yours to bring home! I can never remember a year in which we did not bring home a turkey! Eventually, this tradition was stopped (upon advice from the humane society) and with good reason!

Following the two day celebration, I would lay in bed on Sunday night already planning for the next year. I knew I had one year to figure out a way to win the money and prizes at the carnival. I also know that even today, I cannot eat a piece of turkey without returning, if ever so brief, to that very special time in my childhood.

As mentioned earlier, I felt there was no better place to grow up than where we did. Rose Lake was right in front of our house, offering us all the opportunity in the world for fun—and at a price we could not deny—FREE!! The resorts next door enabled us to acquire lifelong friendships with the visiting tourists. I can remember convincing the young tourists from the South that baling hay and chasing cattle would be great fun . . . their volunteerism didn't last long. There was one neighbor family with whom we played quite consistently with and they were the Sailer family. They lived one-half mile from our house. Their father, Archie, was a teacher, coach, and athletic director at the school. Therefore, there was never a shortage of bats, balls, or other athletic equipment. Steve and I would spend countless hours with the Sailer boys playing any sport that was in season.

The one sport that was played a great deal at our place was basketball. You see, we had an indoor arena—our hayloft! We would place a basket on the side of the wall in the barn's loft. We would stack hay to the ceiling just to clear an "arena" in which to play. The floor was not level, but it definitely served the purpose! The Sailers plus other kids from around the area would show up usually at night and most often in the winter. We would turn on the lights, choose sides, and *play ball!!* We also had a hoop attached to the outside of the barn so that in more seasonal weather we could take our game outdoors. This all came to a halt when our barn burned down. Dad, however, proved to be quite ingenious. He erected two poles on the ends of the concrete where our barn used to be, put up a flood light, and the games continued! We had the best outdoor court for miles around. Most importantly, we learned good sportsmanship and to "make do" with what we had.

Winter - pine trees tipped with dustings of snow; Lacelike webs frozen in time; The torment of the wind as it teases the frosted window panes; The luminous moon as it presides over the ending of day; The howling of the timberwolf as it searches for a midnight companion; The frigidity of the arctic air as it silences response . . . Ahh, the passion of winter. (Moonglow, Julia Zieman)

Many people cannot imagine living in Minnesota in winter. Let me tell you, I cannot imagine a winter without Minnesota! Winter means ice fishing!! Our fish house would be put on the ice at the earliest possible date, and we usually placed it on the bay of

Rose Lake. It was ironic in that, year after year, our neighbors, along with ourselves, would place our fish houses in the *exact* same spots. We all had our "hot" spots, and none of us would even contemplate trespassing on another's territory. We would count off from the shore the paces to our site, and I am willing to bet that the fishing spots were not off by a foot from year to year.

During the ice fishing season, Steve and I would get up early in the morning and have hot oatmeal and cocoa. Mom would pack a lunch and off we would go across country to the bay. Our mode of transportation was our Little A Farmall with a saw rig on the back. We would park the tractor on the hill so that if the battery was dead from the cold (by the end of the day), we could just roll it down the hill to get it started. We brought our lunch, a sack of wood, and matches. Many times we would stay the entire day. A major problem we had was that we would eat our lunch mid-morning and then starve the rest of the day. Yes, we had snacks; we would bring pumpkin and squash seeds as well as corn kernels to roast on the wood stove in the fish house. They were tasty, but that house sure got smoky. When the fishing was good, it was very good. When it was bad, we found ways to pass the time. On the slow days, my brother Steve would stoke up the wood stove, plug the stove pipe, and lock me inside the fish house. It would get so hot and so smoky that if we did happen to catch a fish, it would be instantly preserved! When my younger brother, Tim, was old enough to come fishing with me, I pulled the same trick on him.

Fisherman are noted for telling stories about the "one that got away". Well, I have two stories that would rival any tale told. One particularly frigid day, Steve and I went spearing on the lake in front of the house. Within moments, our dream fish came through the hole. It was the hughest northern pike we had ever seen! It took remarkable precision and strength to bring that fish to its ultimate fate. It was so large that getting it out of the ice hole was going to be nearly impossible; it seemed to drag with it half the lake's weed bottom! The "test of strength" between *man and fish* had quite an impact upon our fish house . . . it looked like the site of Poseidon's Isthmian Games—covered in weeds and mud! Once we got the fish outside, the celebration began! I concluded that Steve was the greatest thing on Earth! I pounded him on the back in adoration, and then we grabbed the fish to go show the world! We went to the front door of our home (usually only acceptable if one is a visitor), and all of the family was there to revel in our heroism. To this day, we wonder how large that fish really was. We had no fish scale, so we weighed it on our bathroom scale—22 pounds!! Thirty years later, I can open my billfold and see a picture of two young boys whose smiles were as large as the prized fish . . . captured forever in picture and heart.

That was the story about the one that didn't get away. This is another true story, but with a different ending. My younger brother, Tim, and I were ice fishing when a *monster* (of a fish) appeared in the ice hole. We both froze from shock at what we saw. What kind of fish it was we will never know; it was not listed in any book; it was huge and so out-of-proportion. Despite our valiant attempts, the fish maintained its freedom. To this day, we still wonder . . . what was that thing . . . and is it still there?

Yes, winter did provide the opportunity for creative fun. We would create our own ice tracks by carrying pails of water from the pump to the hills overlooking Mud Lake. We'd throw the water on the hillsides, wait moments for it to freeze, and then proceed to ski and slide. Sometimes, we would tie a rope to our horse, Scout, and take him out on the ice to pull us on skiis. We also built magnificent snow forts and tunnels. The Sailer boys liked to come over for our famed snowball fights. Steve and I were more often than not the victors. Little did our "foes" know that the reason our snowballs hurt so much when they hit was because we had dipped them in water to freeze—thus, they rivaled the impact of a small cannonball.

Some of our more peaceful winter fun consisted of making fish decoys by hand. Dad and the boys would go in the basement and whittle basswood to carve into decoys. We would spend many evenings down there shaping our projects, using snips to cut the fins from tin. We painted them (that's the extent of our artistic merit!)

and concluded the projects by carving a hole on the underside of the decoy in which to pour hot lead for weight and balance. Dad was very patient with us. We did end up with some very strange shaped decoys. I know now that Dad had spent many hours afterwards adding the final touches so that they would actually work. The basement also served as an arena for boxing. Our father had been an athletic specialist in the U.S. Navy during World War II; therefore, we learned firsthand the fundamentals of boxing and sportsmanship. It also proved to be one of many lessons in humility.

So, getting back to the question again, "Did we ever have any fun?" I can only conclude by saying that when I close my eyes at night, I can still feel the thrill of the carousel; I delight in the curiosity of the stars; I hear the laughter of a child within my heart and yearn to share the warmth it emulates. The joy I experienced while engaging in family endeavors and neighborly fun is a priceless gift that will always warm my heart.

CHAPTER THREE

The mediocre teacher tells.
The good teacher explains.
The superior teacher demonstrates.
The great teacher inspires.

-William A. Ward

Henry Adams stated that a teacher affects eternity; he can never tell where his influence stops (*The Education of Henry Adams*). The teachers from my grade school years and beyond were not simply individuals who imparted knowledge upon the students; they directly influenced the development of our values, attitudes, beliefs, and aspirations.

I was very fortunate in that even though we lived in the country, our travels to school did not include walking a great distance; the country school we attended was only one hundred yards from our house. The four older children in our family, myself included, attended the Rose Lake Country School. Ironically, this same country school was also the basis of learning for our dad and his brothers and sisters—65 years ago!

Grades 1-6 were taught in the same one room class. Kindergarten lasted one day. Actually, my kindergarten experience was even shorter; it lasted one-half day. I was very scared of our teacher, Ms. Antonsen. I had to go to the bathroom very badly that first day, but there was no way I would ask her for permission; therefore, I wet my pants. My older brother and sisters were very impressed, along with Mom, when I was sent home. They thought it was because I was too advanced for kindergarten. Now the story is told!

The school was approximately 20 feet by 40 feet in size and situated on a two acre piece of land. The outside grounds consisted of an outdoor toilet, a water pump, and a wood shed. Dad hauled wood to the shed and, at times, would start the fire in the schoolhouse stove as well as pump water for the day. However, for the most part, the boys of the school were responsible for hauling the wood to the school as well as pumping the drinking water. At times, Steve and I had to bring hot water from home to prime the pump. The outside recreational facilities consisted of a softball field, a swamp, and a swing set with an accompanying teeter-totter. When it came to "physical education", running races and softball were high on the list. When we played softball, the teacher always had me play right center field because if the ball was hit out there, it was headed for the swamp. She thought I had good orientation and wouldn't be afraid to get a little wet if necessary; plus, I had a strong arm and could throw it the distance to the plate!

Inside the front door of the school, there was a cloak room for our boots and jackets. Additionally, there were designated slots built into the wall to place our lunch pails. In the rear of the room, a pot-bellied wood stove was located. A large milk pail, with a dipper hanging on a hook, was also found in the back of the room; it held our drinking water. The six grade levels were designated by the four to six rows of desks facing the front of the room. The desks were made of wood with wrought iron accents on the sides and an inkwell on the top. The teacher's desk was located in the front of the room with a table and chair on each side of her desk. Ms. Antonsen would call the younger grades to the front for their lessons while the rest of the class would work on assignments.

My class had three members: Ray Osterman, Marie Molzan, and myself. Ray Osterman came to be a dear friend of mine. I think our friendship was established when I offered to trade my meat sandwiches for his ketchup sandwiches. Interestingly, for three straight years, Ray and I managed to draw each other's name for the school Christmas exchange. We gave each other a jackknife every year. His family consisted of twelve children and they lived across the lake from our home. Just about every member of the family had a nickname; in fact, I really don't know many of their "real" names. I simply recall them as "Fuzzy, Ogie, Punker. . . .

"In the winter, the Ostermans used to walk from their place across the ice to school. They would walk in one long line—oldest to youngest. They were a super-talented family who would give you the shirt off their back if they had one. They were highly intelligent and extremely artistic. They also knew how to take apart any type of engine imaginable! In their yard, they kept many junked cars and trucks. Whenever Dad or anyone needed a spare part for something, it could probably be found there! Most of the kids our age had toys of some type; the Ostermans didn't need them. They were always rolling tires around the yard and playing with car parts! I loved going to their place!

Mike was the oldest in the Osterman family and he had a huge crush on my sister, Judy. One day he showed up at our house looking like Elvis and tried to win her heart by playing his guitar and singing. It was a remarkable impression! As we grew older, Ray and I used to hunt together. Many times when I would be at his house, his mother (Blanch) would bake bread. She had to make so many loaves and sometimes it would end up the most unique shape. But she would slice off a big hunk and cover it with butter and honey. I thought it was the best bread I had ever tasted! I can recall staying overnight with them only once. All of the children shared bedrooms upstairs and due to the large number of children, not everyone could sit at the table at one time to eat a meal. In the winter, there would always be a hog hanging in the entry with an axe beside it. When it was dinnertime, the father (Billy), would use the axe to cut off a piece of meat. Billy really loved his children. He was a hard worker and extremely musical. In fact, he was able to magnificently play a fiddle (no musical lessons whatsoever) that only had two strings! He used to pay his grocery bill by using the barter system. Many people did this—one's word of honor was worth more than any other agreement. People in the town of Vergas used to tell the story about one of the local grocers in town. It seems that the grocer, Ambrose, would usually have a big barrel of nuts sitting out by his grocery counter. Billy really loved those nuts! However, when Billy had all of his teeth pulled out, Ambrose thought his nut-eating adventures were over. Surprisingly, once his teeth were gone, Billy ate more of those nuts than ever!!

One Christmas, Ray was given a motorcycle. I can still see him coming across the ice on that cycle, wearing no hat or gloves, to show it to me. Yes, they were a fine family who did not let hardship get in the way of happiness until tragedy struck. One of the younger boys accidently hung himself in the barn. Billy threw the television through the picture window because he believed that the youngster had gotten the idea from watching westerns. Billy died a short time later; they say he died of a broken heart.

Our grade school teacher, Ms. Antonsen, was also very memorable. She lived down the road with her brother, Gib. He would bring her to school each morning in his car. During the heavy winter snow season, she would arrive at school in a horse-drawn sleigh. She had white hair and was usually meticulously dressed in a long demure dress. Most of the children were afraid of her because of her strict demeanor. She was not afraid to use the ruler on those who did not behave nor did she hesitate to twist an ear when one was not paying attention to her lesson. Consequently, discipline was not a classroom issue. However, I do recall one student who tested her "policy". Forrest Mitchell took his inkwell and dipped the pigtails of the girl sitting in front of him in it. I can still hear Ms. Antonsen's black heeled shoes on the wood floor as she quickly rushed back to his desk and struck him hard on his knuckles with a yardstick. In retrospect, I admire her dedication to the teaching vocation. She taught during a time when there were no "school budgets". I know her lessons plans and the materials she used required a great deal of ingenuity on her part. Plus, she taught every student every subject—and she did it in a one-room school. Today, the country school building still sits on the exact same spot; however, it is no longer used as a school.

Yet, whenever I glance that way, I still "see" Ms. Antonsen guiding us through the lessons of the day and the lessons of life.

I went to the Rose Lake Country School for three years until the country schools closed in our area. I then went to the Vergas School to complete my elementary educcation; my class size was now doubled—six students! My junior high years took me to the Frazee School, and it was there that I experienced cultural shock! We now had eighty students in my class and, for the most part, they came from all different directions! The students who came from the Wolf Lake area were Finnish; the Vergas group was German; the Frazee bunch was quite mixed—mostly Scandinavian. Talk about the "Melting Pot" theory coming alive! Each of the groups definitely formed a distinct clan. These clans would change over the years except for the Finnish students; they remained intact, "till death do us part".

There were four Courneyas who got on the bus every morning for the trip to Frazee, and there were rules we were expected to follow: 1) Our sisters were to be treated as ladies and to let them get on the bus first; 2) Always be waiting by the road when the bus pulled up; 3) Treat the bus driver with the utmost respect. These rules and more applied to our behavior in school. The administrators, teachers, coaches, cooks, janitors, and helpers were to be treated with equal respect. Additionally, if we ever happened to get into trouble while at school, we knew enough not to whine about it or to shift blame to another; the fault was ours and ours alone. The punishment that awaited us at home did not compare to what was dished out in school. Finally, we were expected to be nice to everyone but especially the less fortunate. As our parents reminded us, "This group needs friends more than the fortunate. Also, they will stick by you to the very end."

What an eye opener the first day of junior high was for me. To my surprise, my homeroom teacher was my grandmother, Mrs. Bjorge. She had taught at Frazee for a number of years and was a legend when it came to discipline and professionalism. She was not only my homeroom teacher, but also my Social Studies teacher for the next three years. She had graduated from Carlton College when it was not fashionable for a female to further her education or to demonstrate a desire to be independent! She graduated Cum Laude and spent her summers working in Yellowstone National Park commuting via stagecoach. I marveled at her stories of how her parents came from Norway to America on a clipper ship. Education was high on their list and the children in their family were responsible for assisting one another in attaining a degree. Grandmother Bjorge was born twenty years after the Civil War and lived one year less than the century mark. She witnessed remarkable changes and could "roll with the times". To the last of her days, she remained sharp as a whip mentally, especially in the subject area of History. I truly believe that she was one of the most important people in my early years to influence my decision in becoming a History teacher many years later.

Junior High provided an array of opportunities for growth. Not only was I elected President of my class in grade seven, I was honored with that office for the next three years. Additionally, Junior High meant an opportunity to participate in organized sports. It was a dream come true to be a part of a team, to play and compete against rival schools, and to wear the school uniform with pride. From participation in sports, I learned the value of togetherness, to depend on your fellow teammates, and to dedicate yourself to a common goal of being the best you could possibly be. Was I an athletic star? I have no idea, for you see, we were taught by our parents that no one was better than anyone else. Sure, some individuals had to work harder, to do more, but the chain is only as strong as the weakest link. To this day, I have discovered that I can count on the blue collar worker- the one who digs to the depth of his soul to give all that is possible- more than one who feels he's "God's Gift" to life.

The coaches that I had in the early years were disciplinarians both on the field and in the classroom. Coach Holmes, the football coach, was also my Health instructor, and he taught the entire class the value of following the rules. He instructed us to sit straight in our desks, eyes ahead, and no talking whatsoever while a test was in progress. I will never forget the time when one student did not follow his instructions. Mr. Holmes told that student to stand and face the class from the front of the room, then to bend over and grab his ankles. He then hit the student in the butt with his hand. The force was so great that the boy shot down the row and passed by my desk with unbelievable momentum. From that day forward, everyone adhered to the philosophy of Mr. Holmes.

Another memorable coach of my early years was Mr. Lassila. He later became very influencial in my high school athletic experiences. It is interesting as to how Coach Lassila happened to come to Frazee. As stated earlier, a large group of the students were of the Finnish nationality. Many of these students actually preferred speaking Fin over the English language. Needless to say, they could carry on a conversation that no one could decipher . . . including the teachers. Well, Coach Lassila was a full-blooded Finlander who clearly understood and could speak the language. He was built like the Rock of Gibraltar with a temper to match! My Finnish friends no longer had an edge. Gone were the days of having fun at the teachers' expense. Mr. Lassila was tough, and it was nothing to see him use force to capture a student's attention. He was teaching the importance of discipline and respect. One lesson was enough.

My Freshman year was one of the greatest because, for the first time, we could go out for a varsity sport. Yes, football was my favorite sport and, finally, we could wear the "official" school uniforms—the "magic" of the green and white Frazee Hornets! I would ride my bike five miles to and from Frazee to attend the August practices or hitch a ride with the Sailer boys. At one hundred and forty pounds, I certainly did not punish any upperclassmen but, to me, I was part of something very special—Frazee Pride.

The Senior High experience was equally exciting. For the first time, there were a variety of classes and the earned freedoms from advancing through the system. However, the initial highlight of this passage was getting that driver's license. My behind-the-wheel training instructor was our neighbor, Archie Sailer, who, as I mentioned earlier, was also a long-time coach and athletic director at Frazee. My driver's training schedule consisted of checking out the local duck sloughes or looking for deer throughout the countryside. The day before the test, I finally was taken around the actual driving course and told what the officer would look at and grade. The next day as I passed my test, I knew that I had come one step closer to adulthood and independence.

One particular day in my Sophmore year stands out more than most. We were sitting in Mrs. Bruhn's Speech class when we were notified that our President, John F. Kennedy, had been assassinated in Dallas. The class was stunned and many wept openly and without shame. To the Americans, we knew we had lost our esteemed leader. To my family, we had lost a great role model. To say the least, our family would be considered staunch Democrats. We file into the same category of thought exemplified by my grandpa, Louis Courneya. When he was asked if he was a Republican or Democrat, he would reply, "I vote for the best man, but it always seems to be a Democrat!" Yes, it was a tragic day for everyone when we lost our President. Almost as vividly remembered is that two days later as my family was watching television, we witnessed Kennedy's suspected assassinator, Lee Harvey Oswald, being shot by Jack Ruby in a police station, of all places! It was just the start of the turmoil of the 1960's. We thought we were so safe living in a semi-remote region of Minnesota, but the television brought the world into our living room.

For the next three years, I would grow both physically and mentally. I particularly enjoyed my History and Speech classes, and my parents expected us to devote as much attention to academic excellence as we did to athletics. Fun for us was athletics, but also going to the Sky View Cafe following the games or going with a group of friends haunted house hunting. Topping the list of social events was going to the famed Pavilion in Detroit Lakes. Enroute to this great dance hall, we would drive down Washington Avenue. It would be bumper-to-bumper and kids would jump on the hoods and trunks of cars just to get a ride down the avenue.

It was at the Pavilion that we witnessed the emergence of 'Rock-n-Roll' and the frenzy it could create. Top stars that appeared there were Bobby Vee, Fabian, Bobby Vinton, Paul Anka, Paul Revere and the Raiders, the Hulaballoos, the Uglies, and more. We also enjoyed the drive-in movies. We would pile in as many kids as we could in a car, as well as sneaking some friends in by hiding them in the trunk, to see the latest Elvis Presley movie or anything with Robert Mitchem or John Wayne in the starring role. Not all of my friends were top athletes or the most popular in the class; they were just plain good people. "Friends" meant a girl like Karen Franklin who was a kind as they come and who saved me a seat on the bus each morning for six years; "Friends" was a boy named Everett Davis who loved life, but died tragically in a motorcycle accident; "Friends" was a guy named Larry Golkowski with whom I could count on to be there when he was needed—on and off the athletic field. I have to admit I was particulary taken in by the Finlanders. To me, they were the most expressive and the most fun loving people I could imagine! They were the Koskis, the Hendricksons, the Ahos, and the Nelmarks from the Wolf Lake area. Sure, they did not always follow the straight and narrow path, but they were people you could count on to stick with you to the end.

My high school coaches all shaped by life and philosophy of coaching in one way or another. Coach Smith, whom I still call "Coach", taught me to find humor in one's self and to never find fault with any of my teammates; Coach Sailer, my baseball coach, taught me the idea of what it meant to be a dedicated athlete and to be professional through and through, and finally my basketball and track coach, Mr. Lassila. I told you earlier that he was tough, but he treated everyone the same . . . 'black was black' and 'white was white' . . . there was no in-between. I especially remember my Senior year when we were having basketball practice during Christmas vacation. The "writing was on the wall"—our team was not going to be outstanding. He blew his whistle and motioned for us to gather around him. He said, "Men, we're looking at a long season; the chances for success are slim, but not everything in life is determined by winning or losing. There is 'inner' satisfaction of being part of something great—of being in the best physical shape of your life. Sure, you won't win many games, but you will be able to run forever and you will be able to watch the opposing teams suffer with pain while you do not feel pain. This will be your greatest reward". Following his speech, we ran and ran and ran forever. Some of the players started crying, and Lassila screamed "whimps" in their faces as he ran beside them. He didn't care if you were the poorest kid on the block or the school administrators' kids; you were all treated the same. He spoke of having pride and the desire to go the extra mile—the internal strength—the development of character. In the end, he was correct. It felt so good watching our opponents suffer with exhaustion, even though the scoreboard indicated differently!

Mr. Lassila was also the back coach in football. I recall one time when he went berserk because of our poor tackling. He took the ball and, wearing no pads, ran right over the players—he was like a bulldozer clearing a path. In a scrimmage between the offense and defense, he decided to demonstrate how a running back should perform. He took off with a vengence, and everyone was afraid to tackle him, but guess who chose to tackle him . . . me! I hit him so hard, knocked him to the ground, and he jumped up and screamed in my face, "That's the way the game is played!" To those who feared him, he was a demon; to me, he taught me the meaning of performing to the best of my abilities. There would be other coaches along the way who would have a great impact on my life, but none more than Coach Lassila.

From day one, my parents were there to witness our extracurricular participation. There were always suggestions on how to improve my game and advice on how to demonstrate good sportsmanship. They would never second guess a teacher or a coach, and we were expected to accord the same respect. We never were allowed to dispute an official's call nor make faces of disgust or pain. We were told to look the coach straight in the eye when he was talking and to run to the huddle. If, by chance, we were injured during a game, we knew we would be expected to get to the sidelines by our own efforts. As Dad reminded us, "There better be a real good reason for them to stop the game because of your injury." My mom had the same philosophy—give 200%—and her sense of competition was as keen or more than Dad's.

I know that kids are always told to cherish their school years because nothing can even come close in comparison to the opportunities for growth: fun, leadership, challenge, and lifelong friendships; it is true. Americans can be very proud of the public school system. Granted, schools are criticized severely at times but, in essence, parents form a partnership with the school in raising a child. In no other country of the world are parents given the opportunity to be as closely involved with what goes on in the schools as in the school systems of the United States. The real key is knowing when to step back and allow the child to pursue his/her own dreams—self direction. The overall development of a child is like lighting a lantern. First, you strike a match, then you light the wick. Briefly, the match and wick burn together. However, as the match is removed and is extinguished, the wick continues to glow and, finally, the lantern lightens the room. When I think back to the days of my school years, the "light" I feel within would illuminate the entire cosmos.

CHAPTER FOUR

One drop of blood drawn from thy country's bosom
Should grieve thee more than streams of foreign gore.
　　　　　　-Shakespeare, *Henry VI, I, III, 3*

Benito Mussolini once stated that war alone keys up all human energies to their maximum tension and sets the seal of nobility on those peoples who have the courage to face it. When the subject of the Vietnam War arises in conversation or text, the word n*obility* is not often included in the descriptions. The Vietnam War was definitely one of the most controversial events in the history of the United States. The American involvement in the conflict began with Truman and continued through Democratic and Republican administrations alike, with the largest escalation taking place under Lyndon B. Johnson. From the very beginning, American policy makers viewed Ho Chi Minh's government in North Vietnam as part of a Communist conspiracy directed by Russia and China. American officials claimed that the collapse of South Vietnam would lead to coordinated communist domination of all of Southeast Asia—"The Domino Theory." So, to prevent the collapse of South Vietnam, the United States directly entered the war in 1965. . . . a decision that was "controversial" at best.

As our involvement escalated, so did the number of American advisors. Under President John F. Kennedy, the number of American advisors rose from 650 to 23,000. I often wonder how many of the 23,000 military "experts" ever asked an eighteen-year-old draftee or enlisted soldier, "What's your opinion on our involvement . . . what's it like over there?" Even though President Kennedy reportedly devised a disengagement plan before he was assassinated in 1963, followed by President Johnson's vow, "We are not going to send American boys nine or ten thousand miles away from home to do what Asian boys ought to be doing for themselves"—by 1967, more than 500,000 American troops were fighting on that distant foreign soil. Eventually, the United States dropped as many explosives (in this war) as it dropped in all theaters in World War II, and we were spending over $2 billion per month on the war.

Following more than a decade of direct American involvement in Vietnam, the casualties of the war consisted of the deaths of over 55,000 American soldiers and the injury of 300,000 more, countless prisoners of war, over 1.2 million dead Vietnamese soldiers and an ancient culture destroyed . . . the *nobility* of war.

When I graduated from high school in 1966, the United States was in a state of great turmoil. I was caught in the midst of a cultural revolution—the "counterculture", the civil rights movement, the New Left, the women's rights movement, and the war in Indo China. Even though all of the above profoundly affected what we thought and how we lived, nothing could compare to the impact of the Vietnam War on my family and on my country— "the nightmare of Vietnam".

We had come from a very patriotic family; for the most part, we did not question the government of our country. We felt it was our responsibility to support the judgement of our leaders (especially if they were democrats) when it came to military decisions. My grandfathers had served in World War I, my father in World War II, my uncle in the Korean War, and now my brother, Steve, and I would honor the family military tradition with our service in the Vietnam War.

I enlisted in the U.S. Navy on April 2, 1967. I went to boot camp in San Diego, and it was there that I first came to realize that the discipline and work ethic emphasized at home would come to be very beneficial. I thought the rigorous training and expectations of the military to be actually quite easy and fun, but there were a number of my fellow seamen who did not share my views! It was actually quite simple, the U.S. Navy had rules and you were to abide by those rules . . . no questions asked.

Interestingly, it was the Navy custom to punish *all* for the poor judgement of *one*. For example, one of my fellow mates did not like to wash his bedding at regular times. Therefore, as an example to all of us, our drill instructor closed the drains in the showers, poured boxes of soap in the shower, and turned on hot steamy water to a height of six inches. He then ordered us to take off all of our clothes and to throw them in the shower. The next step was to lock arms and form ranks inside the shower (100 men) and to march around and around, washing our clothes with our feet. As we marched, we were required to chant "swish-swash-swish-swash . . . "in cadence for over four hours. There were a number of lessons that I learned through this experience: 1) look out for your fellow shipmate, 2) a person's feet can get very white and wrinkled by constant immersion in soapy water, and 3) it is virtually impossible to say "swish-swash-swish-swash . . ." for an entire four hours!

Yes, there were countless lessons we had to learn. When we were told to tell our parents and friends not to send us cigarettes or candy, they meant it! For those individuals who did receive boxes of chocolates, they were forced to eat the entire box in front of the entire company! For the cigarette smoker, what a great way to stop smoking; smoking three cigarettes at a time until the carton was finished sure beats a commercialized nicotine patch! I really agonized when my little sister, Julie, would send me a stick of Juicy Fruit gum with her letters . . . I often had to share it with many!

It seemed that everyone got in trouble at one time or another, and I was no exception. In the eyes of the military, I made a horrible mistake the day I wore the wrong T-shirt at inspection. They decided to make a spectacle of me. I was ordered to strip down from the waist up in front of the entire company. They screamed in my face, riduculed me, and finally stuffed the whole T-shirt in my mouth while they continued to inspect the rest of the company. For some people, this may seem like harsh consequences for an innocent mistake, but not nearly as harsh as it was for the poor guy who wore the wrong undershorts!

Our boot camp lasted thirteen weeks as they were pushing recruits out at a record rate due to the war. In fact, during the summer of 1967, draft calls exceeded 30,000 per month, and a 10 percent surtax was initiated to cover the increasing costs of the war. President Johnson talked obssesively about Communist "aggression" in Vietnam and how he couldn't depend on the United Nations to act—"It couldn't pour piss out of a boot if the instructions were printed on the heel." I think the American people were not aware at all of the incredible stealth of our involvement in the war. The public was just misinformed. Perhaps, the greatest misinformers were our governmental officials who lied about the costs, casualties, victories, and build-ups.

Strangely, even though I joined the Navy, I never was permanently attached to a Navy base. I qualified for aviation school in Memphis, and then I was stationed in Yuma, Arizona for one year and Albany, Georgia for one year—both were Marine Corp bases!

Finally, my orders came for overseas duty—the next fourteen months I would be directly involved in the U.S. war efforts . The Kitty Hawk (carrier) became my sister ship and also my home base as I spent a good deal of time on land in Southeast Asia. I became a crew leader and a member of a RA5C squadron. This was an elite photo-reconnaissance plane of limited supply to the U.S. Navy. It definitely was a high-tech plane and extremely valuable to the war efforts.

I saw first-hand and experienced first-hand the tragedy of war. Sadly, the American soldier did not understand his role in this war nor did he understand the lack of commitment of the South Vietnamese soldier. Yes, we knew we were in Vietnam to stop the spread of communism but also to fight for the independence of the nation itself. The impression that was given to us by the South Vietnamese was that they were standing back and were content to let the United States fight their battle. We did not describe our counterpart (South

Vietnamese) by using the words "herosim" or "comrades". Of course, our politicians had all the answers. I can recall them trying to appease the American public by talking about the "deescalation" of the war . . . a pulling back of troops and bombings. I found it so ironic that this was stated the very day the Kitty Hawk set the highest record ever for the number of bombs released. We would read, "The U.S. is centering their efforts and actions in the country of Vietnam"; yet, this press release occurred when we were flying over Cambodia and Laos. The "credibility gap" was alive and well and was one of the reasons for the riots and spiraling crime rates in the United States—a total disenchantment with the "ideals" professed by our government. Still, the American officials tried valiantly to persuade themselves and the world that progress was being made. To further assure the American people, President Johnson stated, "We are not going to yield; we are not going to shimmy. We are going to wind up with a peace with honor which all Americans seek." The war continued.

As with just about anything, there is always another side to the coin. Consequently, some of my finest memories are from my Vietnam experience. Nothing can compare to the friendships I acquired during the war and the vital necessity for trusting another human being. Dwight L. Moody (*Sermons*) stated, "Character is what you are in the dark." Some of the finest and most trustworthy individuals I have ever had the privilege of being with were my comrades in the war; they had strength of character. The word "I" seized to exist. They became my family. We would share the many "care packages" from home. It was this new family that waited each week for my mom to send me the local newspaper from home, The Frazee Forum. These friends from Atlanta, Miami, New York City, Los Angeles, all waited to read my hometown newspaper— news from a town of 1200 people! They particularly enjoyed the gossip section of the paper . . . "Did Mr. and Mrs. Smith visit Aunt Helen this week? . . . Who won the high-low at the Senior Citizen Whist Tournament? . . . Who hosted the monthly Homemakers' Club meeting, and what was served for lunch?" All of this might seem trivial to the average person, but to us it was a touch of reality, an anchor, a hope that all would soon return to "normal". My mom never disappointed us; she sent the local newspaper faithfully for four straight years as she had done the four years previously for my brother Steve.

It is also during times of trouble that one comes to appreciate all those individuals who have been instrumental in life—grandparents, parents, brothers and sisters. I would spend many sleepless nights reminiscing about the good times at home and those closest to my heart. I thought about my grandparents, Louis and Marie Courneya. Grandpa Courneya, a full-blooded Frenchman, had taken part in the "Great War"—World War I. He served in the Argonne Campaign, and his stories would rival any told by historians. It was through him that I "felt" what the Depression was like, the "dirty-thirties", and love of family and heritage. Then there was Grandma Courneya, a French "saint". She had a smile for everyone, a warm heart, and a lady who may not have had all the "riches" in life, but who made life richer. If I could inherit one trait from her, it would be her inner goodness.

As French as my father's parents were, my mother's parents were as Norwegian—strong willed with extreme pride in their roots. As noted previously, my grandmother, Marie Bjorge, was a lady before her time. She continued to aspire to new heights throughout her life. At an age of 99, she requested, "Do not ask how old I am, but rather how young I be." I came to be especially fond of my grandpa, Albert Bjorge, because my family was given the opportunity of having him live with us for five years. I'd like to say that he had a huge impact on all the kids in the family, but none more than myself. He had an extremely sharp mind and was keenly interested in the sport of baseball. Just as I had grown up with heros such as Mickey Mantle and Willie Mays, he had grown up with Ty Cobb and Babe Ruth. He and I would talk for hours about the good old days and the present days. People say that Americans today do not have time for the elderly and, for the most part, do not want to take the time. However, my family took the time to be with those who were instrumental in our development of character—my grandparents. I believe we inherited their appreciation for life. It is through my grandparents that the word "dignity" takes on an added dimension.

Yes, I also spent many a night thinking about my parents and brothers and sisters.

When I thought about Mom (Margaret) I was reminded of the term "unconditional love". She was a supporter of her children no matter what the circumstance. Whatever the situation, she always tried to make it better or to make everyone happy. By today's standards, her role as a mother, wife, disciplinarian, money-manager, and foreman is worthy of the utmost respect. She worked harder than any person I know, and she never complained about the hardships of life. I thought about how beautiful she was on the outside and also within. It is through her that we learned to have compassion for others. As for my dad, Jerry Courneya, I feel an overwhelming sense of pride and respect for what he believes in and what he stands for. He, along with Mom, taught us the value of honesty and integrity by example. He, too, exemplified the honor in working hard, and never complained about the "cracks" in the road. He taught us that life is what we make of it, not what someone else makes for us. They say in America that we no longer have heroes; I disagree, my dad is a hero.

Judy, my sister, was the oldest in the family and, by a vote from all of us, the "nicest". We nicknamed her "the Saint". You name it, she had it: beautiful, intelligent, great personality, and family devotion. She set the standards for the rest of us to follow, and it sure wasn't easy! Next in line came my brother, Steve. Many of my family memories include adventures with Steve. He had looks that would "kill" and a sense of humor that was unparalleled. He also worked extremely hard, yet he knew how to live life to the max! So much of my work ethic came from Steve. I was his shadow growing up and words need not be spoken to prove our friendship . . . such things are just known.

My sister, Cathy, and I had a strange relationship and, at times, I could have killed her. The truth was, she knew how to push my bottoms . . . she enjoyed it and was good at it! She was notorious for making faces at me, kicking me under the table with her feet, switching the dishes of sauce so that I got the smallest, and just trying to make my life miserable. Yet, my memories of Cathy were extremely warm. She was a "knock out", athletic, and generous to a fault. When I thought of her, I was reminded of the laughter and the closeness of family. Tim, my younger brother, and I did the same things that Steve and I had done. We would hunt, fish, and just have brotherly fun. From a very young age, I could see that he had a great deal of natural ability as he was fast, coordinated, and very strong. I would spend hours trying to refine his talents. I would make him play baseball until he cried, and his pitching talents set him a stride ahead of the rest. Tim was disciplined in thought and in action. Julie was "everyone's little sister". She went by many names, but most of us called her "Little Indian Dolly" because of her dark skin and black eyes. I had the opportunity to spend a great deal of time with Julie. She would tag along with her older brother and always "pay" her way. You see, when you took Julie fishing, she would always surprise you by having her pockets full of cookies or candy. She would be the one to crawl up on your lap and make you feel like you were the most important person in the world. She was notorious for setting goals for herself . . . the word, "lazy", was not in her dictionary. Despite her acclamation in academics and beauty pageants, I know her dream was to be an olympic runner. I designed workouts, obstacle courses, and rigorous training so that "we" could achieve her dream. We fell a little short of our goal, but the bond we developed was incomparable. Family . . . it is what keeps us going; it gives us a sense of belonging and, most importantly, family becomes the memories of the heart.

Was the war wrong? Who am I to say? Perhaps we should ask the families of the 55,000 who came home to their loved ones in a pine box. Maybe we should ask the veterans what it felt like to be called "losers" or "failures" by the welcoming public. Maybe I should ask the wife of my friend to whom I delivered a hand written note in which he professed his love for her and their six-year-old daughter . . . written before he lost his life in Vietnam. These are the tragic consequences of war . . . ask them. I personally believe in the quote, "If the men who start the wars would have to fight the wars, there would be no wars."

We Americans always believed that we not only could create a perfect society at home, but that we were also responsible for maintaining peace and freedom worldwide. Our involvement in the Vietnam War deeply scarred and cruelly disillusioned this vision. However, when it comes to disillusionment, nothing can compare to the emotions felt by a Vietnam veteran who opens a high school history text only to discover that more pages are devoted to the War of 1812—a war that occurred nearly two centuries ago and killed approximately two thousand Americans. Disappointment is the sentiment used when hearing about the responses of college freshmen who were asked, "Who fought in the war in Vietnam", and 25 percent answered, "North and South Korea." Sadness is the term used to describe the feeling of watching Florida's Disney World's exhibit, "American Adventure", a twenty-nine-minute history of the United States, and to note that the Vietnam War is completely left out of the exhibit.

Yes, we can question the wisdom of our leaders during the war, and we can question the morality of the war. However, what is beyond question is that the American soldiers did not question their duty to their country. I think the greatest tribute we can give this group of heroes is to make a point to visit the Vietnam Memorial in Washington D.C. . . . trace the name, etched in granite, of a fallen soldier . . . remember to honor the VFW when they march in the parades . . . sing the Star Spangled Banner with conviction . . . place your hand over your heart when you see the American Flag . . . bow your head and pay homage to our veterans . . . say a prayer for those who are still missing in action. We should honor all those individuals, who put country over self; those same patriots who have been omitted from history texts. Maybe then, we will become a part of the true *nobility* of war.

*   Historical information on the Vietnam War was ~~attained~~ *obtained* (16)
from the following sources:

American History, Alfred A. Knopf, New York, 1987, pgs.
872-880.

Lies My Teacher Told Me, James W. Loewen, The New Press,
1995, pgs. 234-243.

Portrait of America, Stephen B. Oates, Houghton Mifflin
Co., 1987, pgs. 410-425.

CHAPTER FIVE

The first thing to do in life
is to do with purpose what one
proposes to do.

- Pablo Casals

I returned from the service with no real plans for the the future. However, I definitely noticed the profound changes in fashion, music, and morals that had occurred during my four-year absence from civilian life. There appeared to be a general revolt against the traditional values that had previously characterized American life. A lack of respect existed between America's youth and America's establishment. The slogan, "Don't Trust Anyone Over Thirty", was counterattacked with describing the younger generation as "druggies . . . hippies . . . radicals". Despite it all, I was glad to be home!

I worked that first summer and, in reality, it was a great time—to be young, strong, and willing to work, along with spending time with family and friends—it just didn't get any better! One of the activities that I particularly took time to enjoy was hunting. From a young age and on, Dad had taught us to respect nature and to enjoy what nature had to offer. Thus, we learned the art and the thrill of the hunt! Some of my greatest memories, past to present, centered on the topic of hunting.

I laugh when I think of the miles and miles that Steve and I, as youngsters, would trek in search of prey that was in season. By far, the greatest distance was covered in the pursuit of ducks. There were endless amounts of pot holes, bays, and lakes for ducks to sit in, but Steve and I knew of these spots also . . . it was not to be a safe haven for fowl! One of our favorite tricks was to sneak through the woods much as the Indians did to close the distance and to get within range. Once in range, Steve would try to line up two or three ducks and pull the trigger. This was known as "pot shooting"; in other parts of the country people would say, we "Arkansawed them". Once the smoke cleared, it would be my turn to shoot the maimed ducks. So in reality, even though I was very young, I could say that I shot some ducks too. The real challenge, however, was how to retrieve the ducks once they were shot. Sure, there are a number of methods: wait for them to blow to shore, use a long stick, or if all else fails, take off your boots and pants and go get them! Always, in the back of our minds, was Dad's rule: "Never leave anything lay . . . always make an effort to retrieve every duck".

When I think back to one of the strangest memories of my early years hunting, I recall the time that I thought I was "dead as a duck". Steve and I had left in the early morning and, again, had eaten our day's lunch by 10:00 am. Following a late afternoon snack of basswood leaves and slippery elm leaves (and little luck with the hunt), we headed for home. It was getting late, and I was so hungry and tired that I thought I was going to die! We were walking through a swampy area, and I decided that I just couldn't go on. I collapsed on the ground and dramatically informed Steve, "I can't go any farther." He took one look at me and nonchalantly said, "Well, this is where you are going to die then", and he took off walking for home. For some strange reason, I found the strength to follow him.

Of course, deer hunting was also high on our list. The two most anticipated days of the fall season were the opening day of deer hunting and the following day. The opener always took place on a Saturday, and it was one morning that Dad took off from work. We have a family ritual that has been followed throughout the years on "opening day" of deer hunting. Dad would be the first to rise (or so he thought . . . actually, I rarely slept all night in anticipation of the big opener). He would cook a big breakfast and pack a huge sack lunch for each of us. I knew that when I opened the sack lunch later that I could always count on finding one of those big thick Hershey chocolate candy bars on the bottom. We would then get dressed and let me tell you, we wore layers upon layers of clothes. We looked like mummies, and by the time we got to our deer stands, we were so hot and sweaty!! We knew enough not to strip off the layers because, within an hour or so, the sweat turned to ice. Those layers of clothes suddenly didn't seem so bad.

To us, our dad was a "Daniel Boone"—the greatest shot on earth! I can remember standing by him when a deer would approach, and I know that no one could replicate his precision. Some years, Dad would have to go back to work after our morning hunt because a Saturday meant time-and-a-half in pay. One particular year, Steve went with him back to work. Dad was grubbing out in the woods on a D-8 cat, and Steve stood close by looking for deer. Steve caught Dad's attention when he pointed down into a swamp where a buck was running. Dad grabbed his gun, pointed it towards the swamp, and shot the deer in its tracks. I lived the story as if I were there. Yes, Dad said it was a lucky shot, but as a youngster, I viewed it as another example of his "supernatural powers".

One of our favorite night time hunting activites was coon hunting. Just think about it—the thrill of a hunt . . . the adventure and mystery of the night darkness . . . and the possibility of making a little bit of money in the process! Yes, hunting raccoons was an unforgettable experience. The basic idea of this type of hunt was to approach a cornfield very quietly and turn your dog loose to catch the scent or sounds of the coon. The fights that came to be between our coon dog and the racoons were unrivaled. A forty-pound coon can definitely inflict a huge amount of pain on a good dog. When arriving at a scene between the two, one was immediately astounded by the quickness and power of both . . . and the bloodcurdling sounds of the fight. The biggest challenge was not accidently shooting your dog while trying to shoot the coon! Once the coon was shot, off the dog would go trying to find any remaining raccoons. But I'll tell you one thing, after all of the commotion, more than likely, those remaining coon were long gone! However, our coon dog would trail them as long as it took . . . through the swamps, across pot holes . . . you name it. Sometimes we would track the coon for a couple of miles only to discover that they were in a hollow tree or had crossed water where the dog would lose scent. If everything went right, the dog would tree a number of them up in one tree. But now the big question, how do we get them down? Remember, it is very dark, and this is their domain. Sometimes they would be extremely high in a branch and the wind would blow, causing the coon to sway. A good flashlight, a 22-caliber, along with nerves of steel become your "friends of the night". I have shot as many as seven coon out of one tree. Yes, the hunt is super exciting, but it is also nerve-wracking, and it is work!

None of my memories of hunting occur without thinking about our most infamous family member: our dog Captain ("Cap"). Mark Twain must have been thinking about old Captain when he said, "If you pick up a starving dog and make him prosperous, he will not bite you. That is the principal difference between a dog and a man." (*Pudd'nhead Wilson's Calendar*). Steve found Captain and brought him home. That dog asked nothing from us except for cookies and adventure! I truly believe in reincarnation, because this dog was half-human. He was a big dog with loose skin, gigantic feet, and droopy expressive eyes. He was our coon dog, our duck dog, our cookie-eater, and our friend. He lacked one thing and that was ambition. However, this dramatically changed when it came to coon hunting. He hated coon with a passion and he knew how to hunt them. His ears were proof of his many battles with coon and, luckily, over the years he did discover which end of the coon would bite back.

There were times when we thought he was "wonder dog", and there were times when we wished he was a "dead dog". For instance, if we shot four ducks, he would retrieve two and we would retrieve two. To him, it was a 50-50 proposition. Interestingly, bravery was not one of his greater qualities. This became quite evident during one of our coon hunts. My friend, Ray Osterman, and I were coon hunting in a small field that was bordered by a large wooded area. Walking along the edge of the field, a bobcat let out a shrill scream that chilled us to the bone. Ray and I took off running across the cornfield to the pickup truck. We both arrived at the same time and tried to get in the same door . . . just like in the cartoons. As we both clamored into the front seat, guess who was waiting there for us . . . Captain! Apparently, we had left the truck window open and he had beaten us to safety!

That same field seemed to have "my number" when it came to instilling fear. A few years later, after coon hunting late at night, I walked back to my truck only to discover that the battery was dead. There was only one thing to do—run the two miles home— and get help. To make my load lighter, I locked the gun and the dog in the front seat. It was a beautiful night, the stars were shining brightly, and I was young and fit! There was a large soil bank field (meadow grass) that bordered the woods and this was my pathway home. With not a care in the world, I ran with the wind at my back . . . wild and free. Then, suddenly, my world changed. As I was running, I stumbled and fell forward onto an object that became huge, hairy, and brutal. I thought I had run into Sasquatch (the legendary Big Foot). I didn't know it at the time, but a stray work horse was laying out in the meadow grass and I had piled into him. He was as surprised as I was. He jumped up with me hanging half-way on him, and he was kicking and snorting. I found my running legs, and I took off at a clip that would rival an Olympic champion. I know that I set the world record for the two mile run! Even to this day, I have never been that scared in my entire life!

That fall when I returned from the service, I spent many moments recapturing the thrill of hunting and reliving its priceless moments. But I also knew, that it was time to think about my future. My younger brother, Tim, who had just graduated from high school, had made plans to enter Fergus Falls Community College and also to play football. He convinced me to meet the coach and to take a look at the college with the idea that both of us would attend the same college and play football together. Prior to going into the service, I had not given college a great deal of consideration, as I knew the military and the draft loomed in front of me. At that time, there was little choice for high school graduating males. However, after taking a look at the college and meeting the coach, I decided to give it a try. Money was not a problem because of the G.I. Bill. It turned out to be a momentous decision.

I had always loved football in high school, and Mom and Dad provided great encouragement then and now. Dad was also a wonderful role model in that he had been an outstanding athlete playing football for North Dakota State University and later, following his time in the Navy, he was offered a scholarship to play at the University of Mississippi and at Notre Dame. Yes, I knew that I would love playing football again, but I also found that I truly enjoyed the education—the "learning"—at Fergus Falls. I had always been interested in our environment, so I decided to explore the field of Environmental Studies. Football may have been my initial passion, but as time went on, my educational studies became its equal.

Football at the Junior College was in the developmental stage, and it was a learning process for our entire team. Success cannot always be measured in wins and losses; the will to succeed, the acquired friendships, the drive to succeed, and the commitments to teamwork, all made up the learning process. It was quite a thrill playing alongside my brother, Tim, for those two years. It gave us time to know each other and to become the best of friends. Football opened many doors for my future. I was fortunate in being honored with a number of awards, and with these awards, came the opportunity to be recruited by some four-year colleges and to receive financial help in the process.

It was in my second year of college that I met and married a girl from Fergus Falls, Susan. Together we looked at the colleges that were recruiting me to play football. Finally, we narrowed our choices down to two: Gustavas Adolphus and the University of Minnesota, Morris. Both of them had an outstanding academic reputation. Finally, we decided on the University of Minnesota, Morris. My brother, Tim, also chose to continue his education at the UMM. We continued to play football together our junior year until he transferred to North Dakota State University to finish his major.

It was during my junior year that I made a decision which greatly impacted my future. I decided that I would become a teacher and a coach. Yes, I changed my major, and it was a decision that I never regretted. I had always been enthralled with history and, needless to say, athletics had always been a big part of my life. I was excited about my future and I knew that I was going to do all I could to be the best teacher and coach I could possibly be.

I truly enjoyed my two years at Morris—both in the classroom and on the field. I was proud to play for the Morris Cougars and especially grateful that my parents and family were in the stands watching my efforts. I tried to learn and gather as much as possible from those individuals who were instrumental in my educational and athletic growth. With each coach for whom I played, I took a piece of their philosophy and vowed to use it to the best of my abilities later in my career. Coach Molde (UMM) was the most detailed-oriented person that I had ever known. His practices were down to the last seconds and his scouting reports were precise. He taught me to believe in the quote, "You have to look good to play good." To him, taking a picture of the team for the local newspapers was like running a perfect play—detailed to perfection. We were to be on the practice field at 4:00 and calisthenics ended at 4:21 precisely! When we left for an away game, the bus would leave at 3:07, arrive at our destination at 5:08, eat at 5:09, and so on. His famous one-liner was, "You men are so privileged to be able to play this game of football." We were privileged to have him as a coach.

I cannot think of my years at Morris University without remembering my good friend and teammate, Lars. He had come as a freshman from Herman, MN. He was definitely one-of-a-kind. He was not into fanfare nor into being a showboat. He would come in to get dressed for our games wearing no shoes and wet up to the waist (from hunting, etc.). Yes, even by his definition, he was a little "woodsy". For that reason and more, I took an instant liking to him and vice versa. He was a great athlete and held the

UMM field goal record—50 yards—for many years. Through thick and thin, we supported one another, and his parents proved to be just as loyal later in my life.

I had to attend college an extra quarter because of my change of major. It was at that time that I was given my first opportunity to coach. I was asked to be the assistant coach of the Morris High School varsity football team. The head coach was a former coach of Frazee, Jim Satter. This man ate and slept football! He was wound tighter than a clock! I admired his attitude and his desire. He was by far the most emotional coach I have ever worked with. His entire life was dedicated to the sport. Everyday, he would say to the squad during practice, "Isn't it a great day to be here!" I witnessed then and there how monumental a coach's attitude is in providing motivation for his team. To me, he epitomized what coaching was all about and what a coach should be. He was a testimony to the phrase, "You have to be willing to go the extra mile". He did that and more.

I graduated from the University of MN, Morris in 1975, and I had two immediate job offers, Mapleton and Barnum. While I was deciding which one to take, I received a call from the Superintendent of Hancock School, Cecil Halliday. He asked me to come over for an interview. I told him that I already had two job offers, but he convinced me to come over and take a look at Hancock, a small town just to the east of Morris. When I went to visit the school, I had an interview with the superintendent and two board members. I was offered a contract on the spot. After discussing the options with my wife, Susan, and knowing that we were expecting a baby in the fall, we decided to take the Hancock offer.

Little did I know that this town so typical of rural America, a town with two gas stations, one grocery store, one liquor store, two cafes, a VFW, and a major employment establishment—Hancock Concrete, would come to be my home for the next twenty-two years. It was here that I hoped to build my career and build my dream of becoming the best teacher and coach. I knew in my heart that I could make a positive difference. I had faith in my abilities as a teacher, coach, and as a viable citizen of the community.

Faith . . . *The reason why birds can fly and we can't is simply that they have perfect faith, for to have faith is to have wings* (J.M. Barrie). 1975 . . . the sky was the limit . . . I had wings . . . I could fly. My goal was to empower those with whom I was fortunate enough to work with and teach, to have *faith* in one's capabilities . . . *wings.*

CHAPTER SIX

One mark of a great education
is the ability to lead students out . . .
to new places where even the educator
has never been.

-Thomas Groome

Every teacher at one time or another has been asked about their philosophy of teaching. Mine would not be easy to explain. I believe that learning must be fun, yet there must be structure . . . teaching from the book is important, but teaching from the heart is even more important. I quickly discovered from "Day 1" as a teacher that educators were required to be a "Jack-of-all-trades". We were leaders, counselors, substitute parents, sounding-boards, coaches, and doctors. Our day did not end at 4:00 in the afternoon. We were on-call . . . day and night. A good teacher listens and cares, encourages and befriends, and more times than not, has shed many a tear in shared anguish with a student. Teachers are entrusted with not only imparting knowledge, but also are responsible for reminding students of the brilliance of life. Did I acquire this wisdom from a college text or from an inspiring lecture? No, my dedication to my chosen vocation- teaching—came from my love of life. Yes, I taught from the overflow of life . . . from the heart.

My teaching assignment for the Hancock School consisted of teaching six classes per day to students in grades 7-12. The average number of students in each class varied, but was approximately 13-20 per grade level. I can remember walking into my classroom at Hancock for the first time. I saw the rows of desks closely aligned with no space whatsoever separating the desks—front to back. I knew that I would have to command their attention and gain their respect to maintain discipline in such close quarters! I thought of the many teachers who had brought me to this point in my life, and I drew upon their wisdom and example. I realized that if I were to survive in this challenging profession that I would have to accord respect for the subject and respect for the learner. No, I did not demand respect from the student . . . I earned it.

I taught classes in Social Studies, American and World History, Civics, Sociology, Psychology, Economics, and Political Science. I made every effort to bring the subjects to life! We would have panel discussions, mock trials, debates, creative demonstrations, improvisations, projects, and so on. The classroom became an arena for discovery! Most students became enthusiastic learners and open-minded. One apparent exception to this, however, was when one boy told me (after a lecture about World War II) that the German Nazis did not persecute the Jews and that the "stories" about the Nazi camps were all lies; his parents told him so. I knew that I and the history books would not be able to change his or his parents' minds; therefore, I simply stated, "I guess alot of history books will have to be rewritten." Other subject areas that created student and parent unrest were topics about evolution, Darwin, and Freud. In addition to my teaching and coaching duties (which I will expand upon later), I was a class advisor as well as an advisor for plays, prom, fund-raisers, skits, etc. Teachers were expected to go beyond what was written in their contract . . . to go the extra mile for students. The pay was not great, but the rewards of working with young minds went beyond any job description.

I truly loved teaching and I loved my students. I believed in and always expected the best from my students. I knew that my work would be in vain if I did not have a true interest in their overall well-being. Therefore, I was there to greet them each morning—to extend a warm hello or to give a friendly hug. Compassion can go a long way in proving that you, too, are a caring human being . . . beyond the book. Students would seek me out if they had had a bad day and if they had had a glorious day! They shared their fears, their failures, and their moments of triumph. I saw pictures of their family celebrations from weddings to births—and I made a point to make them feel like, no matter what, they were the most important person in the picture—they were special. I genuinely cared, and they knew it. If a student was sick or hurt, I did not hesitate to call them at their home to find out how they were doing. As I said earlier, a good teacher does not close the book at 4:00. You have to genuinely care about the well-being of your students.

I do feel that my title as "teacher" was stretched at times especially when I was asked to be a fashion consultant of sort. Now, this is totally out of my domain of expertise! Yet, many girls would come and ask me what prom dress to order . . . they never knew that this was definitely "out of my league!" I gave it my best shot! I can remember telling some girls that they were already beautiful individuals and, oh, how they would smile! You would have thought that it was the first time anyone had said something nice to them. Many had such low self-esteem, and I did what I could to elevate their sense of worth. I wanted them to know that they were unique and valued. I can remember one student in particular that stated, "Mr. Courneya, you use the word 'love' so easily and it seems so natural. But you know something . . . I have never told my parents that I loved them and I can never remember them telling me that they loved me." It was my hope that my example would encourage this student to extend love to her family.

Who received the most attention from me? Any student, boy or girl, who needed it. The "A" student . . . the student who struggled to get a "C" . . . the girl who was never asked to the Homecoming Dance . . . the boy who didn't have enough money to hardly buy a lunch ticket . . . There was one particular boy who waited by my door many mornings before the start of the school day. His mom and dad were having a tough time getting along. He and I would make small-talk each morning until, finally, he confided in me. He shared his anguish and his fears. I gave him some advice, a hug around the shoulders, and told him, "I care". I now had a friend for life . . . built on trust. There was the girl who shared her apprehension about joining a church and actually asked for my approval. I told her that it was a decision that only she could make . . . to look into her heart. She joined the church. Many students came to look upon me as family. I was asked many times to stand up for them at parents' night when their parents did not or could not attend. I did it with pride and esteem. I was further honored when the students dedicated the yearbook to me in 1983 and also in 1997. My interaction with students was one of high standards, high expectations, and a willingness to create situations in which the students would profit from their mistakes as well as their successes. They expected the same from me.

There were so many memorable moments with my students. It was wonderful sharing in their growth and success. There were many times in which we shared laughter over their blunders as well. Notable statements (by students) that I will never forget include the following:

* "I got so embarassed, I got beet as a red";
* "25,000 people were slaughtered in the battle and they all died";
* Question from me, "How many people live in the Twin-Cities?"
  Student response, "100,000".
  Follow-up question from me, "So, how many live in Minnesota?"
  Student response, "75,000".

Of course, there were a variety of excuses for missing assignments: "My dog ate my homework . . . It blew out the window . . . I dropped it on the way to the bus and my dog picked it up and ran away with it . . . My dad used it to start a fire . . . I couldn't find a pencil . . . "Yes, teachers must learn to be empathetic but not naive! Additionally, a good sense of humor goes a long way in the classroom!!

For the most part, the parents were grateful for my commitment to their child's growth.

I particularly remember two parents telling me after their children had graduated, "Thanks for raising our kids. It's the first time our kids ever heard the word 'no' and it was meant!" Other parents confided, "You have had such a positive impact on my child- thank you", and "How do you get them to work so hard for you? We can't get them to do anything at home." I have chosen not to use the names of the parents mentioned above . . . it could be anyone. They know who they are, and I am grateful that I was able to be a part of their child's life. Was I ever criticized by parents? Of course. I cannot think of a teacher who has not had a conflict or two with one of their student's parents. One thing I do know is that the parents knew I was approachable. I was always willing to discuss their child's progress—good and bad. My door was an "open door"—open for communication.

There were so many people at the school who made coming to work a "unique" experience. When I began teaching there were seventeen teachers. For the most part, our secondary teaching staff was a close-knit group. We would celebrate any and all occasions: first day and last day of school, first snowfall of the season, Super Bowl, Homecoming (with faculty skits and parade floats!), Irish Day, Dane Day, etc. One of our more festive faculty celebrations was in honor of Norwegian Independence Day—complete with costumes, food, and Norsky music! Ruthie Dahlseg, a teacher on staff, was a true Norwegian and we "felt" her pride in heritage. She helped remind us of the importance of our roots and the necessity of honoring our ancestry. Yes, we were commited to educating the youth, but we also knew how to have fun! We were not above dressing up like chickens from head to foot and strutting accordingly during a Homecoming festivity . . . we were not beyond taking part (in character) in skits before important athletic events . . . we were not deterred from attempting to play the school song in front of the student body knowing that few of us had any instrumental ability whatsoever! We were humble and we were human.

Despite our ability to unite in fun, we did not have a strong local teacher's union. I served a number of offices in our union as well as a negotiator, but we were, as a whole, quite weak. Our meetings were random and sometimes quite pointless. Many of the union offices were unfilled. I cannot remember having a teachers' rights chairperson serving in our local or ever discussing union policy. I guess we just always felt that our "teaching world" at Hancock School was safe, and that no occasion would ever arise requiring us to unite and face adverse circumstances. As the years passed, the faculty became less close with one another. Some of the teachers retired, and some of the new teachers had different ideas on how a teacher should act. Some felt that we should distance ourselves from the students—rise above them . . . not with them.

As in all walks of life, a few individuals prove to be more memorable than some. I am reminded of one of our earlier science teachers who claimed he had the power to make a bomb and could easily blow up the school if he chose to do so. We believed him. Interestingly, the school bought out his contract. There was the coach on staff who would throw green gum to the students at pep fests and say that our opposition was nothing but "green snot" and that "we were going to chew them up!" Some athletes also told of the time when this coach was taking them to a competition and they happened to stop at Kentucky Fried Chicken. Once on the bus, he discovered that he hadn't been given a fork or spoon in which to eat his mashed potatoes and gravy; thus, he pulled out a comb from his pocket and ate with it instead!

Another highly memorable individual was the custodian who basically "ran the school". Most of the staff and administration were afraid of him. He cleaned when he wanted to clean, and if he ever got mad at you, your room was never cleaned! I chuckle when I think of the teacher who asked for assistance in replacing a lightbulb in a ceiling fixture that was located ten feet above. The teacher was given a bulb and a response, "Here is one, do it yourself." I actually got along with our custodian and was able to visit his "office" in the school. It was a real eye-opener! I never asked him to do anything out-of-the-ordinary for me; plus, I supplied him with fish and ducks! The school did utilize his talents. He was an excellent carpenter (saved the school money by doing repair work, etc.) and he had the "coveted" boiler license.

Individuals whom I came to value very highly were the school cooks. They were genuine people and very dedicated. I looked forward to seeing their smiling faces each morning as they prepared the day's meal. Dorothy Zeltwanger, Arlene Greiner, Vonnie Thielke, and Lamae Pieske were the *salt of the Earth*. When I arrived early each morning, they would often have treats for me. I also enjoyed giving them "advice" on meal planning! I knew which dishes were my favorite! Their school meals ranked very high, second only to my mom's cooking. When I would bring Arlene some tomatoes or asparagus, she would reciprocate with a freshly baked pie! I know I got the better of the deal! Vonnie did a lot of canning for me, and we would split the results. Arlene's sister, Lamae Pieske, worked as a substitute in the kitchen, and she ended up canning just about everything for me. Sometimes I would give her my excess garden produce, and she would repay me with homemade soup. Wow! Sometimes she would even put the soup in my pickup when I was on a road trip with my teams; therefore, when I returned late at night, I would be able to have something to eat when I finally made it home. One of the school secretaries, June Pearson, and maybe one of my all-time favorite people, Doad Greiner, also "bartered" for my garden vegetables. June would bring pies to my house, and Doad even gave me a rain suit for fishing. The word *kindness* takes on added dimension when I think of all of these women. Their deeds of kindness enriched my life and my heart.

During my twenty-two year teaching career, I basically had three superintendents and three principals. The first set was very conservative and probably due to that particular period of time. Additionally, the religious climate of the community had much influence with the financial decisions of the school. With the last set of administrators, we noticed a definite communication problem between them and the faculty. Throughout the year, there were few teacher meetings (just one or two yearly), and many times the teachers would be the last to be informed of pertinent educational issues. The administration ran a "loose ship" and tried to avoid controversy. I can remember when some parents came to look at our locker rooms and noted how filthy the rooms were. The administrative response was, "We are not running a hospital here." It seemed that the school received public complaints about being dirty every year. Nothing was done about it. With regards to assistance with discipline, the teachers were supposed to handle their own problems with the students. Additionally, teachers were told not to bother the administrator with early morning telephone calls. If we were in need of a substitute teacher to take our place for the day, we were expected to find our own replacement. As for teacher evaluations and observations, I was observed and evaluated frequently in the early years. I saved the evaluations and at times would remind myself of what was recorded in my file by an administrator, "Dennis Courneya is a master teacher." During the last ten years of my career, I was observed only twice. However, I made a point to invite the administrators into my classroom quite often to take part in class activities. Therefore, they did visit my class and were able to witness my teaching style . . . upon my initiative.

Teaching and coaching became my life, and it was during my first year at Hancock that my strength and commitment would be tested. It was during that first year that I and my wife got divorced. My son, Jerid, had been born and I thought life couldn't be finer! I enjoyed parenthood and all the challenges and joys that it brought. Yet, my wife and I had different views of the future. I was content with my job and location . . . she was not.

My marriage ended, and I was left with the nails on the wall, my clothes, a digital clock radio, and a 48-Dodge pickup that did not run. This was the most painful journey of my life. I couldn't bear to look at my son's vacated bedroom, so I closed the door. However, I remained committed to being a good father and did all

I could to visit Jerid when allowed. Despite it all, Jerid and I remained close throughout his childhood, and he eventually came to live with me when he was a teenager. Those years with Jerid were the best of my life.

To say that I was poor during those first years of teaching is quite an understatement. I did not fare well with the divorce and, despite what many think, a teacher's salary must be stretched to the max! I decided it was vital for me to take on a second job. I would teach and coach during the daylight hours and then I would go to my night security job in Morris. Many times, I would arrive home from my night shift just in time to get cleaned up and ready for my day of teaching and coaching. I did this double shift for two years.

Over the years, I lived in a number of different places—from renting an apartment to renting a couple of houses near Hancock. One place in particular will never be forgotten nor repeated! The house I rented following my divorce was brutally cold . . . I'm talking frigid! I did not have enough money to buy fuel for heating so, needless to say, the heat was turned down low. It was so cold in this house and so poorly insulated that when the wind blew in the winter, the drapes would stick straight out! The bathroom was upstairs and during the winter was not usable. In the mornings when I went to shave, my shaving cream would be frozen. At night, I would move a cot into the kitchen to be close to a source of heat. I did save money on fuel. That year I spent only $35.00 on oil for heat, and that was for the oven. I learned to economize and to be grateful for the simple things in life!

They say that adversity builds strength of character. I can't say that it weakens it, that's for sure. However, I have my own version of what makes one happy and strong. It is not what one has or what one takes from life. Strength of character comes from what one *gives*. I was an integral part of the most honorable profession—teaching. I wouldn't trade one moment for all the money or fame in the world. I *gave* my heart and soul to education . . . to the future. I have no regrets. I wonder how many others can say the same? *What* you are takes precedence over what you *say* you are. I am, and always will be, a *teacher*.

CHAPTER SEVEN

The best theology would need no advocates;
it would prove itself.

-Karl Barth

I was told when I arrived in Hancock that there was a "different religion" that pervaded the town. Yes, there was, along with many different religions. Hancock, with a population of 860, had six churches within the city limits and an additional three churches in the immediate surrounding area. All churches were a denomination of the Lutheran Church and/or Baptist Church. There were no Catholic churches in Hancock. I came to discover that the church to which an individual belonged was the determining factor as to whom your friends were . . . and how you lived your life.

One of the strongest churches in the area was the Dutch Reform Church; 99% of its members were of the Dutch nationality. Working, play, recreation, etc. were all prohibited on Sunday: "Work on Sunday, Break down on Monday." This rule was not bent. I can recall when the father of a friend of mine wanted to use a piece of machinery from one of his neighbors. They, as neighbors, had traded machinery back and forth and helped one another out quite often. However, the piece of machinery (which was owned by a Dutch Reform member) could not be lent or used on Sunday if it was going to be utilized for work . . . even at a friend's request! This particular faction reminded me of the Finlanders near Frazee in that they really stuck by one another, and pity the individual who tried to win any election in which they were also a candidate!

Despite the strength in numbers of the Dutch Reform, nothing could compare to the strength of *thought* found in the

Apostolic Christian Church. Little did I know how greatly this group of people would come to affect my professional life . . . my personal life . . . my future.

The origin of the church dates back to the 1830's when a young seminary student in Switzerland experienced a Biblical conversion. Feeling "led of God", Samuel Froehlich, began preaching the simple truths of the Bible. Hence, the name "Switzers" became the pseudo-name for the followers of the Swiss-born religion which accords God the glory for all accomplishments. The Apostolic Christian Church established its presence in America in 1847 and, initially, the churches grew primarily in the fertile farming areas of the midwest. However, from the 1920's and on, most of the new churches formed in metro-politan areas because the church's offspring sought occupational op-portunities in areas other than farming. Yet, most of the larger churches are still found in rural America.

The Switzers in the Hancock and Morris area were extremely influential. They owned a great number of the main street busi-nesses in Morris. Additionally, they owned huge farms and placed great emphasis upon building successful family-run farms and businesses. Many of my students were from families of the Apos-tolic Christian Church. I had to learn to adapt to their belief sys-tem and how it influenced their customs, their actions, their judge-ments.

In order to understand the influence of the Apolostic Chris-tians on the school and community, one has to become familiar with their beliefs and customs. Much of my knowlege regarding their beliefs came from multiple sources: conversations with mem-bers, observations, their written doctrine, and through research reports by students in my classroom. According to the beliefs, an individual is not an official member of the church until baptism which generally occurs from seventh grade and on. Non-members and the young children are referred to as "Friends of the Church". The church believes in adult baptism or "believer's baptism" as opposed to infant baptism. As a new creature in Christ, the be-liever is expected to reflect the Light. Inward holiness is comprised of gentleness, goodness, meekness, and temperance (Gal. 5:22-23). Outward holiness is distinguished by restraint, discretion, and moderation in attire. Costly array (1 Tim. 2:9) and conformity to fancy and ridicuous styles in clothing are avoided. For the women, outward piety is reflected by a chaste, non-sensual appearance. They gather their long hair in a modest style and refrain from cosmetic enhancment and jewelry. Men, too, maintain an outward demeanor that is consistent with simplicity. They contend that a respectful appearance reflects a heart that is of spiritual sincerity.

Ministers of the church are not trained at seminaries or Bible colleges. The church feels that one's faith should not stand in the wisdom of men, but in the power of God. Worldly knowledge is not deemed important (1 Cor. 2:5; 1 Cor. 1:17). Therefore, the elder (bishop) and deacons are chosen from the congregations. It is they who serve as the administrators of spiritual matters and perform ministerial duties. However, it is the elder that is responsible for administering discipline in the assembly of believers.

Prepared sermons are not used for the worship service, but rather the Scriptures are opened randomly and used as the text. It is their contention that God knows much better than the minister what the congregation needs to hear. The worship is simple as is the singing—"cappella" fashion. The intent of the worship is not to entertain. Therefore, there are no individual soloists, no choral groups, and no instrumental accompaniment during the worship service.

Female members wear a veil during prayer and worship as a symbol of their submission according to God's order of Creation; male members pray with their heads uncovered. Additionally, men and women sit separately during regular worship services. Gender distraction is to be avoided. It is customary to have two worship services on Sunday. A noon lunch is served between the morning and afternoon service. Members attend both worship services as well as a Wednesday evening service.

A close fellowship is very precious to the Apostolic Christians. Members greet with a holy kiss (within their own gender). The church believes in the teaching of unity and oneness. Individualism is in conflict with the truths of a unified brotherhood. The Bible gives the church great authority, not only to "bind and loose", but to instruct and encourage. Believers are to keep the same spiritual judgements and walk according to the same rule. Discipline of erring members is administered for their own spiritual welfare. With regards to *Hope*: The goal is to reach the portal of heaven. The importance of material and earthly things, such as wealth, status, and ease will erode one's spiritual resolve. Therefore, affection is set on the things above, not on the things of the earth (Col. 3:1,2).

So, what does all of this have to do with me? Almost consistently throughout my teaching years, 50% of the Hancock School Board members were Switzers. Most of the remaining board members were employed by a Switzer. On the average, 25-30% of the student body was also Switzer. Did this have an affect on my teaching? As long as I stayed away from controversial subject matter, I met with semi-approval. I recall in my initial years of teaching, I made a mistake of talking about Karl Marx and his views on social classes. I simply commented that a governmental system in which there were no social classes had an element of merit. I was called a communist. I also know that the DARE Program received heavy scrutiny because the program colors (T- shirts) were considered to be "colors of the Devil".

I later realized that I should not have encouraged the students to strive to be individuals . . . nor commented on how remarkable they had become intellectually or personally . . . I should not have advocated that learners need to be "finders" of information rather than constant "receivers" . . . I should not have allowed them to see that teachers, too, are vulnerable caring individuals . . . I should not have professed the necessity for gender equalilty . . . and I should not have led them to believe that they have an inner strength and a capacity to make a difference in this world. I guess I was supposed to remind them that they are followers, pilgrims, strangers . . . not leaders, and that there is only one path . . . and it is a narrow one.

The "First Generation" Switzers (the Believers during my first years of teaching) were, in general, a very supportive group of individuals. They did "practice what they preached". This initial group of Apostolic Christians was very school-minded. They hardly ever missed a teacher conference. They also told me to call them if I had any problems with their kids, and they respected the discipline I maintained in the classroom.

How did the religion affect the students? Once an individual joins the church (baptism), they can no longer participate in athletics or any other form of competition. Prior to their baptism, many of my students excelled in extra-curricular programs and athletics. Interestingly, many of the parents were not allowed to witness their child's accolades because it was against the church doctrine to attend and witness competitive endeavors. Some of the students did postpone their formal entry into the church until after graduation. Yet, I noticed that the following occurances hastened their decision to join early: 1) An unexpected death, usually of a non-member; 2) If there appeared to be peace in the Middle East; 3) Signs that the world was coming to an end (the "world was coming to an end" many times during my teaching career); 4) Boyfriend-girlfriend problems; 5) Parental pressure; 6) When a powerful church leader visits (Kansas) and scares the "Hell out of them".

In the quest towards formal membership, the individuals are required to ask for forgiveness from anyone they feel that they may have sinned against and to make restitution. One of the local grocery stores made $150.00 from two boys who professed that they had stolen a great deal of candy over the years. I have been approached many times by would-be-members asking for forgiveness. I found it interesting that forgiveness does not have to be granted; the fact that it was requested is enough.

I noticed quite a difference between the "first generation" Switzers and the "latter group" (offspring). When it came to athletics, the latter group was much more opinionated. They also did not become as involved in their child's education at the school; yet, they became more critical of me and my teaching style. I only wish that this had been brought to my attention during teacher conferences, etc. However, less and less parents attended class functions and school conferences. Jealousy became more evident between the parents and between the students—especially with the females. Additionally, I noted that those youngsters who were about to become full-fledged members certainly did not hesitate to "sow their oats"—they knew how to party! The "First" group expected discipline and accountability, and they expected it of everyone . . . including their child. Many of the "latter" group expected it only of the teachers.

I highly respect the Switzer parents I came to know during my first years of teaching.

They exemplified qualities we deem necessary for the betterment of society: humility, compassion, and self-sacrifice. Yes, time changes . . . and people do too. I have attended the weddings and the funerals of their family members at their huge, modern churches; I have shared in the joy of graduation celebrations at their homes and ate the banquet meals that were "fit for a king"; I have painted their beautiful houses that would rival those seen in *Lifestyles of the Rich and Famous*; I have marvelled at their expansive farms which hailed only the finest of equipment; I have secured my money in their elite banking institutions; I have, undoubtedly, purchased many luxury items and sporty attire in their wonderous retail stores; I have substituted for them at "Parent's Night" because they would not attend the function with their child. I can call many of them *friends*.

I have come to the conclusion that religion should be an *experience of the heart and soul.* If the goal in life is to reach the portal of heaven, I believe the first step is to have a humble and compassionate heart. It is at this portal that our true heart will be fully revealed. The determination of entry will not be according to whether we memorized a doctrine, but rather by the *unity* of our heart and soul.

On the stage . . . masks are assumed with some regard to procedure; in everyday life, the participants act their parts without consideration either for suitability of scene or for the words spoken by the rest of the cast: the result is a general tendency for things to be brought to the level of farce even when the theme is serious enough (Anthony Powell).

I intend to greet my *friends* at the portal of heaven . . . I will not be wearing a *mask*.

*   Information on the Apostolic Christian Church and their *Statement of Faith* was attained from the following source: http://www.bibleviews.com/AC.html 9/28/99

CHAPTER EIGHT

If you achieve success, you will get applause,
and if you get applause, you will hear it.
My advice to you concerning applause is this:
enjoy it, but never quite believe it.

- Robert Montgomery

A true athlete is a good person on and off the field. In terms of athletics, Hancock had never been known as a sports-minded school. When I began my teaching and coaching career with the school, girls' sports were in the infant stages, and the boys were known for their achievements off the field (drinking, party-goers, etc.). My first challenge as a coach was in the sport of football. For the first few years, I served as an assistant coach under Dave Schoeck. Dave was a fine person through and through. Even though we had different philosophies on coaching, he and I remained friends throughout my years at Hancock. He earned my respect, and I believe he respected my coaching philosophy as well.

I can recall those first days of coaching football as if it were yesterday. The athletes showed up for practice when they felt like it, and they were as "soft" as freshly-baked bread. I quickly established some rules: An excused absence resulted in double conditioning, plus enduring a linemen's challenge "obstacle course"; an unexcused absence meant the same but the conditioning and obstacle course challenges lasted for one week! For the first time in their lives as an athlete, they were to be held accountable . . . they were each a very important link of the chain. Setting these examples definitely helped when the first day of school came around.

The word got out that I was tough but fair. Therefore, the stage was set for the classroom as well as the athletic field.

Giving a 100% effort is not a choice. As a coach, I had so many ideas that I knew would lead to a successful season. After a few years as an assistant football coach, I was assigned the head coaching position. Many challenges lay ahead! One of the greater obstacles was our facilities! The football game field was a disaster. It was "rough" to say the least. It had peaks and valleys, and the lighting system was designed for night baseball. In fact, the lighting system was so deficient, that our field was dubbed "candlestick park". We prayed for no rain because the bulbs would pop! Initially, the practice field was also supposed to serve as the game field, but this idea was abandoned a few years earlier because the field consisted of "fill": scrap metal, dirt and concrete, and weeds growing profusely! Ironically, I discovered that my coaching job description also detailed that the coaches were responsible for mowing the playing field, putting the lines down manually, and taking care of the priceless practice equipment: two blocking dummies! Eventually, the custodian assisted with mowing the field. However, he got angry at me about something and refused to mow the field. Guess who assumed the job once again . . . me. The administration was aware of this conflict, but did nothing about it. The word "crude" described the entire football program. I intended to change it all step-by-step!

To get beat physically is a part of life, but to get beat mentally is a disaster.

My first goal was to have the school hire an assistant coach that would help our team rise to the ranks. Little did I know that the person who was hired would end up being the finest friend anyone could ask for: Gregg Hills. He was a great friend and an offensive genius. He and I put together a playbook filled with offenses and defenses that many had not dared to attempt! Much of the offensive schemes were ones that I had known for years; some I had gathered from watching college/pro football on television; the majority came from my mind! Both the offense and defense were patterned after a blitzkrieg approach, and this would be my philosophy for all sports in which I coached . . . "Strike quickly, cripple your foe, and then . . . finally the *kill*." My first season as head coach was a dream come true; we finished 7-1, and the foundation for a successful athletic program was started. Following that first year, the name Hancock started appearing in the top ten in the state rankings. The program continued to progress to the point of winning a conference title, to playing in the section finals, and finally advancing to the state level.

Never envy anyone . . . be just like them. What was the key to our success? Number 1: Our practices were tough and discipline was demanded; Number 2: A weight program was instituted and we became stronger—mind and body; Number 3: The kids were made to feel special. We would have a season preview at the start of the season. The athletes would dress in uniform, and we would show the parents and fans a number of basic concepts. There were picture-taking sessions and, finally, everyone enjoyed a pot lock supper which was organized by the captains' mothers.

In the beginning, the fan support was sparse as Hancock was much more known for its baseball and boys' basketball teams. However, soon the fans came in droves . . . the football games were the place to be! The teams had come a long way because of discipline and pride. Gone were the days of "talking a good game" and party antics.

Some parents still tried to impress their children with stories about how "they used to do it . . . how we played the game . . . this is where we used to party . . . "They no longer impressed anyone. Records speak for themselves, and as I reminded my athletes and the "would've been, could've been, should've been" parents, "Excuses are like butts; everyone has one."

There can be no greater glory than to lay on the field of battle exhausted . . . but victorious. I have been asked many times as to what was the most memorable game? There were so many, but there is one that stands above the rest. It was a home game against our arch rival, Starbuck. It was for the conference championship and bragging rights—winner takes all. Starbuck had had many outstanding teams, and I considered their coach, Bill Bailey, to be the finest coach around and in the same league as two other exemplary coaches, Neil Hofland of Chokio Alberta and Keith Swanson of Hoffman.

Our home field was jumping, people stood in long lines waiting to get in, and the fans were packed ten-deep on the sidelines and in the end zones. The game was a see-saw battle and as dramatic as any Super Bowl ever televised. Starbuck had taken the lead late in the game, and with less than two minutes remaining, we scored to go ahead. I'll never forget the vision of our running back, Boyd Malo, disappearing into the throng of fans in the end zone. Victorious, our players walked into a maze of fans waiting for them in the gym. The players and fans shed tears of jubilation. They had become "someone" . . . they had "paid the price" . . . they were "winners".

People fail everyday, just don't be like them. Looking back, those were glorious times. I had two of the finest assistant coaches and friends that anyone could ask for, Greg Hills and later, Scott Carbert. The athletes worked hard for me, and I worked hard for them. Yes, I pushed them to the limit and beyond, but I was also there to give them a hug or words of encouragement when the times got tough. Hancock was no longer a school of "big talkers" but, rather, a school of "doers". We had a new field, a new lighting system, a new scoreboard and, finally, a team that was ranked Number 1 in the state the entire regular season. Additionally, I no longer had to mow the playing field (although, I still had to mow the practice field)! What made my coaching position even more memorble was when my son, Jerid, came to live with me when he was a teenager. I loved being a full-time father and being able to coach your child in a sport creates a bond that is indescribable! I felt that my life as a teacher, coach, and father couldn't get any better!

There were so many notable athletes that I was fortunate to coach. Athletes that exemplified "class" on and off the field included Rob Payne, Scott Carbert, Boo and Cory Schoeck, Jere Hanson, Shane Joos, Keith Hanson, Chad Nuest, Justin Thielke, Tim Kraemer, Chad Solvie, and many more. These boys not only had talent and commitment, they also knew that no one individual can be more important than the team. *There is no "I" in the word Team.*

Being average is no goal; average is as close to the bottom as it is to the top.

After the first few years coaching at Hancock, I knew that if we were to get ahead, our kids had to get stronger—boys and girls. We needed an organized weight program. The major problem was money. The school would not help with financing the program because the school board had other priorities, such as the music program. I felt so strongly about the concept of weights that I went and ordered $1200.00 worth of weights and, needless to say, I did not have the money to pay for them. I approached a couple of parents and professed, "You know what, we need a booster club." The fire was lit! We started off with 12 members and tried many fund-raising schemes. All along, I did not let them know about the weights until finally at a meeting, I brought up the idea of, "Success through Strength." They agreed to my goal and now I had the money to pay for the weights!

The next challenge . . . where could we locate the weight room? There was a small storage room (12' x 15') off the stage. It had nothing but junk from bottom to top. I transported seven pickup loads of junk out of that room! I went to the carpet store in Morris and purchased two pieces of remnants for $15.00. I installed the carpet and then I went to the art teacher and suggested a good class project for the class. They painted the walls with athletic pictures and slogans. I furnished the paint. We now had a full-fledged weight room. I was there at 6:00 am every school morning and from 7:00-9:00 at night to supervise the program. I did this for fifteen years—free of charge. Finally, in 1994, we were asked to find another place for our weight room. The Superintendent suggested we use the back part of the stage area, but we would have to build a petition to enclose it. Additionally, we needed a lock system. The big problem again was money. I formed an "All School Athletic Club" and we managed to raise $6000.00! The success of

22

the program convinced the school to chip in a small amount as well. We spent over $5000.00 on weights and replaced my carpet remnants with mats. It was impressive. Eventually, the program was taken over by the Community Education Program during the summer months. I was given the approval to hire two athletes to supervise the sessions. Three goals were accomplished: The weight program was year-round; the gym had to be open at the same time; my former athletes now had an opportunity to pick up a little money supervising the weight program!

You have to get off the steps if you want to run with the big dogs! In addition to coaching football, I also was assigned to coach track—boys and girls. Needless to say, the track program had a distance to go in order to achieve acclaim. Just to give you an example, at our first conference meet, we scored 2.5 points. The number of participants was low, and the talent was even lower! In fact, in the initial years, we brought our entire team to meets in a station wagon. Was I jealous of the teams who had thirty members or who scored a hundred points at the meets? No, I was not; I was determined to be just like them . . . only better.

Where does one start to build a program? I started by convincing a number of talented girls and boys that track would be the foundation for their other sports. They would gain strength, endurance, and discipline. I was totally confident in this belief. We were very fortunate in that a couple of my new track recruits were also leaders, and this is what Hancock had never had before. When these leaders took the first step, so did a number of their friends. We were now on our way. No, success did not happen immediately. It took a great deal of time; plus, the athletes had to see *proof* that track was instrumental in their other athletic endeavors. They saw it. The first three All-State Football players were track athletes; additionally, 70% of our All-State Football players were track athletes. The reciprocal benefits were even more impressive when it came to Hancock girls' basketball. Of the top ten career scorers, nine were also track athletes. Every girl from our school who was eventually selected to the Minnesota All-State Basketball team was a track athlete. As far as individual record holders, 97% of the record holders were track athletes. Records don't lie.

Be gracious when you lose . . . and humble when you win. One of my most cherished moments occurred while coaching track. I will never forget when we won our first conference title. Tears rolled down my face as the trophy was handed to our captains.

I saw visions of our humble beginnings when we scored only 2.5 points. I saw a team that practiced on an old dirt track with ruts, weeds, and pot holes and seldom complained. I saw a team that had to sell pizzas to raise money for uniforms and equipment. Again, one of the dreams I had for my track team was to see them advance to the state level. This came true as our girls' team in 1989 became the first Hancock team to place at the state level. An important point to remember is that our school, with an enrollment of 70-plus in the top three grades, was required to compete against schools with an enrollment of 400-plus in grades 10-12. Another memorable moment occurred when our boys' track team took 2nd in the District Meet with only five athletes scoring! When the photographer came to take the team award picture, he inquired, "Where is the rest of your team?" The team replied, "You're looking at it."

From our humble start as a "station-wagon" team, we grew to a combined 50-plus participants. The success was because of pride and individuals who were committed to personal and team growth: The Hansons (the parents as well as Keith, Boo, and Kim), Micah Grafenstein (also a collegiate runner as well as a Boston Marathon competitor), the Goll families, the Griener sisters, Shane Joos, Shawn and Shelly Nohl, Heidi Picht, Shannon Solvie, Lee Schmidgall, and so many more. However, the overall success of the track program was due to a willingness by the athletes to *go the extra mile—success starts in the heart.*

To the victor go the spoils. In 1996, a number of kids who were not volleyball players and who were runners kept asking if the school would ever have a cross-country team. I volunteered to coach it for the first year (no salary) until a coach could be hired. I saw it as a good extension for conditioning and as a prelude to the basketball program. In addition, I was already coaching football; therefore, I would simply utilize the entire practice field for both sports! I had it all figured out—I would schedule their early August practices after our morning football practice. Once school started, I would have the athletes in both sports go through the same calisthenics and agility drills, and then I planned individual running programs for each. The cross country meets were scheduled for Mondays, Tuesdays, Thursdays, or Saturdays. I managed double practices and attended the majority of the girls' meets between football commitments. I had excellent support from Steve and Connie Nuest who volunteered to transport/chaperone the cross country team when I was unable. In 1997, the school still did not have a coach, so I volunteered once again, free of charge. I purchased "Cross Country" sweatshirts for the team members. It was in this second year that we had enough members to compete as a team, and we scored very high in a number of high-powered meets. I bought awards to acknowledge their accomplishments and their initiative. It was my goal to bring this team to the state level. I had no doubt that this goal, too, would be attainable. *Believe.*

Small thoughts come from small dreams. Girls' Basketball. I basically "inherited" the title of girls' basketball coach at Hancock . . . it was a "why don't you fill in for a while . . ." offer. This "fill-in" assignment resulted in twenty years as head coach. When I met with the very first team, I immediately noticed that many were physically and fundamentally weak, and most of all, I noticed that being an athlete was not high on their list. Where does one start? Discipline and a solid work ethic were high on my list, being punctual, and giving 100% was a start! Surprisingly to many, we actually won a number of games that first year. However, I was not just concerned about the present state of girls' basketball at Hancock, I was even more concerned about the future. I knew that the program could not be built in a day and that the future depended on those kids in the elementary. Therefore, I went down into the elementary grades, introduced myself, and asked them to be a part of the future. We started a Saturday morning elementary basketball program. I supervised this program for ten years before turning it over to my varsity players. My contact with the younger kids was not just limited to Saturdays. I used to go through the lunch lines at school and single out those elementary players who wanted to help Hancock become renowned in basketball. I would check their muscles and tell them to eat their food so they could get big and strong. I would get them so keyed up that the elementary teachers dreaded seeing me come into the lunchroom!

The big turning point in our basketball program began with a young eighth-grade girl, Lois Schmidgall. I saw her as the young athlete that I would build our team around and, more importantly, she was the role model every coach looks for. She was a bright girl who was gifted both in the classroom and on the athletic field. More importantly, she had character. Her family had a large outdoor court, and she and her friends would turn on the outdoor lights, crank up the music, and play ball! I'd stop by their place and just sit and watch them enjoy playing the game! She was a leader and she was committed to excellence in all facets of her life. Her enthusiasm was contagious! What impact did Lois have? When she was a senior, a group of sixth-grade girls came into my classroom after school and asked which desk belonged to Lois. When I showed them where, there was a mad scramble for the coveted seat! Yes, the program was well on its way!

Someone is going to lose . . . make sure it's the other person. Our entire basketball program was built on speed and the ability to press and run for four quarters. This was our trade mark for twenty years. Even after the "Lois" era, we kept producing outstanding teams for many years to come. For ten years, we averaged over twenty wins per season. We won fifty-six conference games in a row, and we had an unbeaten streak at home of over sixty games! The keys to our success included our strength program, our hard work, our commitment, our discipline, and a string of great role models. Our press and style of play became infamous; we basically ran the other teams to death! Additionally, I expected the team members to be "quality" on and off the court. They were not al-lowed to argue with the officials; they had to give 100% every trip up and down the court; they were expected to maintain top grades academically. As a coach, I never made excuses, and I did not tol-erate it from the players either. We never said that it was a "re-building" year; we just said that we were "re-loading". I never had a young and inexperienced team because I felt that after one game they were all veterans.

Just because you don't feel well, they wouldn't stop the war. There is no doubt that we would have been undefeated during the regular season year after year if we had been resigned to playing our con-ference schedule. However, this was not our goal. Our goal was to play the strongest competitors, even if we lost. Therefore, we played schools who had a city population and school enrollment at least ten times greater than ours: Alexandria, Fergus Falls, and Moorhead. We also played the powerhouse teams of Tracy-Milroy, New Lon-don-Spicer, and Minnewaska. We loved those games because we would "turn up the heat" in more ways than one! We would run—run—run! Our game play was not much different than our prac-tices . . . run—run—run! We not only exemplified talent, we had style. When we came on the court, the fans said we reminded them of the Golden Gophers' basketball team with our flashy warm-up uniforms. Plus, our pre-game was a combination of the Harlem Globetrotters and Hancock flash. We captured the attention of the audience immediately and held it for the entire game.

If winning is not important, why do they keep score? We were admired by many teams, but hated by more. Yes, we were accused of "running up the score", but I can honestly say that this was not my intention. Our style was to press and to fast-break. The scores could get out of hand quite quickly. Coaches and fans from the opposing team could not understand why we would keep a star player in the game when the "writing was on the wall" for their team. My answer to these critics was fast and clear. My "star" play-ers had sacrificed a great deal to get to this point in their career. They had worked hard; they had spent a great deal of time and money at summer camps; they chose to put in extra hours of practice; they had *gone the extra mile*. Therefore, should I *reward* their efforts by jerking them out of the game and substituting a player who did nothing? Look at the message there: Let's reward everyone, regardless of effort and sacrifice. Sorry folks, my response instead is this, "Turn up the heat!" Oh, you say that it's not fair? Well then, maybe you should stop throwing the ball into your 6'2" center and I'll tell my 5'4" players to stop running.

Who were our "star" players? They were the leaders . . . the Picht girls, the Greiner sisters, the Dejagers, the Golls, the Versteegs, Shawn and Shelly Nohl, and Shannon Solvie, Lois Schmidgall, just to name a few. What did they all have in common? They knew they were no more valuable than the tenth player on our team . . . "team" came first to them. I think each morning they must have gotten up and said to themselves, "Today I'm going to do my best. I'm not going to take the easy road; I'm going to give 100%." It is this kind of commitment that distinguishes a "star" from a bench sitter.

Some people say, "We are just happy to be here . . ." a loser's comment. From day one, I was a "hands-on" type of coach. In practice, I was not a chalkboard artist. Until my weak knees made it physically impossible, I demonstrated the skills and would become another player on the team—defensively or offensively. Believe me, I have had many a coach who could "talk the game"; I knew that developing skill levels and confidence depended upon a coach who was willing to "play the game." The girls learned to be aggressors on the court! Many things enter into the development of confidence with the greatest factors being experience and success. Throughout my twenty years of coaching, I have had only one six-foot tall player. Our teams were always typically short in stature. Therefore, many times I became the six-foot opponent they would undoubtedly meet in the conference, sectional, or state game. Why not just practice a new maneuver against one of your same stature? That's not how you develop skill . . . that's not how you develop confidence . . . that's not how you achieve success. The girls never complained about me becoming another player during practice. In fact, the good ones demanded it.

What kind of relationship did I have with my athletes? They knew that gender was not a crutch. The female athletes were as capable as the male athlete. I asked one thing and that was for them to give 100%. They also knew that I would be there for them whenever they were in need, and was this ever tested! My role as a coach went way beyond description. An example that comes readily to mind is when two girls from our school got themselves in a precarious situation with some minority students at the University of Minnesota, Morris. One of the girls was a good basketball player; the other girl was not a dedicated athlete. The issue was first brought to my attention by the athletic personnel at the Univeristy. They gave me an indepth account of their *activities* with these boys. Our school counselor also knew of the situation, but indicated to me that she would feel very uncomfortable bringing it to the attention of the parents, especially one of the fathers. Interestingly, I received another notice about this issue via an anonymous letter placed under my classroom door. It explained in great detail the particulars of not just the event at the University, but many other incidents as well. I showed this letter to the counselor, but she continued to profess that she would rather not face the girl's father. Therefore, I wasted no time in addressing the issue with the girl. I simply told her that I would not hesitate to tell her father if she continued this course of action. I also spoke with the other girl. Their controversial activities ceased. All was back to normal.

When it comes to determining the "greatest moments" of the basketball program, I wouldn't know where to begin. The first District Championship would be high on the list as well as the Regional Championship over Perham which gave us the right to advance to our first state competition. Perham was loaded with talent and they dwarfed us with their size. I guess we wanted it more badly than they. Following our fourth trip to a state competition, a lifelong dream came true when we won the State Championship. When I close my eyes, I can still see each member receiving their gold medals. I can see the face of our student manager whom I gave my medal as she walked out to the center of William's Arena to receive her acclamation. She was a sixth-grader . . . she, too, represented the future.

Yet, the game that left an impact on me and everyone in attendance was our District title win over a very talented West Central team. They had beaten us earlier in the regular season, and on paper there was no doubt that they had the most talented team. We had only one senior on the team, with the rest being eighth, ninth, and eleventh graders. The annex was filled to the rafters; many came to see Hancock's reign come to an end . . . or so they thought. Yes, with three minutes remaining in the first quarter, it looked like we were headed home. Our talented point-guard, Shannon Solvie, blew out her knee. Her good friend and teammate, Caron Goll, rose to the occasion. She took charge of the game! She was unstoppable and basically "carried" the team until the unthinkable happened—with five minutes remaining in the game, Caron blew her knee out in the exact same spot on the floor as Solvie. When I walked out to look at Caron, the referee commented, "No one ever said life was fair." Our two stars were now wrapped in bandages and sitting on the bench. We were forced to use the eighth and ninth graders. The time-out was reminiscent of a funeral; the younger players were crying and the crowd was speechless. My comment to the team was, "No one has died; it's time to repay Caron and Shannon for all they have done for this team." A young ninth-grader, Gwen Greiner, gave the "thumbs-up" sign to the fallen soldiers, and took the game in hand. It was a great victory and a reflection of the success of our entire basketball program—commitment, dedication, sacrifice.

With over thirty-five championship titles encompassing the Conference, District, Region, Holiday Tournaments, and State level, one would think that *support* for the girls' basketball program would be "*a given*". Think again. There were so many negative comments about the girls' program from the top on down: "I thought they were supposed to be good" . . . "Girls sure do funny things" . . . "Girls can't handle pressure" . . . "The cheerleaders are just as good an athlete as your basketball players" . . . "If your girls keep lifting those weights, they're going to start looking like men" . . . "Those girls are going to be all flab when they get older" . . . Many of the negative remarks about the girl athletes came from the community, administrators, and also from a number of female staff (school) members. They did not feel that the girls should be told by a man (their coach) what to wear and what to look like (for games, etc.). I admit it, I did not want the basketball girls to wear makeup during the games or to wear fancy hairstyles. They were there to play the game, not impress the audience with fashion statements. The players did not have trouble with this request; some faculty members did. I was also advised by my female counterparts not to treat the girls on the team like boys, "You must know that girls get so emotional . . . don't yell at them, they'll cry . . . they can't take it." As far as I am concerned, the only irrational females I ran into were those trying to give me advice.

I wish more female faculty members would have chosen to be positive role models for the female athletes—to express support and affirmation. I viewed it as a total disgrace that these adult females had become so absorbed in the wonder of themselves that they couldn't see beyond their perceived self-image. Oh, if only mirrors could talk, I would surely ask, "Mirror, mirror, on the wall, who's the vainest of them all?" I already knew the answer . . . she was on staff.

I also know that our team would have appreciated greater support from the administration. I was a committed fan of the boys' athletic programs and followed the teams diligently; however, there were some noticable differences in recognition given to the boys. Many times the scores from the boys' games would be in the school bulletin, but not the girls' score. It was the girls that brought this to my attention. The praise and ceremonies for the boys greatly outshined that given to the girls. Come to think of it, I cannot remember being congratulated as a coach for winning a Sectional or State game. I can remember being told, "Boy, I bet a good B-Squad boys' team could beat a varsity girls' team." This challenge was "put to the test" and consequently "put to rest" . . . Catch my drift? It was never suggested again.

We had many great supporters over the years, but the best and most loyal had to be Jim and Gail Hanson. Their children, Keith, Kim, Carrie, and Kurt, were all dedicated athletes and, eventually, valuable friends to me. They would prove to be there when I most needed them. My heartfelt "thank you" would never be able to convey the gratitude I owe this family. The continue success of the program was also possible because of my assistant coach, Ken Grunig. He was also the band instructor as well as the coach of the seventh, eighth, and B-squad basketball team. I never had to give him "orders"; he, too, knew that the success of the team depended upon discipline and commitment. He was a valued friend and instrumental in our successes. However, during the last six years of my coaching career, an individual came into my life who came to be one of my best friends. Don Bulluyt entered the picture when there was an opening for a seventh and eighth grade coach. He took on the task and also helped me with my varsity practices. I had discovered that my mobility was declining because of poor knees; therefore, Don was "put to the test" during our offensive and defensive practice drills. He continued to fill any void we had from keeping stats, to summer coaching, to helping with transportation. Don was there . . . unconditionally. Later, too, when I needed a true friend, Don was there . . . unconditionally.

Yes, when I think of the faithful parents, I think of the Versteegs, the DeJagers, the Pichts, the Greiners, the Hansons, the Solvies, and so many more. But as the years went on and the expectations for success became even greater, a jealousy factor amongst the "newer-generation" parents became apparent. It usually started in volley-ball and carried over into basketball. Every parent thought their daughter should be the star, and if she wasn't, it was because I didn't give her the chance or because some other player was "hogging the limelight." There were even accusations that I favored some of the players because their parents gave me pork, beef, or milk! The most venomous critics were those parents who had never attained athletic success themselves. They tried to uplift their self-esteem by living their dreams through their children. It was not a healthy situation for the parent, nor the athlete. I can recall vividly Ken Grunig saying to me, "It sure is easier building a program than trying to keep one." It got harder and harder.

O beware of jealousy; it is the green-eyed monster which doth mock the meat it feeds on (Shakespeare). Yes, the green-eyed monster showed its ugly face within the ranks of my team prior to our state championship year. It all began when the Basketball News Magazine, statewide, ranked our team Number 1 in the preseason picks. Reporters from all arenas of the media wanted to know about my "Starting Five"—those five girls who had demonstrated noticable leadership and talent. I had always tried to give my entire team credit for its accomplishments, but statistics don't lie. The media wanted to focus on those five who had achieved statewide name recognition. To add "fuel to the fire", the state tournament sports' anchors dubbed the same group of girls as the "Iron Five" . . . tough, dependable, merciless! It was at this point, that some of the younger players (non starters) demonstrated a total lack of class by bad-mouthing the leaders and the starting five. I found it interesting that the girls who were expressing their envy were players I had not brought up to play at the tournament level or had openly displayed hatred of the concept of discipline. To top it off, one underclassman stated, "I hope the team does well, but I hope Gwen (our dedicated player) breaks her leg." Their words exemplified their lack of commitment to the team and demonstrated their true character. As Longfellow stated (*Hiawatha),* "All your strength is in your union, All your danger is in discord." Needless to say, the "Iron Five" and the remaining talented team members rose above it all to show what *commitment* and *character* can achieve. The *green-eyed* players had to be content with watching the victory from the bench, on television, or in the audience.

When I think about the media nicknaming the five girls "The Iron Five", it was actually quite appropriate. So many of my athletes and students had become accustomed to nicknames.

They had nicknames for one another (as well as me) and I dubbed them alias names as well. Some of my favorites were: "Shadow" (Heidi: She came out of the "shadows" to win—track); "Bird" (Shelly: she ate like a "bird"—thin, small-boned); "Silk" or "Down Town" (Caron: On the court, she moved effortlessly—"smooth as silk"; "Down Town"—named after Willie Brown, a pro player who shot from a long distance);

"Sudden Sam" (Sandi: Someone else had nicknamed her "Sam", but I added the "Sudden" because she could strike so quickly and totally devastate the opposition). We had many more nicknames that were used on and off the court, such as "Primetime", "Blonde", "Jo-Jo", "Gopher", etc. Did the names have a double meaning? Most of them were said in jest, to lighten the moment, to correlate with a pro-athlete's name, or to inspire.

We were always expected to be the best—regardless of the talent level—and it became quite a burden. The audience really became "experts" on coaching. . . . "Why didn't you do this. . . . ""How come she shoots the ball so much?" . . . "You sure didn't play very good, did you?" My favorite comment from a parent was this, "Well, you finally did it"; this was said prior to our fourth trip to the state tournament! Yes, we had created a successful basketball program, but we had created a *monster* in the process. In my last years of coaching, I found that I needed to distance myself from the parents and the celebrations. One reason for this became quite apparent when I commented (to a parent) following a great victory against a tough team, "I don't want to have to go through that again . . . "Her *respectful* response was, "You didn't do anything but sit on your butt." When I would encourage a athlete to "keep going", this particular parent would reply, "If it's so easy, you go out and do it." I wonder how any child in a family can learn the meaning of *respect* when a parent openly degrades coaches and teachers. In the end, I would always take a deep breath before walking into the gym and I would say to myself, "It's time to try and please them all again."

There were a great number of coaches that I came to admire

and respect during my years at Hancock, representing an array of schools and sports: Earl Steffens (Wheaton), Terry Coulhane (Tracy-Milroy), Mike Frisch (West Central), Ed Loeffler (Hoffman-Kensington), Arden Hyland (Minnewaska), Dick Simpson (Brandon-Evansville), Neil Johnson (Wheaton), and Gary Gillis (Storden-Jeffers). Did they all achieve state success? Some did, but that is not what impressed me the most. What I admire in a coach is leadership and commitment to the game. They all were professionals through-and-through. They loved and *lived* athletics. I also came to admire and appreciate "quality" journalism. When Kevin and Linda Simonsen were affiliated with the Hancock newspaper, it was "class" all the way. The same can be said of the sports' editor for the Alexandria Echo Press, Larry Halverson—top notch all the way.

A highly acclaimed professional coach once stated, "The primary challenge of coaching is to get people to do what they don't want to do in order to achieve what they want to achieve." How in the world does one accomplish this task? *Motivation.* This is the key to getting the best out of people. There is no basic formula . . . no magic hocus-pocus on motivating an individual. However, I do know one thing, when you expect only the best from an individual, you will seldom be disappointed. Why did I continue to coach for over twenty years? I truly loved athletics and I admired those individuals who were inspired to "go the extra mile". Was it for the extra paycheck? Well, look at it this way, after buying all of the awards for the end-of-the-year sports' banquets (out of my pocket) for twenty years, I had invested over $17,000.00 in acknowledging our athletes with trophies and etc. This "donation" came to be expected; I seldom received a thank-you. I averaged earning about 50 cents per hour for the time I committed to the girls' basketball program. No, it was not for the money.

The answer to the question, "Why Coach?", is perhaps best answered through this letter that I wrote to my athletes after they had won the State Championship title in 1997: "Words cannot describe the feeling . . . You have all been an extension of a great tradition that has been built for the past twenty years. Yes, it's true, but you carried it one step further; you dared to be the best and accomplished our goal. I must be the luckiest coach in the world. I have had the opportunity to be around the classiest athletes that Hancock has ever had. . . . Thanks for the memories." I considered them "family" . . . I was fortunate, indeed.

In the course of life, there will always be adversity. This is certainly true for those who choose to coach. I don't claim to be the best coach there ever was. I do claim that I gave my entire being to the art of coaching and to the athletes. Through it all, I discovered that "fame" is fleeting . . . records will be broken . . . there will be new heroes and heroines. However, there is one quality that cannot be replaced: *Character*. Horace Greeley provided a poignant reminder when he said, "Fame is a vapor; popularity an accident. Riches take wing; those who cheer today will curse tomorrow; only one thing endures—character."

CHAPTER NINE

He who has a thousand friends has not a friend to spare,
And he who has one enemy shall meet him everywhere.
                                        -Ralph Waldo Emerson

A note to the reader: It is at this point in our journey that I have chosen to refer to certain individuals by a designated alphabetic letter (letters have been randomly selected and have no intended relevance), rather than their real names. Why? There are a number of reasons: 1) I wish to protect my family from any further heartache or injustice; 2) I do not want to give these individuals additional "glory" in seeing their name in print; 3) My integrity . . . "to do injustice is more disgraceful than to suffer it" (Plato).

October, 1997. It was a Thursday morning. When I awoke, I did not feel well at all. I felt dizzy, short-of-breath, and I had chest pains. I attributed the symptoms to the fact that I had been feeling run-down, stressed out, and I hadn't been getting enough sleep. Actually, these symptoms were nothing new as I had experienced them before in the past two years and had even been hospitalized twice. I told myself that the continual expectations and challenges of teaching and coaching were just taking its toll, and I wasn't getting any younger. I went to school and began my day, as usual. However, by 10:00 am, the symptoms had not subsided; in fact, they had gotten so bad that I thought I was going to pass out. Therefore, I went to the office to see if anyone would take me to the hospital. The superintendent indicated that he would take me to the Morris Hospital.

This man, whom I considered a friend, had little to say. He dropped me off at the hospital and departed. However, I thought it very strange when he said, "When you come back to school, stop in and see me."

At the hospital, it was determined that I had heart-related complications, and I was to be transported by ambulance to Abbott-Northwestern Hospital in Minneapolis. Before I left, Mom, Dad, and my brother Tim, arrived. They were very concerned, as was I. At Abbott-Northwestern, I was put through a barrage of tests, and it was determined that I had a stess-related condition. I was given a medication that was supposed to counter the stress levels. Again, my parents and Tim, as well as my sister, Judy, and her husband, David, were there to offer support and reassurance. I was very worried about my health but, ironically, I was also thinking about my football team who had competed in a game that afternoon. I could not be with them. This weighed heavily on my mind.

At the suggestion of my family, as well as the medical personnel, it was determined that I should spend the next few days at my parents' home to try and regain my strength . . . and to be watched carefully in the event of medical complications. On Saturday night, I received a call from a former student, Shawn. She was crying and saying, "I don't believe what they are saying . . . My family doesn't believe it either . . . "I could not make sense out of what she was talking about. I particularly did not want to alarm my parents, so I did not ask any questions of Shawn. However, I thought about her comments all night . . . I couldn't sleep. I also knew that I needed to keep myself as calm as possible. I did not want a relapse and, consequently, another trip to the hospital!

On Sunday, I called my good friend, Don Bolluyt. He informed me that a girl, "Z", had accused me of an incident out on the practice field during cross country practice—an incident that she described as having sexual overtones. I was virtually speechless. I could not believe that anyone, especially "Z", would ever accuse me of such a thing. She was a student athlete who experienced a tough time in academics and athletics. Nothing came easily for her, and she struggled a great deal in both realms. "Z" was on the cross country team, and everyone knew that she truly disliked the sport. Why did she continue to participate in cross country? Was it because of pressure from home? I do not know. Throughout my years of coaching, I have come to realize that some parents put undo pressure on their children . . . to match their (self-professed) accomplishments or to achieve what they could not. This girl, in particular, appeared to live in the shadow of her mother who placed herself up on a pedestal. Another parent who is known for her Christian values confided that the reason "Z" was making such horrific accusations was because she wanted to get back at her mother. The mother of "Z" had been a student in my class. She had come from a wealthy family and, following her marriage to a man from Hancock, they both joined the Apostolic Church.

I guess it would be quite a strain for any young girl to try to live up to a mother's (or any parent's) heightened self-perception. Some of the other teachers also expressed concern about the emotional well-being of "Z". One teacher commented, "Have you noticed how strangely she has been acting? She just stares out the window and doesn't seem to care." I do know that I tried to encourage her, as well as the other athletes, not to be a quitter. Yet, she seemed to get so "down" because of her lack of success, and she did not hesitate to tell me about all her problems. I gave her as much attention as I gave any athlete. She, perhaps, wanted more attention.

I decided that I best head back to Hancock. After returning to my home, Don came by and we talked for hours. We talked of the past, the present, and the future. We both knew that accusations such as this, even when unfounded, can totally destroy a person's life. My concerns became even more accelerated when I received a letter from the school indicating that I had been placed on administrative leave . . . pending investigation. Investigation of what? My question was answered when I received a visit from the Hancock Superintendent, Principal, and counselor (she apparently wasn't too "uncomfortable" to face this controversy). When they arrived, they acted like they were attending a funeral and it was me in the coffin. They informed me of the accusations. My first response was that this had to be some kind of big mistake . . . a joke, right? I commented to the three visitors, "Those girls trust me with their life . . . "I was in a state of total shock. I looked at the three individuals confronting me, my *friends*, and I noticed that there was little support. They had become stones. I simply said, "No matter what, I will not cause any embarrassment to the school or to you." Some might view such sentiment as blind loyalty; call it what you may . . . that's how we were raised and how I lived my life . . . the value of loyalty is above rubies.

Where does one go from here? I was devastated over how this was going to affect my family . . . how should I tell my parents? However, I knew that the clock was ticking and I best concentrate my efforts on finding legal assistance. My first course of action was to contact the Minnesota Education Association (MEA). I, like most teachers, believed that the MEA/NEA (National Education Association), would be able to provide the legal advice and representation as provided through our liability insurance. I quickly located a pamphlet that we teachers receive each year regarding our guaranteed insurances. As stipulated in their "Certificate of Insurance" Coverage A-C: Coverage A—Educators Liability— $1,000,000 per member per occurence; Coverage B—Reimbursement of Attorney Fees for Defense of a Criminal Proceeding— $35,000; Coverage C—Bail Bond—$1000 per bond. I was under the presumption that the MEA/NEA would be there for me.

Think again.

The Regional MEA Service Representative informed me of my legal rights and advised me not to talk to anyone. I was also informed that the MEA would pay for legal costs **IF** the attorney I used was affiliated with or endorsed by the MEA and **IF** I was cleared of all charges. I scheduled a meeting with one of their endorsed attorneys. At the initial meeting, he looked at the charges which he described as "flimsy", and proceeded to ask for my side of the story. I indicated that I could not understand "Z's" accusations. I tried to explain the incident from my perspective. The alleged incident had reportedly happened on a Monday. The cross country team was stretching-out on the field during a joint practice session with the football team (approximately 30 athletes). "Z" had acted extremely depressed in school that day, and she was behaving very despondently at the practice as well. She, along with all of the others, was sitting on the ground stretching her muscles. I came up behind her, touseled her hair, and said, "You just need a little lovin". This is a comment that has been said to me by the players when I was having an "off" day, and I was known for saying it back to them as well. After the comment, I gently pushed her head with my hands to signify that she should "snap out of it" and get ready to practice. I then said, "Just forget it . . . it will get better." I walked away. I proceeded to talk to both the girl and boy athletes on the field and tried to "fire them up" for practice. I am not known for trying to "baby" any athlete; if this is what "Z" wanted from me, she was sadly disappointed. I was not going to let her mood swings (or anyone else's) deter me or my team members from accomplishing the goals at hand. However, even after her "accusations", I couldn't help but pity her. When I told the attorney that there was no way that I wanted to put "Z" on the spot or ridiculed, he said, "Just forget that thinking; she's out to get you."

I left the attorney's office feeling confident that I at least was going to be represented. When I returned to Hancock, there was an overwhelming amount of supportive calls, messages, and visits. The support came from all directions: students, parents, athletes, former acquaintances, former students, area coaches, and community members. The captains of the football team, on their own initiative, came to my home. Another student stopped by to deliver sub-sandwiches that I had bought earlier from a club that was trying to raise funds. I did call two members of the cross country team to give them a workout for the weekend. The team was preparing for the Sub-Sections, and they had no coach . . . they did not know what to do (Remember, the cross country coaching position was not salaried). I kept telling myself that this would all work out . . . "Z" would realize that the attention was not worth the deceit . . . I still had confidence that there exists an inner goodness in all of us . . . *character* will prevail.

Friday morning. My brother, Tim, had come down to do some pheasant hunting with me. I had alerted him to the accusations.

He, too, had shook his head in disbelief. Following the morning's hunt, we came back to my place to have some lunch. As we looked out the window, the Sheriff's car pulled into the driveway. Two officers came to the door and said that they had a warrant for my arrest. I cannot recall being read my rights, nor told why I was being arrested. They took me to the courthouse and proceeded to book me . . . fingerprints . . . pictures . . . etc. To further the degradation, they handcuffed me to the wall while they went to dinner. Finally, they told me that I was being arrested for trying to influence witnesses, or as they said, "Get to them . . . "They informed me that I was to appear in court, but because of the upcoming weekend, a judge might not be available. However, they found an available court in Willmar and I was scheduled to appear in two hours. My first concern was how I could get my attorney there in time for the court appearance. He was in Detroit Lakes—three and a half hours from Willmar! I called the MEA Representative and he lined up an attorney from New London Spicer (twenty minute distance from Willmar) to represent me. I also managed to call Tim to tell him what was going on and where I was headed. The officers cuffed me and we headed to Willmar.

When I was escorted into the courtroom, my newly appointed attorney was waiting for me. He had a copy of the charges ("Z") and the latest alleged infraction, "Influencing Witnesses". I asked myself how in the world could I be charged with influencing witnesses? The only explanations I could find were that the charges must have been filed due to the voluntary visits from the Hancock football team members and the individual who delivered my submarine sandwiches, as well as the suggestions I had given some of the cross country team members regarding their continued workouts. Interestingly, these individuals had nothing to do with the case. My attorney looked at me and stated, "You'll be ready to coach basketball by the next season." It was quite apparent that the female assistant prosecutor had other plans for me. She tried to portray me as the most powerful person in the world as she explained to the judge the state championship and the "power" I held. If I had believed everything she said, I would have thought myself to be "God on earth". My attorney argued that I had an excellent reputation in the community and that I was on paid leave from the school. He assured the judge that I would have no contact with the kids, etc. I was unaware of the stipulation that I had been prohibited from having any form of contact with students. I was hearing it now.

The judge released me on a number of conditions: no contact with students, no leaving the state, etc. My brother, Tim, was in the courtroom witnessing the proceedings. As we were leaving, he said to me, "Get your bags packed; we're getting out of town. These people are out to get you and nobody can be trusted anymore." I could not believe it had come to this point. Every teacher and coach realized that there had been a recent *epidemic* of accusations nationwide by students against teachers, coaches, clergy, daycare providers, etc. It was in every newspaper, television, and portrayed in movies. I now was a part of the *epidemic*.

I asked Tim to drive ahead of me and forewarn Dad. My biggest fear was telling my mother. How does a son confront their parents with news such as this? They had been supportive parents and supportive fans of the Hancock School as well as the athletic program. They were infamous for their sportsmanship and their devotion to the Hancock athletes. They had not hesitated to drive hundreds of miles in blizzard-like conditions to show their support for my teams; they had acted as sponsors for many of the girls; they had given the entire team money to buy lunch following championship games; they had opened their home to visiting athletes, parents, and administrators from Hancock; they had attended the graduation celebrations as well as the weddings of Hancock students. Mom and Dad greatly admired the athletes and families they had become acquainted with, and they considered them to be family. They would be devastated to hear what had just transpired. How could I tell them that we were about to enter *Sudden Death, Overtime . . .* and this was no game.

CHAPTER TEN

When sorrows come,
they come not single spies,
but in battalions.

-Shakespeare

Longfellow professed that *some days will be dark and dreary . . . into each life some rain must fall.* The *storm* in which I found myself could only be described as torrential—turbulent, sudden, and overwhelming. I no longer faced the potential destruction from just one girl's accusations but, rather, a deluge of charges . . . coming from all directions . . . and more unbelievable and devastating than the original ("Girl Z").

Following the report to the Stevens County Sheriff's Dept. on October 9, 1997, by the Hancock School Counselor of the possible incident of sexual contact involving "Girl Z", I discovered that during the dates of October 13-23, at least fifteen additional students had been interviewed by the County Sheriff and Social Worker at the school or at the Sheriff's Department. Following are excerpts from the voluntary (documented) statements by some of the girls in which they cited instances where I allegedly demonstrated sexual intent or misconduct; documented questions by the County Sheriff and/or Social Worker are also noted:

"Girl Z": "He comes up behind me and he put his two legs on the sides of my shoulders . . . he's leaning over, kind of . . . and he starts rubbing his . . . his dick . . . against my back from my-right by my head to probably the mid-part of my back . . . He was just rubbing it up and down and over . . . "(allegedly during

cross country practice while the girl was sitting on the ground stretching out. . . . in the presence of the entire football team and cross country team)

(Question): "And when he was rubbing and going back and forth, about how long do you think, time wise, that this occurred? Was it seconds, or a minute, just an estimate I think."

(Response): "I would say, together, it was about a minute and a half or something."

(Question): "Is this something that happened to you before or anybody else on the cross country team?"

(Response): "It's not exactly, it has happened to us before . . . we'll be sitting in our desk, straight, you know, look like this, and he'll come up behind you, in your desk, and he'll also rub his dick against his-your back . . . and just start massaging you and rubbing against you and everything."

(Question): "Getting back to the incident that happened last Monday, and again you indicated that his penis was probably erect, you're pretty sure, and the same kind of thing is happening in the classroom as well?"

(Response): "Yeah."

". . . there's like two girls in my school and me, he has done the same things to . . . just a tish different, but they're exactly the same, and we've been talking about that . . . we were discussing it and they agreed with me that he's done the same things to us all."

(Question): "I have a couple of questions that come to mind. What did Coach Courneya have on, what was he wearing ?" (*Referring to alleged cross country incident)

(Response): "Some tight sweat pants and like a t-shirt or a sweatshirt. I can't remember."

(Question) ". . . you mentioned that you could tell that his penis was hard. You could feel that."

(Response) "Mmm, hmm."

(Question) "Could you tell in the classroom?"
(Response) "Yeah."

*Note: "Girl Z" went on to profess that due to the alleged cross country incident, she was crying. A few days later, a teacher, "P", noticed she was crying (in the classroom) and engaged her in a conversation. Consequently, the incident was brought to the attention of the counselor and the report was filed.

"*Girl Y*": ". . . and like, okay, one time like last year or whatever, I was wearing a tighter shirt and he was like 'a little nippy', I don't know what he meant . . . you know what I mean. He always just like relates to something else perverted . . . "; ". . . he called me the night before I went to the hospital and he was like telling me how, I don't know—well he, 'cause I had nose—I broke my nose, and he asked me how it was . . . and then he was like, 'well, you'll still be gorgeous no matter what, you know.' It's not his place to tell me this stuff."; ". . . yeah, he rubbed me once in a desk, that I can remember. I can't even remember all the times"; "Like my parents knew he was perverted, you know."

"*Girl X*": "Well, this year like last year towards the end of the year, I don't know, he just totally started ignoring me"; ". . . he like played defense on us (describing a basketball practice session) . . . and he would play defense on us and then we would—he'd like be standing there in the defense position and we would have to go like-kind of sit on his knee . . . yeah, he was kind of like squatting and we were like squatting and pushing against him to like get up to the bucket . . . I just felt like his leg was always in my crotch area . . . "; ". . . he'd like push against you so that you'd have to use power. I don't know if he was doing this for, you know, his joys or what . . ."

"*Girl W*": ". . . he'll come and grab my arm . . . feeling your muscle or whatever . . . he'll like his fingertips would be rubbing, you know, the breast part"; ". . . he's like, 'you're an exceptional person, athlete,' just stuff like that . . . he's like, 'you have a lot going for you, you're really talented, you're beautiful'. . . ."

"*Girl V*": "Yeah, yeah just comments like, 'oh, you're looking nice today' or I mean, he looks—like when he says it, he's looking up and down so you know he's—I mean, some people when they say it they mean it just in a friendly way, but I'm sure he's meaning it in a friendly way too, but I mean just the way he looks, I mean—"

"*Girl U*": "Yeah, I was sitting on the ground stretching out like bringing my head down . . . and he just came up behind me and grabbed my neck . . . I was trying to get forward so *it* wouldn't touch me."

(Question): "Did his groin area actually touch your back or your head area?"

(Response): "Yeah."

(Question): "When these incidents occurred, whether it was in the classroom, when he accidentally brushes your breast or intentionally, we're not sure, he probably intentionally does, . . . how does that make you feel?"

(Response): "Very uncomfortable."

(Question): "And you girls, have you talked about how that makes you feel among yourselves?"

(Response): "Yeah."

"*Girl T*": "He always—like I wasn't really good at basketball right away and he liked to come and tell me like how I'm supposed to shoot the ball and just show me how, putting his arms around me and everything."; . . . "He'd make you look like a total fool. I mean, during class he'd say something and you wouldn't know the answer or he would just totally ignore you and just—you felt like, dumb I guess."

(Question): "And also, I assume he could probably affect what happens on the basketball court as well?"

(Response): "Yes. Yeah."

(Question): "Maybe he doesn't come out and say that, but does he
     imply that somehow or -?"
(Response): "You don't get to play as much."

The accusations went on and on and on. I could not fanthom
where their dillusions came from . . . nor the physical impossibilities of some of the charges. Was it just my imagination or did the
questions from the County (Sheriff/SocialWorker) "lead" them in
a particular direction (take note of the questioning technique . . .
who was providing some of the information . . . the girls or the
interviewers?)?

The real question was why were they making these accusations? All I could surmise is that these girls (or their parents) must
have an axe to grind . . . or maybe they were enthralled with the
psycho-sexual stages described by Freud! I stand nearly six-feet tall
in stature. If a girl is sitting on the ground, stretching out, and I
am standing behind her as they claim, it would be physically impossible for my groin area to touch her in the back. I am not a
contortionist nor a midget! Additionally, I do not have the capabilities of Spider Man. How in the world could I fit between desks
that are separated from one another by two- to- three inch gaps (at
best) and fit myself and as they described "my erection" between
the slats of the desk chairs and "rub . . . push" them in their
backs . . . and in front of an entire classroom? When I read the
charges, I was astounded, dismayed, and embarrassed. The girls
described in detail my physique when I wore "*tight sweatpants . . .
erections during practices and during track meets . . .*" If I had known
that I was to become an object of imaginative thought, I would
have confessed to my athletes that I actually wore a protective
athletic cup during practices . . . or perhaps, I should have worn a
trench coat to veil all thought! Their descriptions of my so-called
sexual intent were as vulgar as any I had heard.

The newspapers were quick to pick up on the sensationalism
as well. The St. Paul Pioneer Press and Minneapolis Star Tribune
ran some very *picturesque* articles. The headlines, alone, were very

incriminating . . . **Town Talk in Hancock Revolves Around Accused Coach.** One that particularly stands out in my mind read, **Hancock, town of 800, abuzz after coach charged**—*Rumors of sexual misconduct heard for years* (October 20, 1997). The first paragraph of the article read, *For much of the past two decades, people in the little town of Hancock have heard rumors about their well-known coach and his female students* . . . and a quote from a Hancock resident (paragraph three), *"You couldn't really say you were too surprised, because you heard that those things were going on, but you really never knew to what extent."* The district attorney added comment to the article with his encouragement to individuals with more information to call the Sheriff's Department and his following comment, "Not only do they know the person, but he is in a very prominent and powerful position. "The Sheriff also added an interesting conclusion to the article, "He's certainly well-known in other districts as well," he said, "due to his success in sports." Statewide, the newspapers kept me informed of the turn-of-events of my case.

I found it quite amazing that the media knew the *facts* before I did . . . where and from whom were they getting the information? As summarized by an individual (former journalist) residing in Stillwater, MN, in a letter to my family (October 23, 1997), "Here's that terribly misleading 8-column front page banner headline story on Dennis (*St. Paul Pioneer Press*) . . . Somebody in Hancock must want to destroy Dennis . . . somebody must know a reporter . . . this big, sensational item is enough to serve as judge, jury, and hangman to the public. How can a man get a fair hearing after this story? So sorry to see this 'yellow' journalism."

To add to my turmoil, I was also having great difficulty with my legal consul. As mentioned earlier, I entrusted the Minnesota Education Association (MEA) with providing my due legal representation. However, there were so many times that I could not get in touch with anybody who knew anything! More often than not, I would be put "on hold" or told to leave a message . . . I would wait all day for a response. When I did receive a reply it was to be informed that they were out of the office. I learned to never call on a Friday . . . they were out of the office until Monday. As the legal charges against me accumulated, I felt it became extremely difficult to get in touch with anyone from MEA legal services! Interestingly, my first MEA endorsed attorney left on a hunting trip during the stage when my case became classified as a "criminal" case. With the onset of a November pre-trial date, I found I was without an attorney at all! An assistant attorney took over my case, but he made me feel like I best find a window to jump out of . . . and it better be a high one. Again, I was reminded by the MEA legal staff that the only way I would receive repayment of my legal costs (and only a portion thereof) was if I won the case and was cleared of all charges. I knew I needed legal assistance quickly and with consistency. That is when I turned away from the MEA services and to the public realm.

My family and I went on a search for an attorney who would represent me to the end. My sisters, Judy and Julie, searched via the yellow pages and advertisements for a criminal attorney . . . and we selected a Twin Cities firm that had experience and success with cases such as mine. I now had legal consul . . . a chance. However, my new founded legal representation was going to cost me. The fee agreement which I entered into with the Law Offices of Kurzman, Grant and Ojala required me to make a down payment of $20,000.00 which would be applied to the hourly fees for legal services rendered. In the event the down payment was used up and there was additional work to be done, we committed to the premise that we would forward additional increments of $5000.00 as requested. When Court proceedings were scheduled, we agreed to forward an advance of $2750.00 for each anticipated "hearing/trial" day as requested by the law office. We were informed that the legal representation would probably cost $20-30,000.00. As I listened to the quote of costs, I thought to myself, *I wonder exactly how much money I had paid to the MEA/NEA in twenty-two years of monthly dues? I was under the impression that teachers would receive legal representation, if necessary, from our union . . . if not, what purposes were the monthly dues?* Well, no time to lament about wasted money . . . We wrote the check.

November was to be the month of the pretrial or omnibus

hearing followed by the trial in February (1998). However, there came to be a series of postponements . The trial originally scheduled for February was pushed back to April; the pretrial was now scheduled for February. I received notification of the postponements via a friend who had "heard" it . . . the media again. The reason given was that the girls (accusers) would be involved in tournament play during the late winter months, and it would be too much pressure for them to also deal with a trial at that time. In other words, it appeared to me that the athletic program took precedence over the legal process. Being a History teacher for twenty-two years, I had taught the basic concept of the U.S. Constitution and the basic rights of a *speedy trial by jury* and *one was innocent until proven guilty.* With the postponements, the continual media coverage, and my professional/personal life torn completely apart, I felt that my inallenable rights were being denied. I continually wondered *why* the accusers were making such atrocious accusations . . . Were they being coached? . . . Was it the sole action of one student affecting the thoughts of the others? . . .

Was the administration, or some faculty members, trying to open old wounds or hoping to appease those in a position of power? . . . Did someone want to make a name for themself? . . . Were the accusations riddled with jealousy? . . . Did the relationships among the accusers themselves promote similar thought (One of the girls was a cousin to three other accusers; two sets of accusers were sisters; five accusers were children of Apostolic parents or affiliated with that church)? . . . Was there a more *powerful* force behind it all? All unanswered questions.

After the additional charges became media headlines, I felt that there were few people whom I could actually trust. Therefore, I decided to move from Hancock and live with my parents in Frazee until the nightmare was over. I'll never forget the day that I locked the door and departed. I had spend twenty-two years in Hancock— it was my home—and now I was leaving and not because I felt I had a choice. My good friend, Don Bolluyt, my son, Jerid, Dad, and my brother, Tim, and his sons assisted me in the move. People from the town would drive by in their cars . . . but no one stopped, except two individuals: Larry and Marsha Picht. They were parents of three children whom I had taught and coached . . . they were a part of the "rags to riches" era of the Hancock athletic program. They dared to drive up and wish me well. They were true friends . . . *class* all the way. I will never forget their goodness of heart. At that point in my life, it meant more than I could ever convey. It was people like them who gave me the strength to endure.

I was to face another challenge, and it concerned my livelihood, my occupational status. When the initial charges surfaced, I was placed on administrative leave. It was my understanding that I would be on paid salary from the school until the trial was concluded . . . after all, we are innocent until proven guilty . . . right? I would find out that this was another fallacy or dillusion of our legal system. I was notified that the school was seeking to terminate my position at the school. I thought of the countless hours I had put in at the school with athletics, teaching, volunteerism, parental conferences, painting, building, chaperoning, donating materials, etc. I was not even given the benefit of the doubt . . . they wanted me gone.

I was particularly dismayed with the apparent attitudes/actions of the two administrators. I had considered them to be friends of mine; I respected them. One administrator was a good friend to my parents, and he had even sat at our family table sharing lunch. I knew that other faculty members felt that they had been treated unjustly by the administration. Two examples that come to mind include the teacher who was "pressured to leave" after she had received a divorce (she was no longer a good role model . . . "rumors" about her misconduct). The other example concerned one of the most successful coaches in the entire state, the Hancock Wrestling Coach. He was "forced out" because some members of the community felt that some of his tactics were not appropriate. Ironically, the multiple wrestling awards and statewide acclaim were "appropriate" . . . yet, he was not? He was a superior coach who helped the athletes develop into tremendously talented wrestlers. Inappropriate, I guess.

Despite the cited instances of unfair judgements, I felt that the animosity of the administrators towards me had to have deeper roots . . . were they feeling the *heat* to get rid of me and from where? Was it a financial decision (a bond issue was on the upcoming November ballot and a great deal of money had to be generated)? . . . A personal issue (one of the accusers had a parent serving on the Hancock School Board)? . . . A religious concern (five of the accusers had parents/relatives who were either members of the Apostolic Church or Friends of the Church. The Hancock School Board was also comprised of Apostolic Church affiliation)? . . . Was it an "inside" move (my basketball coaching position was not given to the man who had been the assistant coach for fifteen years and who was also the highly successful B-team coach.)? Yes, the position of head basketball coach was given to the volleyball coach (she wasn't a Hancock teacher nor a basketball coach). However, she was the wife of a school board member. Everyone was aware that the upcoming group of basketball players had more potential than any previously. I foresaw multiple state championships for them in the future . . . talent galore! What an opportune time to take the helm! I dismissed all of the above notions regarding the "why" of my dismissal. I gave them the benefit of the doubt . . . blind loyalty again.

I, once again, contacted the MEA to at least represent me in retaining my job at the Hancock School. Through correspondence with MEA officials, I was informed that even if I was acquitted of all charges, the school could still terminate my position due to probable cause. Yes, the MEA would back me, but I was left with the impression that I should seek another solution. Advice came from all directions . . . "Fight it" . . . "Make them pay through their nose" . . . "You are entitled" . . . The reality was that I was not raised to take advantage of anyone; I was not going to lower my standards to meet their level of disregard. The greatest factor influencing my decision to resign my position was that I had given my *word* to the superintendent (the day of the administrative visit to my house informing me of the initial charges) that I would not take advantage of the school and would bring no shame to the school. Therefore, I asked for my salary including health benefits up through the 1998 school year. They countered with an offer to pay salary through the summer of 1998 and no coaching salary beyond the month of January. One coaching check I would not miss was the cross country coaching salary . . . there was none!

(Ironically, the following year, a salaried cross country coaching position was created).

The ramifications of my professional decision were far reaching. In three years, I would have been able to retire with all the retirement benefits I deemed necessary. I was also aware that if it all ended badly, I would never teach again . . . the vocation that I gave my heart to . . . my soul. What do I have to help me remember those precious years of teaching and coaching? The students . . . the parents . . . the school . . . the town. With just a signature on the dotted line, I gave it all away . . . everything but the memories. They will never die. It is because of the good memories, the good people, that I can still close my eyes at night and re-live the life I loved. Nothing and no one can take that away from me. To teach is to touch and be touched by *eternity.*

CHAPTER ELEVEN

Preach to the storm, and reason with despair,
But tell not Misery's son that life is fair.
- H. K. White, Lines on Reading . . .

George Granville stated that *patience is the virtue of an ass . . . that trots beneath his burthen . . . and is quiet.* I knew one thing and it was that I was going to face this crisis head-on. If they expected me to hide under a rock, they were sadly mistaken.

I had found myself a reputable attorney; I had the support of hundreds of friends and acquaintances—from all walks of life; I had family members who vowed to stick with me to the end. What did we all have in common? We knew the *truth*. However, the challenge of the moment was maintaining patience. Waiting for the omnibus hearing (pretrial), seemed like eternity . . . this *eternity* had already suffered two postponements.

I was anxious to get this nightmare over and done with—to get on with my life. This was not to be the case.

The omnibus hearing took place on February 2, 1998, with both attorneys (my attorney and the County Attorney), the County Sheriff, court reporters, and a few spectators (newspaper reporters?) in attendance. Prior to the hearing, I had met with my attorney (Kurzman) in a private room. His initial response was, "If the judge had any guts, he would throw out this entire case." I liked Kurzman's style . . . his candor . . . his intelligence . . . his respect for my innocence. Yes, I knew that I was paying a great deal of money for his presence; yet, he was a true professional. His *confidence* in me and my innocence could not be *bought*. He believed in me and I entrusted him with my future.

Both sides met in the courtroom and there was a huge amount of "legal" talk. I felt like a bystander . . . watching a television drama. I could not help but notice the difference in the two attorneys. Kurzman was knowledgeable, efficient, and confident. He would site legal precedents that even appeared to take the judge by surprise. In comparison, I did not find the prosecuting attorney (County Attorney) to have an impressionable demeanor. He appeared to be a direct opposite to Kurzman's style and confidence. Yet, I knew he had probably achieved much in his life . . . and this case was as important as any for his continued success. I did have the impression that he and the judge seemed familiar with one another. Perhaps this judge had presided over other cases in which this attorney had been involved . . . Maybe . . . Maybe not.

Kurzman tried to get a number of requests granted; for example, diaries of the accusers were requested, and he moved that the case be dropped due to the fact that no intent was evident, etc. It seemed, however, that his requests were denied even before he could finish his sentence. At times, the attorneys would joke amongst themselves . . . this bothered me a great deal. I felt like they didn't even know I was in the room . . . did they not understand the severity of the situation . . . was I just another pawn in the legal game? I listened to comments by the opposing attorney and I could not believe that I was being referred to so negatively. It was at this pretrial that I entered my plea, "Not guilty."

Again, if I wanted to review any of the court proceedings, all I had to do was turn on the television or read a newspaper. The accounts of the pretrial hearing were headlines . . . statewide. The Morris newspaper, as well as others, had a comprehensive summary, of course, with the Stevens County Attorney providing comment. I don't claim to be vain; however, the pictures of me that were used to accompany the storylines made me look like an escapee from Alcatraz . . . after a long swim. At that time, I was sure glad that the jury pool would not be chosen from the reading area. . . . right? But wait . . . where would they find jury members who had not read the newspapers statewide . . . newspapers that capitalized on the accusations . . . ? Where would they find fair and impartial jurors who had not seen/heard the television reports which, again, focused on the accusations?

The trial would have to take place where I would be guaranteed an element of fairness . . . out of the county. Right? Think again. The issue of moving the trial out of the county became critical. The motion was made by my attorney. Letters were written by community members testifying that I could not receive a fair trial due to all of the media coverage. In an affidavit, a teacher from Hancock professed the following, "I volunteered my view that it would be improbable for Mr. Courneya to have a fair trial in Stevens County. This is due to a number of factors, including a great deal of prejudicial pretrial publicity, the strong sentiment and preconceived notions which have developed in this region, and the rumors and gossip which have run rampant about the matter. It would definitely be prejudicial to Mr. Courneya if he were tried in Stevens County, as opposed to another county. At my mother's workplace, people have talked about the pro-prosecution publicity and bias in Stevens County as well, and people have expressed their view to my mother that if Mr. Courneya was to receive a fair trial, it would have to be in another county." A motion was made for a change of venue: MN Crim. P. 2502 Subd. 3—massive publicity can give rise to a presumption of prejudice. *Sheppard v. Maxwell,* 384 U.S. 333, 1966. Denied . . . Denied . . . Denied. The trial would take place, as scheduled, in the Stevens County Courthouse, Morris MN . . . approximately eight miles from Hancock. Apparently, potential juror members do not read newspapers . . . they do not watch television.

With two months to go before the trial, I thought that I had endured all the adversity and negative media coverage there would be . . . for a time, anyway. I was wrong. Prior to the start of the basketball tournaments, I had written a good luck letter to the Thielke family: Tony and Tracy Thielke—Hancock Public School-

(Contents)—*Tony and Tracy* -

I just want to wish you and your team the best of luck in your tournaments. I've followed both of you and your progress this past season and I'm so proud of you both. Yes you both held a dream in your hearts in 96-97 and your dream came true. Take each game as your last and everything will turn out great. You both are class acts and I wish you only success. No matter what happens, hold your head high, you are Thielkes!!

Say hi to both your mom and dad, and Tony—pull your dad through, he's just a rookie!

Coach Courneya

Tony and Tracy were both seniors at Hancock, and their father, Randy, not only was a good friend of mine, he was also experiencing his first year as coach of the boys' basketball team. Randy and I had played college football together and, later, he had been my assistant football coach for five years. Randy, his wife, and his children meant a great deal to me . . . they were some of the finest people you would ever meet.

I sent the letter to them at the Hancock School because I did not have their home address.

Apparently, someone at the school intercepted the letter and the Sheriff was called to the school. Consequently, the letter was not opened until the parents, the Sheriff, and the administration were in attendance. I heard about the "letter issue" while attending a college basketball game. Randy's wife came and sat by me and told me what had taken place regarding the letter. She mentioned that they thought it was such a nice letter and with such fine intentions. She commented, "We don't want you to think we had anything do do with it. It was such a nice gesture on your part." She further announced that they (the Thielkes) made a copy of the letter so that they could keep it. She expressed her embarrassment of how the whole issue had been handled . . . beyond their control.

I did not know the ramifications of sending the "good luck" letter until a few days later. An officer from Fergus Falls arrived at my parents' home (where I was also living) with a warrant to appear in court. According to the media (again) and the County, I had violated the conditions of my release . . . I was trying to "get to" students without their parents' knowledge. Further accusations from the opposition implied that I had been sneaking around . . . following them. Following who? The letter was intended for the two children and their father . . . it was a letter of good will. These particular individuals were not affiliated with the case. They were my friends . . . the Thielkes.

When I appeared in the Willmar Court on March 16 as summoned, neither attorney was in attendance. Rather, their comments were via telephone in the judge's chamber. The County Attorney argued that I wrote to the kids and sent the letter to the school so that the parents wouldn't see I was contacting the kids. A very assuming question was asked by the County Attorney that I interpreted as "empowerment". The request was phrased something like this, ". . . So, if Mr. Courneya goes against the rules of his release, we can have him picked up?" I wondered whom he meant when he used the word "we"? The judge did not approve that request and indicated that he (the judge) would be the one to decide if I had gone against the provisions of my release.

According to law, I had made a grave error. A release order (dated 10-17-97) stated that I was to have no contact, direct or indirect, with all victims listed in the complaint as well as all students at Hancock School. My punishment for writing the good luck letter was to pay a sum of $1000.00 for my bail. I was released and given a few days to come up with the money. This shouldn't be too big of a deal . . . right? According to the NEA (National Education Association) liability insurance which all teachers (union) are entitled (Coverage C-*Coverages and Limits of Liability*-Bail Bond), $1000.00 is accorded for Bail Bond Insurance. I contacted my sister, Julie, who also happened to be a teacher and a teacher's union president, to check into the matter for me. Again, after many calls trying to attain the necessary information, we were told that the Bail Bond Insurance Coverage did not apply to my situation. Surprise . . . Surprise. My question is, "What kind of situation does warrant the use of our Bail Bond Insurance?" Therefore, I wrote another check . . . brought it to the Morris County Office (where the mother of one of my accusers works) . . . and paid for my *error in judgement . . . my error of good intention.* Yes, I learned a good lesson from this misunderstanding: Trust No One.

We proceeded to prepare for the trial. Letters of support arrived daily as did the legal papers. We prepared our list of potential defense witnesses with Kurzman and Grant (another attorney from the firm) working diligently. Additionally, we were informed of the possible witnesses for the prosecution. During the winter (upon request from my attorney), I had taken a polygraph /voice stress analysis test as well as a comprehensive psychologist evaluation to assess the areas of possible sexual intent, etc.

The results of the evaluations were complimentary to our case. However, we were informed that an order *in limine* was filed from the prosecution which precluded the defense from adducing evidence, etc., or making any comment in the presence of the jury in the trial regarding the taking, the willingness to take, or the results or interpretation of any polygraph or voice stress analysis. Upon hearing this, I wondered what would have happened if I had "failed" the tests . . . Would negative results have been considered admissible in court?

The first phase of the trial dealt with jury selection. My attorney favored the use of an extensive jury questionnaire that would be completed by the potential jurors. However, the opposition declared that they did not oppose the use of a jury questionnaire, but contested that the material Mr. Kurzman seeks was "too far removed from anything relevant to the jury selection process." His contention was that Kurzman's more comprehensive questionnaire could possibility aggravate the jurors. The State proposed the use of a questionnaire that dealt with knowledge of the case, feelings about the case, and sensitive matters that might touch upon a juror's fairness, etc.

It was during the oral questioning of the potential jurors that I came to realize that my life was being entrusted to a group of

My 2B

strangers . . . individuals who may or may not have already determined by guilt or innocence. When I listened to the questions posed to the jury pool by both attorneys, I was aghast at the questioning style (particularly by the prosecution). Examples of questions used were as follows: 1) "Do you think it's right that a History teacher touch his students for sexual reasons?"; 2) "Do you think it would be easy for any young student to tell an adult that they are being touched for sexual reasons?"; 3) "Can you see how students could clearly notice the difference between a bump versus a grab?" It appeared to me that the questions themselves were attempting to provide evidence . . . before the trial even began. After extensive review of the jury pool and their responses on the written questionnaire, the following individuals were selected to decide my fate—(Please note that the designated numbers are used only for chronological purposes; relevance to any particular juror is purely coincidental and not intentional):

(Information attained by the Court: Voir Doir: Court File K7-97-155):

*Juror 1: Female. A student at the University of Minnesota, Morris. She professed that her friend had been date-raped. She also indicated that there had been some sexual abuse involving a family member. She admitted that she is a friend with a boy whose mother is listed as a potential witness for the State.

Question: "Anything about this situation that might affect your ability to be fair-impartial?" *Response:* "I suppose there could be . . . I don't know too much about what this case is going to be . . ."

Question: ". . . Some people think that people don't lie about sexual touchings . . . Do you feel that way?" *Response:* "I think it is probably lied about, but I don't think it happens very often . . . but I'm sure it does happen."

Question: "If a number of people claim abuse?" *Response:* "I—I don't know. I'm sure you're more convinced if there are more people . . . it's still . . . one word against the other."

Juror 2: Female. She claimed no prior knowledge of the case. She indicated that the Sheriff's wife babysits her children. The lawyer for her sister's divorce was the State's attorney. She worked with a potential witness.

Question: "Have you ever been accidently touched while playing basketball with someone's elbows, knees, or arm on your private parts?" *Response:* "No."

Question: "Had that occurred, would you have assumed that the coach was touching for sexual reasons?" *Response:* "Well, if it was a grab, yeah. I would have probably assumed, yeah." (My thought at this time was that the attorney had not used the word "grab" . . . that was not the question. No prior knowledge of the case?)

Question: "Some people think that children would never lie about something like sexual contact. Do you share this belief?" *Response:* "I believe that." (She later added, "I don't believe children at young ages, or whatever ages, would have a reason to lie.")

(My observation was "why have a trial then?")

Question(s): "Would it be hard or perhaps impossible for you to disbelieve a girl who says she was molested?" . . . and *(regarding the number of girls testifying against the defendant . . .)* "What effect on your determination?" *Response.* "I guess it makes you want to lean than way . . . if there's more than one, I guess."

Question: "Anything we should know about you that touches upon your ability to be fair and impartial?" *Response:* "I haven't been sexually abused, but I was in an abusive relationship."

Question: "Anything about that situation that could hinder you from fair judgement?"

Response: "No, I think I could be impartial on that."

Juror 3: Female. She works as an aide in a nearby school. She professed to having heard about the case. Her husband works sometimes with an individual on the witness list for the State. Additionally, she belongs to the same art club as another potential witness (a friend).

Question: ". . . as to whether she had discussed the case prior to today . . . ?" *Response:* "Yes. . . . I haven't lived in Chokio very long, so everyone had to fill me in." She then went on to say, "I wondered if any children were involved like ____'s children" (Mentioned the name of her friend who was listed as a potential witness).

Question: "Did people share with you their own personal opinions as to whether they thought Courneya had sexually abused these girls or not?" *Response:* "No, mainly it was my husband and I looking at it or talking about it."

Question: "Do you believe a girl could be wrong about a man touching them for sexual purposes?" *Response:* "Maybe."

Juror 4: Female. University of Minnesota, Morris student. Her mother is a legal assistant. She claims she had not heard about the case.

Question: "Are you familiar with any other cases of people being accused of sexual misconduct by numbers of people . . . 4, 5, 6, 7 people?" *Response:* "Just what I've seen on TV."

Question: "Are you referring to Dennis Courneya or are you referring to the President (Clinton)?" *Response:* "Well, more the President of the U.S."

Juror 5: Male. University of Minnesota, Morris. He recognized the name of a possible witness (that ultimately testified for the prosecution) and informed us that he serves in the National Guard with the father of a potential witness for the State.

Question: "Based on your knowledge of him (the above mentioned ("father") individual), have you formed an opinion concerning his credibility?" *Response:* "Just that he's a very trustworthy, honest person."

Question: Dealing with this case . . . "A number of people have come forward and it is going to trial; therefore, there must be something?" *Response:* "Well, there's a pretty good chance . . . I mean, we can't assume anything at this point." This juror later admits that three of his prior girlfriends had been sexually abused or assaulted (by another individual) and that two of them still have painful memories.

Juror 6: Female. She graduated from Morris High School. She had heard of the case in the news and media. Her mother used to be a legal secretary in Morris.

Juror 7: Male. He explained that he had been a member of a bowling league with a Morris police officer. He knew of the case via the media (specifically an article in the Minneapolis Tribune). He stated that he knew the State's attorney—" . . . we have children that are both in Scouts, and so there have been some things where we have been at the same function."

Juror 8: Female. She had been employed by a lawyer in town . . . also worked as a bar waitress in town. She professes that her good friend was sexually abused or assaulted and later assaulted and murdered.

Question: Dealing with . . . ". . . interfere with ability to be fair and impartial based upon her experience with having a friend that was assaulted?" *Response:* "I don't think so."

She claimed to have never heard about this case . . . (even though she worked at the same bar as one of the other jurors). She mentioned that she doesn't read newspapers.

Juror 9: Female. University of Minnesota, Morris. She stated that she knew nothing about the case.

Question: "Have you or anyone close ever been accused of a crime?" *Response:* "No, unless underage drinking and driving is a crime."

Question: "A lot of people think that if somebody gets to this point . . . that they probably did something wrong. How do you feel about that (the person being accused in the trial)?" *Response:* "Well . . . I would think there would have to be some kind of evidence that would hold a person this long."

Question: ". . . Would that suggest to you that they must have done some sort of crime. . . . ?" *Response:* "Well, there's a definite possibility of crime."

Juror 10: Female. She has worked at the University of Minnesota, Morris for many years. She professed that she has heard about the case via the media. Her husband's nephew is a judge. She admits that she has heard many people talking about the case—pro and con. She has worked with the parents of two of the girls filing charges in this case and one potential witness for the defense.

Juror 11: Female. She works for the U.S. Dept. of Agriculture working with government and commodity programs. She claims to have heard about the case via the media (Morris newspaper, Willmar and Minneapolis paper, also radio reports). When she was shown the list of potential witnesses, she stated, "I know quite a few of these people through my work, the husband's . . ." She later identified the specific individuals that she knew (parents of witnesses—State and Defense).

Question: (referring to testimony of the girls) ". . . if a witness were to cry, would that have any effect on your weighing or eualuating their evidence or their testimony?" *Response:* "Probably. I don't know."

Question: ". . . If something like that were to happen (crying), . . . you would feel sympathy for the person and thus tend to lean toward whichever side they were on?" *Response:* "Probably."

She admitted her neighbors and friends have taken sides in the case . . . both for and against.

Juror 12: Male. He claimed he had not seen/heard any media coverage regarding the case. He did not know any of the witnesses.

Juror 13: Male. He was aware of the case via the media coverage. He proceeded to describe critical information regarding a family member. Specifically, his statements referred to the mistreatment (abuse) of the particular family member . . .

Question: "Knowing this (referring to the described mistreatment), could it affect your ability to be fair and impartial?" *Response:* "I guess I would hope not . . . we agonize . . . I'm aware of the long term effects (in reference to the family member) . . ."

The juror stated that his wife works for the special education coop that serves the Hancock School District (secretary). He also indicated that he has discussed the case with the pastor in Hancock as a colleague . . . "In the group of pastors that were gathered, we did—we expressed concern for him as a pastor." He later added details about the discussion with the Hancock pastor, "Really all he shared with us was that parishioners were—were coming to him and that he was hearing both sides of—of what seemed to be the prevailing opinions in Hancock . . ."

Question: "If you were to hear—through testimony in this case, from a witness who claims they had been sexually abused, something that sounds like a problem you think your _____ (family member) may have had. . . . do you think this person who is testifying here must have been sexually abused or otherwise they wouldn't be having those kinds of problems?" Response: "I . . . I don't believe so. . . . In my line of work, I . . . do make judgements about those kinds of things . . ., so, I—I may hear more in somebody's testimony than another juror. Yeah, I might."

Question: "Some people think that a teacher or coach should never put a hand on a child. How do you feel about that?" Response: "That's my personal practice."

Question: ". . . how do you feel about others who do things like that?" Response: "It makes me feel uncomfortable."

*Juror 14: Female. She works at the hospital in Morris. She claims to have heard about the case via the media (TV, news). My impression was that she appeared to be quite conservative . . . of the "old school".

Of the mentioned jurors, twelve were selected to serve on the jury with the remaining two determined as alternates. As I reflected upon the jurors' responses to the questioning, I could not help but note critical information that was attained from the 14 individuals:

* The 12 jurors selected: 9 were female; 3 were male
  (Note: Later in the trial, the ratio would change to 10
  females, 2 males)
* 7 jurors were either students or individuals who worked at
  the University of Minnesota, Morris. (I was concerned with
  the "University Connection")
* 7 jurors either claimed to be friends, acquaintances, or
  recognized names of individuals listed as possible witnesses
  for the prosecution
* 6 jurors described cases mentioning family or acquaintances
  who had experienced some form of abuse (physical or sexual
  abuse)
* At least 10 professed that they knew about the case

Yes, the *talented twelve* had been selected. They would determine my fate. They were instructed of their responsibilities . . . a responsibility that I prayed they would take seriously. This was not a game . . . this was not a television drama . . . this was not a classroom presentation. This was life. Their decision meant a determination of truth . . . freedom.

Ye shall know the truth, and the truth shall make you free (New Testament, *John,* VIII, 13). This was my hope and my belief . . . the truth would finally be revealed and this nightmare would be over. The State of Minnesota vs Dennis Edward Courneya was about to begin.

CHAPTER TWELVE

One of the striking differences
between a cat and a lie is that
a cat has only nine lives.

-Mark Twain

The determination of my ultimate fate had begun. There were many spectators in attendance for the opening statements—separated by the customary *isle of justice*. Typically, those who were there hoping for my "demise" sat behind the prosecution. I turned around and looked at this group of people . . . there were no surprises. Interestingly, when I glanced their way, no one looked me in the eyes. I felt sorry for them. How ironic that it was *me* who was on trial.

When this entire nightmare had begun, one of my sisters had coined it as a *contemporary witch hunt*. According to some historians (regarding Colonial New England), panic was often blamed on clerical "bigots" who fanned controversy or excitement to restore their declining power. The resulting hysteria was also attributed to the youth who had become disenchanted and alienated from the world of their parents. The concluding speculation was that out of this spiral of fear and anxiety, came irrational accusations . . . accusations based upon jealousy and deceit (*Portrait of America*, pgs. 76-78). Did I agree with my sister's comparative analysis? Oh, I don't know . . . she's the creative one.

Quite naturally, there was a stark difference between the opening statements offered by the prosecution and defense. I was charged with 28 counts of criminal sexual conduct involving nine high school students. The County Attorney proceeded to inform the jury about several of the alleged incidents both in the classroom and during athletic practices. He vowed that the prosecution would show through its witnesses that my intent was of the sort that justified the criminal charges. He proceeded to tell the jurors what he anticipated the witnesses were going to say in the case. He further assured the court that the evidence would make it pretty obvious that it was for sexual or aggressive purposes and it was no accident. My heart went out to my parents who were sitting behind me. They had to sit and listen to someone degrade their son. No parent should have to bear witness to such debasement. I wanted to turn around and give them both a big hug. I wonder how that would have been interpreted? Instead, I wept . . . inside.

My attorney, Marc Kurzman, maintained his dignity and composure when he stated in defense that while my behavior may not have been "politically correct", never in my 22 years of teaching and coaching, had I ever been told my behavior was inappropriate. He argued that my actions had been misinterpreted by the students. He also stipulated that the evidence was going to show that these girls were under quite a bit of pressure . . . from peers, police, parents, etc. It was during this opening statement that the defense referred to the role of another female teacher (from the Hancock School) in the case, "P": "She doesn't like Dennis Courneya. She personally felt Dennis Courneya was a guy that was a male chauvinish pig; he's a guy who thought that guys are strong and powerful and women can't survive without their help; that she took offense . . . So, when she hears about this discussion going on about a guy who she already thinks is a sexual harasser for the reasons that she'll tell you about, she has a conversation with 'Girl Z'." Kurzman went on to describe the role of the school counselor, the Sheriff, and the school district in the case. In conclusion, he admitted that it was going to be tough for the jurors . . . but reminded them that they have to decide "whether the State has proved beyond a reasonable doubt that he (defendant) acted aggressively and sexually or whether he's a coach that may have been out of his time, but never was warned, never was instructed to do different, and suddenly one day has his life destroyed and comes before this jury for a trial."

I looked at the twelve individuals who were assigned to weigh the evidence. Some of them were taking notes . . . some were not. Some appeared to take a great deal of interest in the arguments . . . some looked like they had had a long night previously and concentrating on anything would be a great challenge . . . much less staying awake.

As for you, the reader, I am asking you to be the *13th Juror*. Please take the place of those jurors who fell asleep during some of the testimony (as told to me by many spectators). Please take the seat beside the jurors who must have had exceptional talents in the area of "memory" as evidenced by them not taking notes through-out the trial. Be humbled, Einstein. Please keep in mind the premise of *reasonable doubt.*

Yes, I had to believe in our justice system. I had to believe that this group of jurors would remain fair and impartial . . . would set aside any preconceived notions they might have about my inno-cence and guilt . . . would refrain from reading the multitude of newspaper articles that emphasized my plight . . . would turn the television off (or not watch it at all) when summaries of the trial were reported . . . would not let any past personal experience in-fluence their decision regarding my innocence . . . would not let their lack of sleep or lack of note-taking interfere with their ability to make an intellectual decision regarding my fate.

Yes, I also had to believe in the integrity of the judge assigned to the trial. I had to hope that he would never slumber during the testimony. I had to tell myself that he would not degrade the severity of the case by turning his back to the court during testi-mony or arguments. I entrusted that he would not misuse the word "over-ruled" when my attorney voiced a legal objection. Af-ter all, as Bacon reminds us in his *Essay: Of Judicature*— . . . *Above all things, integrity is their (judges) portion and proper virtue.* I also had to believe that the County had conducted a fair investigation and that the procedures used were righteous. Yes, I had to believe that our justice system was *just*. What choice did I have?

(Reminder to the reader: Once again, I have chosen to refer to certain witnesses by "alphabetic" notation. Any relevance of the notation with their name is coincidental, not intentional. Additionally, excerpts of testimony cited in the subsequent chapters are derived from the volumes of documented testimony in the case of the State of Minnesota vs. Dennis Edward Courneya; Court File No. K7-97-155.)

Witness: County Sheriff:

The State called the County Sheriff as its first witness. Upon questioning from the County Attorney, he recalled for the Court the sequence of reports/actions that led to the initial investigation of the case. He described the procedures used in the investigation (interviews/taping) and how as a result of the interview with the first girl, "Z", other names of students surfaced that led to the subsequent interviewing of additional students.

As I watched the Sheriff, I could not but help wonder how experienced he really was with this type of investigation. I had read the documented statements given by the girls during the interviews by the County. Were these girls influenced by the questioning techniques?

I will probably never know; I can only speculate. However, when it came time for cross examination by my attorney, Kurzman, he was going to do more than just speculate . . . he was not going to tiptoe around the issue one moment.

His first question dealt with the Sheriff's training in taking statements from adolescents who were suspected of having been sexually abused. The Sheriff announced that he had received training—"I think in part through the Bureau of Criminal Apprehension . . . and possibly there's others as well that I just don't remember." A bit later he indicated that he had taken the training process/courses "four or five years ago maybe. And that's a guess." Kurzman went on to inquire if he (the Sheriff) "believed it's important when you come across evidence suggesting that somebody didn't do a crime—to make note of that?" The Sheriff professed that it was important. However, upon further questioning, "Can you advise the jury how often you did that in this investigation?" The witness responded, "It's hard to put a number on it. I guess there's—there's certainly—some of the context in the interview that I conducted, there's positive things that are said about Mr. Courneya."

Kurzman continued to challenge the Sheriff, ". . . When a child would claim that another child saw something happen and you would speak to the second child and they would say 'I didn't see that happen,' did you do a report about that?" The response was, "Sometimes I did." Kurzman tried to zero in on the questioning techniques used by the Sheriff/social worker during the initial interview of the girls: ". . . In this investigation, why did you decide that sometimes you should use leading and suggestive questions when you were questioning some of these girls?" The witness responded that he didn't believe he was asking leading or directing questions and continued . . . "But again, you know, the statements are taken very well, or they are—they are good statements."

Kurzman continued: "I see. Did somebody review them and give a report to you that they were taken well and they were good statements?"

Response: "Nobody gave me a report, no."

As the defendent in the case and also a citizen of the County, I had cause to be alarmed at much of what was professed by the Sheriff. Yes, I had noted the questioning techniques used when the girls were interviewed . . . I had wondered if and/or how statements could be contaminated, shaped, and changed by the influence of adults and/or peers. Again, I could only wonder . . . speculate.

Another issue of considerable debate with the Sheriff concerned a list of names of students provided to him by the school superintendent. Kurzman questioned, "Where is it? Do you have the handwritten list anywhere?" After agreeing that a copy of some rough notes was in the possession of the Defense, Kurzman examined the notes . . . appeared perplexed and then inquired, ". . . There's a name here . . . Do you see that? . . . Whose handwriting is that?"

The Sheriff replied, "I have no idea."

Kurzman: "Whose handwriting is the list?"

The Sheriff answered, "Well, I assume it's Mr. Larson (superintendent). At least he provided it to me, but I have no idea who actually wrote it."

There proceeded to be considerable consternation regarding whose handwriting was on the note with the Sheriff professing, "There's some writing on here that's my handwriting", but added later in the testimony that with regards to some of the notations, "That's not my handwriting."

In an attempt to emphasize their positions, both attorneys utilized the opportunity to redirect. The Sheriff was on the stand a considerable amount of time. My feelings about the results of his testimony were best stated by an elderly gentleman who had witnessed the testimony. He shook his head in disgust and stated, "For his sake, I sure hope he's (the Sheriff) not up for re-election this year." I questioned whether the Sheriff would ever want to come back to this courtroom again. Knowing Kurzman, however, I was confident that he would want the Sheriff available and present at all times!

Witness: "Girl Z":

"Girl Z" was next on the agenda for the State. The allegations of criminal activity had begun with this girl. As she took the stand, one would assume that I viewed her with anger . . . disgust. No, the word *pity* best describes how I felt towards her. After stating that her mother was a court administrator in this courthouse (where this trial was taking place!), she proceeded to answer the questions pertaining to the alleged incident. When asked what the date was that the incident supposedly happened, she replied, "It was like October 5th or something." Upon further questioning, she professed that she was not sure of the day of the week. Her testimony continued to describe the alleged incident. She claimed that as she (as well as other athletes of the cross country and football teams) was sitting on the field, stretching out, the defendent came to stand behind her, rubbing her shoulders. She continued, "Well, he basically was—he had like two legs on the sides of me, and he rubbed his groinal area against my back, my upper back into my middle portion, and I could feel that he had an erection, and it was—I was really uncomfortable, so I kinda moved forward, and he kinda did it, he just did it a little bit longer, and then he walked away and snickered."

Later, upon request, "Girl Z" demonstrated for the court the way that she was sitting and the kind of stretching she was doing at the time. As I observed her demonstration, I said to myself, "There's that 'midget' theory again." How in the world could I rub her in the back (as she professed) as I stood behind her? Surely, the jurors would see her accusations as totally preposterous! Furthermore, the State requested that the record can show that ____ ("Z") is seated on the floor with her feet drawn up towards her and the bottoms of her feet together and her hands on her feet. Perhaps realizing that the jurors might be questioning the perceived height differentiation, the attorney continued to ask her how tall she was ("five nine") and . . . "were you—realizing that you are maybe a growing person, were you shorter, substantially shorter back in October of 1997?" Upon further questioning in this realm, she indicated to the court that she did not think that she had grown a lot since then. Later, during questioning, she declared that she had talked to some of the other athletes about the incident. "Yes, we were about to go, and I said, I go, 'You guys will never guess,' I said, 'what Mr. Courneya did to me today.' And they are like, 'What?' and I told them."

The questions from the prosecutor continued, "Have there been times in the—in the classroom when there's ever been any sort of physical contact that he's had with you?" The witness, "Girl Z", explained, ". . . and he would come behind you, almost do the exact same thing like on the playing field. He would rub your shoulders kinda and he would rub against you." When the prosecutor questioned, "And where would you be at this time?", the witness replied, "In your desk." The court was then exposed to another demonstration. A school desk with a Resusci-Annie was set-up for view. The witness, "Z", agreed to demonstrate on the Resusci-Annie in the desk, as to how the defendant would come up from behind . . . "can you show us what he would do?" For the record, the witness stepped up to the mannequin in the desk and massaged on the shoulders. However, the demonstration did not end at that point. The witness went on to claim that I would kinda squat down and would start rubbing down here ("Well, you would kinda feel it in the back"). The prosecutor continued, "And you are indicating the back of the seat of the chair?" The witness responded, "Yes", and following a few more questions from the attorney, she continued by saying, "Sometimes you could feel his penis," indicating an area below the seat back of the chair. Upon questioning, she admitted that she did not know how he would manage to get down to that level. I thought to myself, "I would have to be a contortionist to do what she described."

Following this most interesting demonstration by "Z", she also professed during questioning, "—he would grab your muscle and just, you know, he'd say like, 'You've got chicken muscles,' or something. He would just go like and sometimes he would brush across your breast." Again, the court was witness to another demonstration (the alleged brush of the breast). The witness continued with citing examples of comments that I supposedly had made that were "out of place". She concluded with describing how she brought the alleged actions/comments to the attention of one of the teachers ("P"), (a couple of days later, I might add . . .):

"Well, I was sitting at my desk, and the girls in my class started telling the guys in my class, and it was like a big ruckus, everyone can hear everyone telling about it."

When "Z" was questioned, "Telling everybody what?", she replied, "Telling the guys what he had done to me at practice. I could hear them saying, 'Oh, my goodness, that's so gross.' They were whispering, I could hear it. It really affected me. It just . . . I started crying. I just . . . I think it finally hit me that what he did was so wrong, and I felt like I should do something about it, but I was scared and . . ."

The witness continues to explain that the teacher ("P") had overheard and "she goes, she called me up to her desk and she goes, 'Can I talk to you after class?' and I said sure." According to her testimony, following "Z's" discussion with the teacher, "P" (the teacher) inquired if she wanted to go and talk to the school counselor about it. The witness went on to declare that following the discussion with the counselor (with the teacher, "P", in attendance), she eventually told her aunt. I wondered why she chose to inform these people of the alleged incidents before she told her parents. She answered this question later in her testimony, ". . . they (referring to her parents) have had him as a teacher and as a coach, so I just thought that they would think that, you know, I'm over-exaggerating it, or just didn't think they would believe me." This is the only statement made by her that I actually understood.

Truth, crushed to earth, shall rise again; Th' eternal years of God are hers; but Error, wounded, writhes in pain, And dies among his worshippers (William C. Bryant).

Cross-Examination:

It was now our turn (the defense) to obtain testimony from "Girl Z". Kurzman cut "right to the chase"! His line of questioning began with gathering information regarding the classroom. In response to his question of appoximating the size of the classroom, she informed the court that the classroom was a little smaller than the courtroom . . . and later deduced that it was about thirty feet by thirty feet. She went on to respond that there were about thirty chairs in the classroom. Kurzman then proposed the use of a drawing to depict the classroom. He drew a box (Exhibit 4) and requested that the witness assist by drawing some details of the classroom (orientation:door/teacher's desk/student desks).

The witness was questioned as to "how much space" there was between the chairs of the desks. She responded, "Three, four inches. I don't know." When Kurzman furthered the testimony by inquiring, ". . . Could somebody walk from left to right, in other words, go right behind the desks—?" She responded, "Yes." Kurzman inquired once more, "—in that three to four-inch space, if he could do that?" . . . "Girl Z" declared, "Yes."

To emphasize the testimony, Kurzman put forth a follow-up

query, "So your claim would be Mr. Courneya would be in this three or four-inch space and massaging your shoulders and also feel his penis underneath the wooden portion of the chair that comes across; correct?" Her response was, "Yes." Kurzman appeared a bit baffled by the testimony and inquired, "How did he do that?" The witness went on to describe that I allegedly would come behind the desk and rub her shoulders and rub against her. Kurzman finally requested a response to the following, "How did you get to feel his penis all the way down here underneath the back portion of the chair?"

It was at this point in the testimony that I actually began to pity the witness. Her following explanation confounded earlier testimony, "Actually you could feel it up in here. I'm sorry, I said it wrong before. He would come kind of on the side of you and he would rub."

Kurzman challenged, "So you want to change your testimony now?"

She responded, "Yes."

During the next lines of questioning, Kurzman inquired, ". . . Is it possible that what you thought now, or whenever, was a penis, was actually his knee could have been down there underneath the wooden portion of the chair?"

She responded, "It could have been, but I don't know. I could just—I thought it was. I was pretty sure that it was his penis."

The next phase of inquiry concerned the "field testimony"—where upon the girl had claimed in earlier testimony that she was sitting on the field in the butterfly position. The question from Kurzman: "And Mr. Courneya came behind you and you say that he pressed his erect penis against you; correct?" She responded, "Yes."

When Kurzman inquired as to where on her body she thought she felt this, she replied, "It was like the middle back to about right here." At this point there was disagreement from the attorneys/court as how to describe the area in question.

Finally, the Court requested, "Tell us where you believe it was."

She answered, "It was my like the middle portion of the back."

The Court later furthered, "You're indicating in the middle of the back between the shoulder blades?" The witness responded, "Yes."

By Mr. Kurzman:

Q: "How much space is there from the ground to the place that you believe you felt his erect penis in October? In inches approximately, how much?"

A: "Twelve."

Q: "Okay. And think you said you were in the back of a group of people that were all facing forward and doing calisthenics with the captains; right?"

A: "Yes." (She later admits that the captains were facing towards the kids)

After obtaining information from the witness regarding her discussions of the alleged incidents with friends and the teacher/counselor, Kurzman obtained more testimony regarding the "field" incident:

Q: "This activity you describe on the field when you were in the butterfly position, is it your claim that Dennis was standing or he was on his knees?"

A: "He was standing."

Q: "Okay. How did he position himself while standing and you are in the butterfly position so that his penis came into contact with a spot about 12 inches from the ground? How did that happen? Can you—is that physically possible?"

A: "Yes."

Q: "How?"

A: "Well, I'm sitting straight up." . . . "And him having his knees kind of like around my shoulders, and then him rubbing against. It's physically possible."

Q: "Did anybody, the Sheriff, anybody who has talked to you about this ever ask you to try to reenact what you claim happened and see if it's physically possible for somebody to do the things that you described?"

A: "Yes." The witness upon follow-up question, indicated that the County Attorney had asked her to reenact . . . "this past week."

It was also at this point in the trial that testimony provided information regarding "counseling" sessions that were held at the school :

Q: "Is it correct that there's been somebody coming to the school every Wednesday since October to talk with you and other girls about these allegations?"
A: "Yes. We never really talked about the allegations that we made. She was just there to comfort us and everything."
Q: "How did you come to meet her?"
A: "Through the school. Just us girls that were involved in this trial, the school had like counseling every Wednesday after school . . ."
She continued to claim that the sessions started about maybe four weeks before the trial began. She assured the defense that it couldn't have been going on for months . . . and that they basically talked about the trial procedures. The witness also added in later testimony that the "counselor" with whom they met indicated that she worked with a doctor in town.

Following this phase of questioning, the witness also responded (to inquiry) that they had also talked with people who are representing the school district, "Yes, they had a private investigator." . . . "Theresa. I don't know her last name." She also indicated through testimony that she had had two meetings with "Theresa"—once alone and one time with her parents in attendance. She recalled that her parents were at the first meeting. She also indicated that it was at the second of the two meetings that "Theresa" was typing while she was asking questions. I had a strong inclination that the role of the investigator, "Theresa", was one that the defense would address later and more strongly.

I also found myself wondering if we had been given copies of these documented interviews?

There was one last issue that Kurzman wanted clarified for the Court and it dealt with the witness, "Z", and some information she apparently had professed to the Sheriff during the initial interviews (investigative):

Q: ". . . And you told the Sheriff supposedly that he (Courneya) had done the same penis rubbing against other girls in similar situations; right?"
A: "Yes."
Q: "You mentioned two in particular, Shannon Solvie, . . . and Gwen Greiner, . . . ; do you remember that?"
A: "Yes."

Following a series of "Objections" by the prosecution (and "Sustained" by the Court), Kurzman rephrased his next line of questioning:

Q: "What was your basis for telling the Sheriff that Shannon Solvie had suffered the same sexual assault you did?"
A: "I had heard that that had happened to them."
Q: "So you heard it as sort of like gossip, rumor, that type of thing?"
A: "Yes."
Q: "You didn't tell the Sheriff you just heard this rumor about it; did you?"
A: "No."
Q: "You told the Sheriff that it had happened and you gave them those names; right?"
A: "Uh-huh."

Following additional questioning, the witness also professed that the basis for naming Gwen Greiner had also come to her through the rumor mill. While listening to this portion of the testimony, I could hardly wait for Shannon Solvie and Gwen Greiner to take the stand. They would be testifying for the defense, and I hoped that the Court would recognize that they were fine examples of character and class . . . not perpetuators of rumors.

Kurzman concluded his initial questioning with the following request, "You also said that as you talked about it (referring to the alleged sexual assault by the defendent), it made it more real. Do you remember that, Page 9 (in reference to the documented interview by the County)?" Her answer was, "Yeah."

Q: "What did you mean, 'made it more real'?"
A: "I don't know."

As expected, the County Attorney chose to redirect (examination) followed by Kurzman's recross (examination). In my opinion, the more she testified, the more confusing and contradictory it became. I had heard enough. Apparently, one of the spectators in the Court agreed—I heard a long distinguishable yawn. I glanced towards the juror's box . . . one of them was fighting off sleep to the best of her abilities. I wanted to tell this group of people—*the determinators of my fate*—to please take notes . . . please stay awake. I knew that I would endure . . . but would the truth endure?

CHAPTER THIRTEEN

Two things fill the mind with ever new
and increasing wonder and awe -
The starry heavens above me and the
moral law within me.

-Kant, *Critique of Pure Reason*

It took unbelievable strength to withstand the horrific accusations I heard in the Stevens County Courthouse. One after the other, the witnesses for the prosecution attempted to defile my character . . . my name. Again, as I listened to their testimony, all I could do was wonder *Why?* Perhaps, you, the "13th juror", can render an unbiased opinion to my question.

Witness: "Teacher P":
The teacher, "P", whom Kurzman had alluded to in his opening statement took the stand. I was extremely interested in hearing her testimony . . . her explanation of her role in this ordeal. We knew what to expect from this witness. She would offer no surprises; yet, we hoped that she would offer some form of truth. During our pretrial interviews with potential witnesses, the name of this teacher, "P", surfaced time and time again. I knew she did not like me. Would she renounce me on the stand or would she give a stellar performance? Yes, this was going to be very interesting . . . *Don't turn the channel!*

As I listened to her initial testimony, I couldn't believe what I was hearing! One would think that she and I were *friends*: "At times, I felt that Mr. Courneya and I could get along very well. He was very, very kind to me."

Q: "That's okay. Is it difficult to be here testifying?"
A: "A little bit."
Q: "Okay. Do you want to just take a minute?"
A: "Thank you. I apologize. I'm sorry."

The witness went on to profess the following: "I can remember Mr. Courneya asking me how I was and telling me that if I needed to talk to anyone, I could talk to him. Not very many teachers do that. I thought that was very nice. But, on the other hand, we had our disagreements."

I thought to myself, "Disagreements . . ., who is she kidding?" An individual can tell when someone does not like them . . . this teacher, "P", did not like me. I could not quite ascertain the reason why; however, some individuals might take offense to one of my strongest philosophies in that gender is not a determining factor of greatness and success. Everyone has the capacity to "reach for the stars." Yes, I encouraged females and males alike to be strong . . . to be individuals . . . to be unique . . . to be true to themselves . . . to give 200%. Perhaps that was asking too much . . . perhaps that made me out to be a "bully" . . . perhaps that depicted me as being too tough on some students . . . However, I have learned as a teacher and as a coach that if you expect only the best of someone, that is what the end result generally is . . . the best. I could have offended many with this idealistic vision . . . perhaps even other teachers.

As expected, the witness recalled the version as testified by "Girl Z". She offered little *evidence* to the contrary. I was extremely interested in hearing the response from "P" to one of the questions posed by the County Attorney: "Did it appear to you as of the meeting of the next morning (referring to the meeting with the adminstration at the school) that the defendant might be in some trouble with the school?"

A: "It appeared that way."

Q: "How did you feel about that?" . . . "Was that good news?"

A: "For me personally?". . . . "No."

I had a question for the prosecutor I wish I could have asked at that time: "Why are you asking her these types of questions? Did you think she would feel good about another teacher losing his job . . . his good name . . . his future? Were you, too, pondering the possibility of a type of conspiracy?" The defense was certainly thinking about it, I can tell you that. These are questions the *13th juror* should contemplate as well.

Cross-Examination:

As noted earlier, we had copies of pre-trial interviews with some of the witnesses. Therefore, when it came time for Kurzman to engage in cross examination, it is not too difficult to deduce why he asked the following questions, especially when the witness admitted that she, too, had spoken with "Teresa/Theresa":

Q: "Did you assist any students in making complaints about any other male faculty at Hancock?" Upon further clarification of the question, the witness indicated that she had voiced complaints about another faculty member to the superintendent.

Q: "Did you tell Teresa that Dennis Courneya has managed to control and basically brainwash the young women he teaches and coaches through mere intimidation?"

A: "I do not believe I used the word brainwashed."

Q: "Did you tell Teresa that Dennis Courneya has called you beautiful and darky and a brunette bomb shell on more than one occasion?"

A: "Yes, I believe I did say that."

Q: ". . . Did you tell the administration that he had made those comments that you felt were inappropriate?"

A: "I—I don't think I did, no."

Q: "Did you tell Teresa that there was a time when you were walking down the hallway and Dennis Courneya approached you, he wrapped his arm around you and pulled you very close, that he was apparently trying to be kind to you because you were having a bad day, but the incident bothered you because you felt his hug was inappropriate and touching?"

A: "Yes."

Q: "So did you share with your colleague (referring to defendent) that you felt he had engaged in some inappropriate touching with you?"

A: "No . . ."

Later in her testimony, she attempted to clarify how she felt when I supposedly put my arms around her shoulders during her "tough day" incident:

("P") ". . . I would like to clarify that the only reason it made me uncomfortable is that I'm married, it's a small town, and I don't want people to think I'm having an affair with someone, because I'm not. That's the reason. Kids observe things."

Q: "And is it your experience that kids sometimes misunderstand what they see and get it wrong?"

A: "Based on my own children and experience with them, I suppose that would be a fair statement."

Q: "And is it your experience that kids might exaggerate?"

A: "It could certainly happen."

Enough said. Next witness please.

Witness: School Counselor:

Next in line was another of my self-professed *friends*, the Hancock School Counselor.

She, too, explained her role in this ordeal. Apparently, as she testified, the girl, "Z", in the company of the teacher, "P", came to her room after school and told her of the alleged incidents. She also indicated that she told the young girl ("Z") that she was under duty to report what she was professing. The County Attorney asked a very intriguing question when he required, "Did you tell her that before or after she told you what she had to say?"

The counselor replied, "Before."

Follow-up questions: "And was there some reason that you felt that the information she had was of a nature that might be reportable under the law?"

The witness responded, "It is my understanding that I report all of those things."

Question: "At the time that you talked to her about reporting, did you have a general idea of what the subject matter was going to be?"

Answer: "No." The witness continued to explain that the reason she talked about reporting was that "If kids come down with issues, I usually tell them that."

At this point, I was perplexed. Is the witness trying to tell us that she forewarns all students who come to her with "issues" that she is bound to report the information . . . and that she has the ability to ascertain (before even hearing it) if it was going to be a reportable issue? Is this woman a psychic? I feel sorry for the student who makes the mistake of wanting to talk about *nonreportable* issues: graduation requirements, career hopes, credit card dilemmas. Hold on . . . *this could be reportable!* Yes, my colleague of twenty-two years did her job. She listened to the story told by "Girl Z" (with the teacher, "P", in attendance, . . . makes one wonder about confidentiality at this point). She testified that she informed the administration and helped schedule a meeting with the student, the student's parents, the administration, and again, the teacher "P", for the following morning. I have a question or two for the counselor:

1) Who did you call first to report the alleged infraction? The Sheriff or the Hancock Administrators? I'm sure the records can provide that information . . . sorry for asking.

2) Did you ever question the physical impossibilities of the story told by "Girl Z"?

   Oh, sorry again . . . that's probably not your responsibility.

According to her testimony, at this morning meeting, it was she (the counselor) who provided the "retelling of the situation or the incident. . . . I told—I made the statement." She later added, "I told what happened and ___("Z") made comments after I had told them." The witness proceeded to inform the Court that following the meeting, the superintendent called an attorney. Arrangements were made to talk with me at the school about the matter. However, my medical emergency interrupted their plans. Yes, the counselor was part of the trio that came to my home the following Monday morning to inform me of the allegations. I will never forget their demeanor . . . their lack of emotion . . . their *support*. After all, I was just an employee . . . I deserved no better, I guess.

Later in the questioning, the witness admitted that other girls (besides "Z") contacted her about concerns about the behavior of the defendant. I hope she remembered to inform them before they spoke that she was bound to report the contents of their discussions. Interestingly, the County Attorney concluded his line of questioning with the following:

"Did any of these girls talk to you about wanting to get the defendant or get even with him?"

The counselor responded, "No."

Follow-up question: "Did ___ (teacher, "P") ever indicate that sentiment to you?"

Response: "No."

Actually, I have a follow up question for you, the *13th juror*: "Were you wondering if the girls in question and the teacher, "P", wanted to get even with me about something?" This is a question definitely worth pondering.

Cross-Examination:

When Kurzman began his questioning, he was deliberate and straight to the point. He questioned the witness about the individual who had been meeting with the girls on Wednesdays, and she responded that the lady was a licensed psychologist and counselor. She also testified that she had made the intitial call (upon administrative request) to obtain the services of the psychologist/counselor. She further indicated upon questioning that the job of this individual was "to help the students later on . . . in dealing with the situation, . . . and moving forward with their life." (It sure sounded to me like she already had me on trial and convicted.) She acknowledged that letters had gone out to parents to advise them that there was going to be a counselor available for their kids. She stated that she sent the letters. Later she admitted that there were about fifteen students who attended a session in which she was also in attendance. She also indicated that the County Attorney attended one of the sessions ("twenty minute" session) in which the students asked questions about "What does the courtroom look like?" (Again, wasn't the purpose of the meetings supposed to be to "help them move forward with their lives"? If so, why was the prosecutor in attendance? Oh yes, to tell them what a courtroom looks like . . . I forgot.)

Kurzman later asked a question that I found to be extremely pertinent: "Why were counselors not made available to all of the students, including those who might not be making accusations of sexual impropriety against Mr. Courneya?" She was not allowed to respond to the question due to a voiced "Objection" by the State (Sustained).

As with the prior witnesses, the counselor indicated that she, too, had spoken with the investigator for the school, "Teresa", (* Note: the spelling of the name Theresa/Teresa, as taken from Court File No. K7-97-155, was interchanged frequently; however, it refers to the same individual), but admitted that she had not received a written summary of their conversation. Kurzman also attempted to clarify earlier testimony by the girl, "Z", when he inquired, "Do you know when—whether or not ___("Girl Z") started to claim that Mr. Courneya had while checking her muscles . . . touched the side of her breast . . . ?" The counselor indicated that she did not know whether or not she ("Girl Z") had made that claim. I was debating at this moment *when* had "Girl Z" *remembered* the occurance of this alleged action on my part (Recall the demonstration by "Z" during her testimony)? Wouldn't you think that she would have told the counselor of this alleged action during that infamous classroom meeting? Wouldn't you think that the counselor would have remembered that the student stated such . . . if she had?

The testimony became even more confusing when Kurzman asked her the following, ". . . As you are sitting here today, do you agree that maybe you saw it but didn't perceive it, meaning how Mr. Courneya interacted with the student, as being inappropriate touching?"

Response: "When?"
Question: "Now, sitting here now and asking you whether or not you agree with that statement today."
Response: "Yes."
Question: "So when was it that what you had been seeing changed and it became inappropriate touching?"
Response: "When did it change?"
Question: "In your mind."
Response: "It hasn't changed."

I chanced a look towards the jury box. Those who had chosen not to record on paper the testimony were sticking to their resolve . . . no notes. Another juror had slumped to the side of the chair in pure exhaustion. I need not worry . . . they were taking their roles seriously.

Witness: "Girl S":
Next in line for the State was "Girl S" (a cousin to "Girl Z").

The bulk of her initial testimony dealt with her claims that I would come behind her in her desk (in the classroom) and would massage her shoulders, etc. She responded that while I was allegedly touching her shoulders that only my hands would be in contact with her body (shoulders). She also indicated that occasionally I would feel her muscles . . . "just grab our arm, kind of, and check our muscles." The State's follow-up question: "At the time that he touched your muscles, your arm muscles, did he touch any other part of you?" Her response was, "Not that I remember." Upon request from the State, the witness demonstrated via the desk and mannequin in the courtroom how the defendant would check her muscles.

Again, the State inquired, "Now let me ask you something. In the course of touching your arm, your biceps, did any other part of your anatomy get touched?"

The witness ("S") replied, "Not that I remember."

However, the County Attorney continued his line of questioning with the following, "Do you remember giving a statement to Sheriff _____ at some time last fall?" The witness replied, "Yes." The State continued, "And do you recall talking to the Sheriff about having your breast touched?" At this point, Kurzman voiced an "Objection" (Leading, etc.); Sustained. The State persisted and finally produced Exhibit 6, a photocopy of her signed statement (given to the Sheriff during investigative interviews).

The County Attorney referred the witness to a particular portion of the written statement and continued, "Now, after reading that statement, does it come back to you, or I mean is it- it didn't happen, or what?"

The "Girl S", after examining the written document, suddenly *remembered*, "Yes, but it's more confusing because it's—it's not—it's more like right here, not across the whole thing, as it sounds a little different to me (she demonstrated an area that indicated "like right here. Shoulder muscle right here, kind of lower armpit.").

In listening to this poor girl's testimony, I reflected upon her personality. I recalled how "nasty" she had become when I made the decision to keep her on the B-team squad for basketball—and not to bring her up to the varsity level during state play. Another highly valued player on the team told me that this witness was the one that supposedly said, "I hope Gwen G. breaks her leg" (during tournament play). Wow, that certainly was a prime example of good sportsmanship, wasn't it? No, I did not respect the character of this witness. When Kurzman was given his opportunity to cross examine, he must have felt the same. He spent very little time and energy on her. I believe he knew that any witness who suddenly *remembers* information after indicating otherwise had little credibility in the eyes of the Court. Let's move on.

Witness: "Girl R":

The sister to "S" took the stand (and again, a cousin to witness "Z"). This witness, "Girl R", was asked the following by the County Attorney: "Has there ever been a time in the classroom when the defendant had any physical contact with you?"

She indicated, "Yes," and proceeded to explain that it allegedly occurred during the 1996-97 school year. She described that it was on a day when she ws dressed up for a date and was wearing a black and gray baby T-shirt, short shirt and corduroys. She testified that she had asked me a question and that I grabbed her arm after I had answered it. According to her testimony, she claimed that I pushed her arm, squeezed it, and then pushed her arm towards her breast. In doing so, she claimed that I brushed her breast with his fingers. Again, the Court was witness to another demonstration of the alleged "brush of the breast" by utilizing the desk and mannequin in the courtroom. She did testify that she had told her mother (who works at the University of MN, Morris) of the alleged occurance.

The girl ("R") also stated that I supposedly said, "My, you turned out to be pretty good. Who would have thought?" As I listened to her interpretation of that statement, I couldn't believe she thought I was referring to her physical attributes! I wish I could have told the Court that this witness was probably the "crabbiest" student I have ever encountered in all my years of teaching.

I had encouraged her to try and be more pleasant. When I gave the above mentioned "compliment", I was referring to the fact that she was making considerable progress towards becoming a more congenial individual. She went on to claim that I would touch other students in the classroom . . . "at least twice a week." Her memory was quite profound because she was able to recall that I would allegedly touch a student "about the same" number of times during the seventh, eighth, ninth, and tenth grade years.

Kurzman's cross-examination, again, was not extensive. He did take the time to request a clarification of one of her statements, ". . . you were not meaning to suggest to the jury that you saw Dennis Courneya brush their breasts (referring to four girls she had cited) when letting go of the arm, just that you saw come physical contact between Dennis. . . . ; right?" She responded, "Yes."

Witness: "Girl Q":

It was now time for another girl, "Q", to testify for the State. She indicated that she was a friend to "Girl Z". She professed that "Z" had told her about the alleged incident that supposedly had occurred during the cross country practice session. This witness, "Q", was asked by the State to use the easel in the courtroom to sketch a layout of the cross country/football practice session . . . and where people were located. She complied with the request. This witness indicated that after "Girl Z" had told her about what had allegedly happened, there came a time when the incident was discussed "When a bunch of people went and talked to Mr. Larson" (the Hancock School Superintendent) . . . "To tell him what happened."

Cross-Examination:

It was during Kurzman's cross-examination that the role of another adult was introduced to the Court.

Question: "Were there any other adults there besides Mr. Larson?"
Response: "Yeah."
Question: "Who?"

Response: "Jody Holleman."

Follow-up Question: "Who is that? Who do you know her to be? Is she a teacher?"

Response: "She's the volleyball coach and the basketball coach."

(Note: This is the individual who was selected to replace me as coach of the girls' basketball team)

The witness added later in the testimony that Ms. Holleman "joined along the way."

Question: "Okay. Do yo remember how she came? Did she just happen to be walking down the street?"

Response: "I don't remember."

I could tell that Kurzman was very intrigued with ascertaining more about the role of Holleman; however, the witness was having great difficulty remembering necessary information:

Q: "Do you remember anything Mr. Larson said?"

A: "Not really, no."

Q: "Do you remember anything Jody Holleman said?"

A: "Not really, no."

Q: "How did the meeting end, if you remember. . . . ?"

A: "He just said, 'Thanks girls. Don't worry about anything. Everything will be taken care of.' Something like that."

(I wondered to myself what Larson meant by that phrase. . . . "Everything will be taken care of.")

Q: "Did anybody else tell a story about what they claim happened to them to Mr. Larson?"

A: "Not that I remember."

Kurzman concluded his initial questioning with trying to attain more information regarding Holleman:

Q: ". . . Did Jody Holleman say anything after she joined the
    group of girls that were heading towards Mr. Larson's house
    either in route, on the way, or when you were at Mr. Larson's
    house?"
A: "She just kinda comforted ____ ("Girl Z")."
Q: "How did she comfort her?"
A: "Said everything would be okay and work out."

(* Again, I pondered the phrase. . . . "everything . . . would . . .
work out." Hmmm.)

Redirect:
The State chose to question the witness, "Q", as follows:

Q: "Did you visit with the defendant after the time that you
    learned from "Z" what she said happened?"

The witness professed that she did visit me at my house . . . on her
own. She indicated to the Court that she had not been invited by the
defendant . . . but went "to talk to him. . . . see how he was doing."

Kurzman upon redirect gave the witness the opportunity to
explain her visit a bit further: "Did Mr. Courneya ask you to say
anything or be sure not to say anything when you were talking to
people?" She responded, "No."

Q: "All right. Did you by chance deliver a sub sandwich to him?"
A: "Yup."
Q: "And he paid you for the sub sandwich?"
A: "Yeah."

(*13th Juror:* Recall that this is the individual who came to my
home to bring the sandwich that I had ordered from the school
organization (fund raiser) before the accusations surfaced.)

I felt badly that this girl, "Q", was being put in such an uncomfortable position. She was a truly sincere and kind young girl . . . a

fine person. I wish I could have told her what was once advised by Cowper with regards to the selection of friends, *I would not enter on my list of friends, the one who needlessly sets foot upon a worm."*

Witness: Hancock High School Principal:
The Hancock High School Principal Principal was duly sworn in as the next witness for the State.

To me, he appeared greatly nervous and reluctant. I also knew that he was extremely ill . . . time was not on his side. I had come to know this man quite well during the past twelve years that he occupied the position of principal. Granted, we had our differences. I knew his view on athletics . . . particularly, the female athletic program. His view was different than mine. Through testimony, he explained how he came to be contacted with regards to the allegations. He offered little additional information regarding the notification of authorities, etc.

However, I was quite taken back when he responded as follows to a question posed by the State in regards to my medical emergency on the day of the administrative/parental/student meeting:

Q: "Did you ever know the defendant to come to the adminstration on other occasions complaining of chest pains?"
A: "No."

I could not believe what I was hearing . . . he must be gravely ill. How could he not remember the time when I was brought to the Morris Hospital because of chest pains and he had driven me there! (Upon cross examination by Kurzman, he did recollect the following: "I believe, yes, that there was, and it just seems to me that might have been once at a game or a scrimmage . . .")

I was also astounded at the reply that the principal gave when the State asked him the following question, "(Are you aware) of any valid educational reason why a coach would need to have full body contact with a girl (pertaining to basketball practices and coaching demonstrations) when there were other female players available for the demonstration?", and he replied, "No."

I thought to myself, "Ok, I guess anybody can coach . . . you only have to 'talk the game'."

Cross-Examination by Kurzman:

"Do you recall he was actually hospitalized for chest pain before this day in question . . . ?"

A: "I—I can't recall if he was hospitalized. I know that he had undergone some—I believe he had undergone some tests. That's the best I can relate." Well, I am glad that his memory returned . . . I wondered if he remembered that it was he who had taken me to the hospital following that scrimmage in Marshall.

I don't think it was Kurzman's intention to have the Hancock Principal reveal his true feelings regarding girls' athletics when he asked the following:

"And were you aware of what contribution, if any, Mr. Courneya made to the girls basketball program during the time you were at Hancock?"

A: "Well, he was the head coach."

Q: "And so when he made this comment, 'This is the kind of thanks I get after 22 years . . .' how did you take that?"

A: "I think that he felt he had given a lot to our school and the basketball program, and—and that was all shattered, done with this situation."

I wish that I could have asked this administrator if he felt that I had given anything to the school. Is it customary for administrators to take their teachers/coaches for granted?

Q: "Did you get any impressions during the 12 years you worked

with Mr. Courneya as to whether or not it was important to him in his life to be a teacher and to be a coach?"
A: "Yes, it was. I mean, that would be my feeling."

Kurzman concluded with showing the witness a copy of the booklet that was published following the state championships (girls/boys basketball teams). In the booklet that commemorated the championship season and the players, I was quoted as saying, "Words Cannot Describe the Feeling . . . I love you . . ." Kurzman asked the Principal the following:

Q: "Do you see anything inappropriate. . . . in that?"
A: "No."
The witness was excused.

Witness: Hancock School Superintendent:
I greatly looked forward to the testimony of the next witness, the Hancock School Superintendent. Upon questioning, he, too, recited the sequence of events that led to the reporting of the alleged incidents. However, he presented much needed information regarding the "meeting" that took place at his home. He indicated that he had received a "phone call from the volleyball coach, Jody Holleman, who said there was a bunch of girls at school crying their eyes out, and they wanted to come to talk to me." (Hmmm . . . didn't one witness indicate that Holleman "joined along the way"? So what happened here?) He stated that approximately "eight or nine" girls came to his home with Ms. Holleman.

His testimony continued, "We sat in the living room, and basically they were very—they were crying, worrying about what might happen to them in school or in athletics. They said things similar to what ____("Girl Z") had kind of said about Mr. Courneya in their class. . . ."

Cross-Examination:
During cross-examination, Kurzman inquired of the witness,

". . . that meeting at your house the Friday night you told the jury about, have you ever written any notes about that meeting?"

A: "I—I had jotted the names down when they were there."

Q: "You did. Where is that note?"

A: "I have it at home."

Q: "You didn't think it was going to come up at the trial who's at your house that Friday night?"

("Objection" by the State; Sustained)

Kurzman attempted later to also bring up the necessity of the written note:

Q: "When's the last time you looked at that note with the names on it?"

A: "Probably after I got subpoenaed." (He later indicated he was subpoenaed three or four days ago.)

The Court: "We move for production, 612, your Honor, Rule 612." The court demanded the following, "Mr. Larson, you are ordered to bring the note with you tomorrow Monday."

It could have been my imagination, but I thought that the witness was quite "rattled" by the request and the many follow-up questions by Kurzman concerning what was on the note. It probably was just too much to remember . . . to think about. The questions continued in a realm that I was very anxious to hear the superintendent's responses:

Q: "Was Jody Holleman coaching girls, it is basketball that day or was she coaching—?"

(referring to the night of the meeting at the home of the superintendent)

A: "No."

Q: "—anything?"

A: "Well, she was our volleyball coach, in the fall season, our head volleyball coach this year."

Q: "So she didn't become the girls coach until Mr. Courneya left?"
A: "Right."

The questioning later went into the school policy regarding physical contact, etc.:

Q: ". . . did you ever enact a policy that spoke to whether or not teachers should ever have physical contact (with students) in the school?"
A: "No. We have a—we have a sexual harassment policy. . . . We didn't have any special edict that came out that said nobody should hug anybody or . . ."

The questioning in this subject area continued for a considerable amount of time with a culminating request by Kurzman, "Had anybody complained to you about people feeling uncomfortable beause they had been touched in some way by Mr. Courneya?"

A: "No."
Q: "No teachers ever said anything to you?"
A: "No."
Q: "Did any teachers ever complain about any other faculty members . . . ?"
* "Objection" by the State; Sustained.

I would have found his response to the last question to be quite interesting . . . didn't the teacher, "P", testify that she had spoken to an administrator about another teacher . . . oh, I forget. Perhaps I should check with the jurors regarding prior testimony. Oh, that's right . . . not all of them are taking notes. Let's move on. Surprisingly, it was the State upon redirect that asked a question I wanted an answer to for personal reasons (thank you) and felt it to be very important for the Court to hear, as well:

Q: "How was it that you—do you know how it was that Jody Holleman was selected to take over as the girls basketball coach. . . . Do you know whose idea that was?"

A: "I don't know if she came forward . . . but Mr. Clarke (referring to the school principal), whether she called him and said she would take it or would be interested, I don't really remember exactly how that worked out, but we somehow found out that she would do it or be willing to do it for the season."

I noticed that the State's attorney didn't ask him if Holleman had much experience as a basketball coach . . . Was she a teacher at Hancock? The answer is "No." I actually thought of many things at this point. I thought of what an opportune time for someone else to take over coaching the girls' basketball team. They were at a point that I knew would lead to a state berth in the next couple years . . . and, expectedly, a state championship. The young girls on the team had talent and desire galore! They would make any coach look good . . . even a volleyball coach.

Additionally, as I listened to the testimony of the administrators, I wondered if the bond issue had passed. I knew that the proposed bond issue had been a "hot" topic . . . about the same time I came under "fire". Were they going to build a new school? That would certainly be wonderful to have "under your hat" as an administrator.

At the beginning of the chapter, in the sub-heading, I referred to a quote that spoke of m*oral* law. The word *moral*, as I refer to it for this text and in life, implies that which is *good . . . virtuous*. I wish that I had been given the opportunity to ask the witnesses if they felt *good . . . virtuous* after their testimony. Even as I listened to the accusations, to the defamation of my character, to the degradation of my ideals, I knew that I could live with my conscience . . . my *goodness . . . virtue*. I wondered if the witnesses could say the same.

Swedenborg, in his *Arcana Coelesta,* professed that *Conscience is God's presence in man.* For the record, *His* presence is alive and well in Dennis Courneya. Yes, Cicero, *Virtue is its own reward . . .* regardless.

CHAPTER FOURTEEN

The deeds we do, the words we say,
Into still air they seem to fleet,
We count them ever past; But they
shall last, -In the dread judgement
they and we shall meet.

-John Keble, *The Effect of Example*

As I listened to the testimonies of the girls, I found that I actually felt sorry for who and what they had become. They had become people I no longer recognized. They appeared to "glory" in the controversy. Yes, I was concerned about the impact their testimony would have—on my future, but, also on their future lives. Did they truly believe what they were implying? It was also at this point in the trial that I had to find another $20,000.00 to pay for my defense. To date, my legal representation had reached a price of $60,000.00 with an additional $4000.00 in miscellaneous costs. I was soon forced to cash in my annuities and to take a severe penalty for doing so. I no longer had a penny to my name . . . not one cent.

Witness: "Girl W":
The State called another girl, "W", to the stand. I knew quite a bit about her family. Her father had come from a strong Apostolic Christian background but no longer attended. This girl had confided many times to me that she hated athletics . . . she resented athletics and everything it stood for. She had mentioned that no one should push anyone to do something that they didn't want to do. That belief made my job as a coach very difficult! What was really sad was the fact that she never trained; her ability

was all natural. All I could think of was what she could have attained with just a little bit of desire.

The prosecutor asked "W" if she had ever seen the defendant to touch female Hancock students in any way? She responded that she had (including her) "mostly in the hallway and in the classroom." She went on to describe how I would allegedly "check her muscles", etc, squeeze her arms. She further complied with the request to demonstrate (my actions) on the mannequin in the courtroom how I would "touch" her in the hallway, followed by a verbal description:

"I would be facing my locker, and he would come around and grab like this and sometimes his fingertips would brush over your breast before he grabbed your biceps."

Later in her testimony, she also demonstrated on the mannequin how I supposedly would touch her while in the classroom. Her demonstration did not include a "touching of the breast". Kurzman asked that the record reflect (referring to the hand motion) "And that it did not touch the breast of the mannequin, even with the back of the hand."

However, the County Attorney asked the following question, "In the process of doing that, again, did he touch any other part of your anatomy at times?" At this point, the witness added, "Occasionally he would touch your breast, but you just wouldn't think anything of it . . . "She added in later testimony that the defendant would touch the arms of other students in the classroom . . . boys included.

The questioning of "W" took an unusual shift when the prosecutor asked her the following: "Were there any topics that the defendant would bring up in the classroom that seemed to you different from the types of things that your other teachers might discuss?" I thought that my classroom lectures better be different than that taught by the math teacher . . . after all, I did teach social studies. Anyway, the witness went on to explain how I lectured about different people in history and their roles and, "for example, he would be talking about George Washington or whoever and tell us different stuff about him, and he would mention stuff that him and Martha weren't, you know, the perfect couple or whatever, and George would—kind of had other mistresses on the side, and then he would go—'You know what I mean, right, ___?' . . . and he would relate stuff like that, kind of like sexual like or stuff like that to me in class."

I could not believe what I was hearing! Did this witness think that she was the sole point of my lectures? What an egotistical opinion! Number one, trying to maintain the attention of the class, especially her, required one-on-one attention . . . eye contact, voice, and a reminder to please listen!! I wish she would have mentioned the many times she tried to embarrass me! Furthermore, she continued to tell the Court that I would say things to her that were defined as "unusual". However, what totally dismayed me was her interpretation and description to the following question by the State:

Q: "Did you every meet with him alone at the school?"
A: "Yes."

She further explained that the meetings were upon my request and probably during lunch hour in my classroom. She described the meetings as follows, "Nothing that he said made me feel uncomfortable, but I could tell walking in and out of the room, and he'd kinda lean back in his chair and kinda just look at you. . . ." She continued her description, ". . . I felt he was looking me up and down." She had informed the Court that the meetings centered around the subject of basketball; however, I wish I could have added that these meetings had been held for twenty-two years with my starting point guards. As far as giving her a "look"; it was often in disgust or disapproval. She was not a disciplined individual on or off the court. We had many discussions about her behavior. But I guess, teachers are supposed to just teach their subject area and disregard the personal well-being of their students.

I thought I had "heard it all" from this witness until she explained her version of the "car wash" incident. She claimed that she was at the volleyball car wash and I pulled up . . . she came to the truck and I told her to get in, etc. In actuality, I had made arrangements with her on the prior Friday that I would be dropping off my truck to be washed, and that I needed to be brought back to the cross country practice while it was being cleaned ((I needed to get to the practice field). She explained to the Court that I said the following, "You are not going to wash any more cars today, if you know what I mean." She indicated that she sort of laughed at this statement. She did laugh . . . if fact, we both did. Yes, while she was dropping me off she would be "free of duty"— free from the car washing duties, for a bit; however, I guess she interpreted the statement differently.

As she dropped me off at the practice field, the cross country team was there waiting for me. I said to the team, "Right now, _____("W") is my No. 1". Again, she inferred to the Court that I meant something perverse by that statement. I was simply indicating that she had done me a favor. . . . I didn't have to walk to the field! However, she stated under oath that "It just kinda sounded like we went off into, like we drive around in his pickup and we did stuff and that I was probably better than No. 3." What in the world is she talking about? Perhaps I should have been more angered by her interpretation of the "trip in the pickup"; however, I found it to be utterly repulsive and totally dillusional.

Later in her testimony, she admitted that she was part of the group that visited the superintendent's home with the volleyball coach, Holleman. When asked what happened at his house, she replied, "He went around (referring to the superintendent)—we were kind of in a circle, and he went around and asked what girls were willing to talk to the Sheriff the next—or Monday morning, and then he wrote our names down." She indicated that at this meeting she told, for the first time, the car wash story, and the other girls also told him about their experiences. The State concluded its questioning with the following, "How did—how does it feel for you to be, to come here in court and talk about these things?" She replied, "I feel scared and uncomfortable." All I can say to this is that she was hiding her feelings well.

Cross-Examination:

When Kurzman began his cross examination of the witness, "W", he thanked her for admitting that she saw Mr. Courneya grab the muscles of boys as well as girls. He questioned her, again, about the incidents in the hallway that allegedly resulted in the defendant sweeping his hand across the chest, etc. Her remarks became a bit confusing and thus, she was asked to demonstrate the action again. She demonstrated and recited the following, "He'd go, 'How is my girl doing today?' put his arm around you."

Kurzman retorted for the record, "Can the record indicate that your left hand went on the shoulder of the left—" (She finished the sentence for him, "Arm."), and ". . . Your right hand went over to the shoulder to the juncture at the top of the left arm."

I could tell that Kurzman greatly wanted to get into her perception of "intention" when he asked her the following, "Yesterday, if my notes are correct, you also said you felt uncomfortable, you didn't know his intentions; is that right?" She responded, "Right."

He further questioned her, ". . . Has somebody told you since the time these things happened and now how you should construe or understand or interpret what his intentions were?"

She indicated, "Well, now I know that they weren't appropriate."

Kurzman then furthered as to who told her that. She first indicated that she couldn't remember who, but then professed, "Well, Mr. Sayre (the Sheriff) said that this touching, touchings were not appropriate, and I think Charley (County Attorney) said that also, and Laurie Keehn (counselor/psychologist) also said that."

Kurzman shifted to asking her questions about the statements that she had given during the interviews by the Sheriff and social worker. In fact, he supplied her with a written photocopy of her statements.

In reference to her statements to the Sheriff, Kurzman questioned, "And then you tell him about in basketball, 'He's never touched me in any way, you know, that you felt was sexual harassment;' right?" She responded, "Right."

Kurzman inquired further, "Do you still feel that way today?" The witness answered, "Right."

In reference to her statements and court demonstration regarding the alleged brush of the breast in the hallway, Kurzman continued as follows:

Q: "And then the Sheriff says to you, after you finished explaining some things, he says, 'Has he ever touched your breasts when he's doing this?' Do you remember that?"

A: "Yes."

Q: "And then you explained about this turning thing that you told the jury; right?"

A: "Right."

Q: "How he would come up and put his arm around you and that kind of thing; correct?"

A: "Correct."

Q: "And then the Sheriff says to you, 'So you are kind of on the defensive all the time.' Had you told the Sheriff you were on the defensive all the time when—?"

Kurzman continued to interrogate the witness regarding the contents of her statements given in interview to the Sheriff and social worker: "On Page 4 there's a long paragraph. Is there anywhere in this whole paragraph where you are talking where you say anything about him (referring to the defendent) scanning your body with his eyes?"

He continued as follows: "I'm asking if you had given any information. . . . in any part of the statement, your own paragraph or up before there, which talked about scanning your body with his eyes."

The witness replied, "Not yet, no."

Q: And then _____ (social worker) says to you, 'So, do you feel like he when he looks at you you feel like he's scanning your body?' Right?"

A: "Right."

Q: "So is that the first time that it was suggested to you that he was scanning your body with his eyes?"

A: "Yes."

Kurzman attempted to get more information regarding the meeting at the superintendent's home and the involvement of Ms. Holleman. He asked the witness what Ms. Holleman said to the girls prior to the home visit. The witness responded, "She tried to ask what was wrong, and then two were crying . . . And she just suggested that we go get some reassurance that we shouldn't be scared because Mr. Courneya wouldn't be coming back."

The girl, "W", also told the Court later in her summary of the meeting that Ms. Holleman said the following at Mr. Larson's house: "These girls are scared and they need to know, you know if Mr. Courneya is going to hurt them or find out what they said or . . ."

Q: "Did Mr. Larson appear to be taking notes while the girls were talking with him?"

A: "No. He just wrote down our names."

By Mr. Kurzman:

Q: "When he was—when you believe he came into contact with your breast, was it obvious to you that he touched your breast on purpose?"

A: "No."

To, perhaps, emphasize the question of intent, Kurzman later asked the witness, "Do you remember talking with a lady on the phone who represented or told you that her name was Carol Grant and that she was working as one of the lawyers for Mr. Courneya?" (Response: "Yes.")

Question: "Do you remember telling her that it could happen by
    accident, not intentionally?"
Response: "Yes."
Wow. I think the State better get this witness off the stand as soon
    as possible.

Witness: Hancock Superintendent (again):
    The superintendent was asked to testify, again, in reference to
the notes that he had been ordered to bring to the court. Much of
the questioning dealt with him explaining some of the written
notations and the partial quotes that had been noted.
    A particular area of concern was addressed by Kurzman, "Can
you think of any reason why the portion of your note that allegedly
relates to the meeting (administrative meeting with the "Girl Z", her
parents, the counselor) at 8:00 in the morning had been erased and
written over?" The witness replied, "Probably couldn't read my own
writing, try to make it legible." I thought to myself as he was testifying, "I wonder exactly when these notes were written . . . ?" There
was also a brief pause in the court proceedings during this phase with
the Hancock Superintendent. Kurzman was questioning as to where
the original copy of the notes were . . . ? He had been given "copies",
and they were extremely diffficult to examine for *authenticity.*
    My question for you, the *13th juror—the reader,* how much
more of this do you need to hear . . . want to hear? I'll let you
listen to a few more witnesses for the State.

Witness: "Girl Y":
    "Girl Y" began her testimony for the State. Don't be de-
ceived . . . she may profess to be 15 years old, but she acts as if she
were 25. "Disciplined" is not the word that would characterize
this girl . . . Yes, I had many conversations with this witness in
regards to her behavior and her "living on the edge."
    She, too, during the initial questioning indicated that I (the
defendant) would ". . . come up to you and like grab your arm,
and he brushed your breasts and—I don't know." She verified her

testimony by demonstrating my alleged actions on the mannequin in the courtroom. She indicated later that it occurred "a couple
times a week." Later, after professing that I also engaged in another
sort of touching, she indicated, "Yeah. He'd be up against you". . . .
"His midsection, I guess."

When she was asked to be more specific, she replied, "His
groin area." She complied with the request to demonstrate on the
mannequin in the desk the above mentioned touch. The State
continued the questioning, "In the demonstration, _____ ("Girl
Y"), did your groin area touch the mannequin?" She answered, "I
think so." Followed by more clarifications, the State requested:
"And then can the record reflect she did touch her groin to the
upper shoulder area and caused the mannequin to rock from a
side-to-side direction?"

It was a very intriquing demonstration, to say the least. Let's
see, I am nearly six-feet tall and she is about five feet-seven inches.
Knowing the height differential, would you call any demonstration such as this valid? I looked towards the jurors with hopes that
they were also noting this . . . oh, guess what? Yes, I am tired too.

The witness added more descriptive testimony when she stated
that I also rubbed and patted her leg, or would rub legs when
athletes were stretching out, etc. "Maybe he was touchy/feely, maybe
that's just the way he was, I don't know."

I wish I had documented the number of times that athletes
had requested my assistance in "rubbing out cramps" . . . male
and female athletes. Coaches think nothing of it . . . they were
"just athletes".

By the State:

Q: "Did the—did the defendant ever make any comment to you
    about any clothing or that related perhaps to some clothing
    that you were wearing in class?"

The witness proceeded to explain that she was wearing a tighter
shirt and "He came in, he felt the sleeve of my shirt, and he goes,

'Gonna feel a little nippy today?'. I don't know. He goes, 'If you know what I mean.' I think he used 'nippy.' 'Nice shirt you've got there.'"

Yes, I thought to myself, I remember that day quite vividly. I expected my athletes to dress respectfully (to "dress up") on game days. They were supposed to represent "character" as students and as athletes. It was my way of saying that the way she was dressed was totally inappropriate—she certainly did not set the example of "good character." On that particular day, we were headed to an away game. I certainly did not want younger students or even the opposing fans to think that her appearance was "indicative" of Hancock. I expected our athletes and students to be role models . . . at all times.

This was also the girl who had broken her nose. I had called her at her home, following her surgery, to inquire as to how she was doing, etc. This action, on my part, was nothing new. I always made a point to call or visit injured athletes—male and female. During the phone conversation, she was lamenting, etc. Yes, I always thought that she was overly concerned with her looks, her appearance; therefore, I said to her, "No matter what, you'll always be gorgeous." She indicated to the Court her negative impression of that telephone call.

She also was the student who showed me a picture of a family wedding. I made the mistake of pointing to her in the picture and stating, "Yup, that's the best looking one right there." Why did she want to show me the picture? Perhaps, I should have said, "Nice flowers."

She continued her testimony by informing the Court that I called her "Wild Thing." You bet I did! Her shots in basketball came from "No-man's Land!"—Totally impulsive and typically way off target! She interpreted the nickname differently. I wonder if she recalled that I had nicknames for practically all of my athletes . . . and the nicknames applied to their athletic style, not their personal attributes.

The girl, "Y", continued to provide testimony that during

basketball practice when I assumed the role of the defensive player, I would be "very, very close and uncomfortable."

Q: "What part of him would touch what part of you?"

A: "His groin area, probably, like."

She testified that she first told an adult, Ms. Holleman, about my alleged actions during volleyball season this year. She further indicated that Ms. Holleman recommended that she go and talk to Mr. Larson. Thus, this witness was also part of the group that made the visit to Mr. Larson's home . . . with Ms. Holleman.

Cross-Examination:

When Kurzman was given the opportunity to question "Girl Y", he reminded her of the statement that she had given to the Sheriff. After doing so, he asked her the following question:

"And he (referring to the Sheriff) asked you at the end if there was anything else you wanted to add, and do you remember what you said?"

The witness responded, "Yes. I said I just hope he gets what he deserves." She further attempted to clarify the statement to the Court; however, as Kurzman pointed out she had not added those clarifications during her initial statement to the Sheriff.

When Kurzman asked her "What did you think he deserves when you made that statement . . . ", she responded, "That's not not really how I said it. . . . I mean, I don't want him to like go to jail or anything. I mean, I don't—I'm just telling the truth, and I hope he gets what he deserves. Nothing more, nothing less."

Further on during her testimony, she recalled more information that shed light on the role of Ms. Holleman. The witness testified that some of the girls (including herself) had gone to the University (referring to the University of MN, Morris) one day to talk to Ms. Holleman . . . "and it's just—I mean, the things that we said, she couldn't believe it. She is like, 'Oh, my word, you guys have to do something about it.' She was just like, 'If my daughter had a teacher or coach like that, I would, I don't know, take them to a different school or something.'"

Later in the questioning by Kurzman, the witness revealed her personal opinion of me quite explicitly. Kurzman inquired, ". . . It's fair to say that you had the impression that most of the kids really didn't like Mr. Courneya?"

A: "Well, to get along with you, you just have to act like he wants you to act."

Q: "Who—do you know who was voted by the seniors to be the person to dedicate the yearbook to last year at school?"

A: "Yes."

Q: "Who?"

A: "Dennis Courneya."

Q: "And do you know who was voted to be the best teacher of the year at Hancock last year?"

A: "I'm not sure on that one. I'm guessing, but . . ."

Kurzman finalized his phase of questioning by bringing her attention to the statements she had given during the interviews by the Sheriff and social worker. It was easy to ascertain that Kurzman was attempting to pinpoint areas of the questioning technique that may have led to presumptions . . . may have led to a misinterpretation of statements. In my opinion, the responses by the witness were confusing and extremely difficult to follow. I empathized with the jury who had to try and discern information given by the witness. The following example best describes what I mean:

Question: "In the statement that you gave where you say words to the effect, 'Come up and brush my breast. I don't know', what did you mean, 'I don't know'?"

She replied, "I say that a lot of times after I say things. I mean, that I'm just . . . I don't know."

I know one thing; her attitude was a disgrace.

Witness: "Girl U":

The younger sister to the previous witness now took the stand. Let's refer to her as "Girl U". During the questioning, this witness also professed that in the classroom the defendant would "grab your muscles and he'd nudge your breast with your—with his hand." Upon request, she demonstrated the alleged "manner in which the defendant would touch your arm and then whatever else happened in the process" (State request) by utilizing the desk/ mannequin in the courtroom.

She also provided testimony that "physical touching" by the defendant also occurred outside of the classroom . . . "During practices or at meets, track meets or cross country meets." Upon questioning with regards to any specific incident in which she was touched, she gave the following response: "At a Benson track meet." She recalled the specifics of the alleged incident:

"Well, he comes up behind you while you are stretching, laying on the ground or sitting on the ground doing your stretch, and he'd grab your neck and he'd like shake your neck a little bit, and he'd be standing like right behind you where like a part of his body would touch you on like the back of the neck, the groin area would." She further explained, "The groin area would touch you on the back of the neck."

As I listened to her "descriptions", I hoped that the jurors were noting her height; she is maybe five-foot tall in stature. *13th Juror:* Is her description even physically possible? She also professed to the Court that "Girl Z" had spoken with her and had "explained the same type of situation."

The State continued with its questioning:

Q: "Remember how the defendant would be dressed at practices or meets for track or cross country?"
A: "Yes." She furthered her explanation with the following description, "Well, sometimes he would have a pair of shorts on that were fairly tight, and some other times he had wind pants on."

A short time later, the questioning became more specific:

Q: "And was there an occasion you noticed something unusual about him as he watched the girls warm up?"
A: "Yes." The witness continued her explanation, "I noticed that he had an obvious erection, because I noticed it because he had tight shorts on."

At this point, I thought nothing the girls professed would phase me anymore. However, this last tidbit left me totally aghast! Is she claiming that this so-called physical description of my body occurred during a meet with scores of athletes and spectators in attendance . . . and that she, alone, was "witness" to the spectacle? I was appalled and in total shock. What in the world could she possibly be thinking about? Apparently, her mind was not on the running event.

She continued her testimony by referring to an alleged comment that I supposedly had made while she was in the classroom, "And he had made a remark on what a nice young lady I was starting to look like. . . . He was just sitting there. . . ."

Q: "Could you tell where he was looking?"
A: "At me."

When the State attempted to get her to tell more as to what he was looking at, she responded, "No, I could not (tell)."

Later in her testimony, she recalled another incident in which I allegedly stated, "You are looking pretty good today, almost good enough to bring home to Mom." Apparently, the witness did not appreciate the comments.

What she didn't tell the Court was that my mom was a friend of the females athletes. My team loved her and she adored the athletes. Mom was one of their most loyal fans. Also, why didn't this witness inform the Court that the cross country team had been to my parents' home the first week of October following a Perham meet. I had introduced all of the team members, and Mom and Dad then took the entire team out for supper. If I stated such a compliment about bringing anyone home to Mom, I was implying that they were respected as athletes, and that they would be welcomed again. I could not fanthom this girl's interpretation. I turned around to give Mom a reassuring look, she was just shaking her head in disbelief as to what she was hearing from this girl. Mom, and everybody else, was certainly witness to the reverse side of "the coin". How disappointing it must have been for the adults to hear today's youth speak so offensively.

Cross-Examination:

When Kurzman cross-examined the witness, he questioned her testimony regarding the stretching out incident when she had allegedly felt the defendent's groin touch her. At this point, Kurzman requested to use the mannequin. He then attempted to re-enact the action she had described. As I witnessed his demonstration, I told myself, "Finally, this issue is dead and done." Later in the questioning, the girl told the Court that she had told the cross country team about the alleged incident . . . before "Girl Z" had shared her story.

My attorney continued to challenge her further in regards to her testimony about "seeing" my erection during a meet, "And can you describe just how it was you concluded that he was standing there with an erection . . . ?"

She responded, "Well, he had tight shorts on, and he has worn them before, and obvious—it was bigger than it obviously had been before."

Kurzman asked the witness if she recalled sharing her observation with others. She answered that she did and stated as such, "Well, I—saw it, and I said that—I said, 'Oh, no, he's wearing those shorts again.' "And then they said, "Yeah, I know. I seen that.' "She added under oath that there was no conversation about an erection at that time—. The witness informed the Court that she did not discuss with anybody else what she recalled happening . . . "Not even your sister?" Her retort was, "Well, probably, yes. We live in the same house." Yet, during further questioning as to whether she had memory of talking about any of this with her sister, she replied, "I don't remember."

Kurzman proceeded to attack the credibility of her statements given to the Sheriff and social worker. Kurzman particularly asked her to recall the affidavit that indicated she had said the following:

"When he said this to me (referring to the statement,"You are starting to look like a nice young lady"), he was looking me up and down as if he was undressing me with his eyes." She recalled the statement.

Kurzman furthered, "Do you remember Mr. Glasrud (County Attorney) asking you if he looked any place in particular?"

Again, she responded, "Yes."

Kurzman continued his questioning, "Do you remember you telling him he did not look any place in particular?"

She replied, "I said I couldn't tell."

She later clarified her statement by indicating, "Earlier I had said I couldn't tell what he was looking at, but now I'm saying that I felt that's what he was doing . . ."

I could not condemn the juror members for not taking notes at this point; it would have been nearly impossible to keep track of what she was saying.

The State, upon redirect, brought her attention back to the demonstration that Kurzman had re-enacted when he had stood over the seated form of the Resusci-Annie. Questions about the height differential between Kurzman and myself were brought to light. Therefore, upon request, Kurzman and I stood back to back to demonstrate our height. We both welcomed the opportunity! The State requested, "Please. Can the record reflect that Mr. Kurzman appears to be an inch or two taller?"

As I returned to my seat in the courtroom, I noted how concerned the State appeared to be whenever the "height" question arose. Do you think that they, too, were realizing the physical impossibilities of the testimony? As the witness was excused, the Court reminded the jurors not to read anything about this case or listen to any news media reports or anything like that.

Witness: "Girl T":

Let's take note of the next witness for the State—a cousin to "Girl Z". This young girl, "T", was also asked about any possible physical touching between the defendant and herself.

She stated, "He would touch our—my arm and feel my muscle." When the State furthered as to whether anything else happened in the way of touching, she added, "He would sometimes feel my breast." Again, the desk and mannequin became the source of demonstration by the witness with her brushing the breast of the mannequin with the backs of the fingertips.

Later in her testimony, she also reflected that the ones the defendant touched were "People that—girls that were in sports or were one of his favorites or something in their class often did." She also added upon questioning, "You got better grades, got a little bit more help maybe."

When she was asked about the first time she told an adult of the touching, she indicated that it was "after it was reported and stuff." When questioned as to why she didn't tell any adults sooner, she replied, "Cuz, I didn't feel comfortable and didn't know if it was that bad that it was needed to be told, I guess."

Cross-Examination:

Upon cross-examination, she indicated (through the questioning) that the Apostolic Christian was "our church." Even though the defense wanted to delve into the issues of that particular religion (beliefs, standards, etc.), we knew we would be met with considered objections. Therefore, Kurzman continued his inquiry into the "muscle checking" incidents. She professed that she saw Mr. Courneya check boy's muscles in classrooms "Once in awhile."

Kurzman particularly wanted to address this girl's testimony in which she had stated that the kids he (the defendant) favored would get better grades, etc. He asked her the following, "Isn't it true that last year's team which won the state championship in basketball lost the team academic championship because of grades received from Mr. Courneya?"

She responded, "I don't know." (Actually it was the team of 1992. Yes, they lost the award because of my scrutiny over their classroom grade.)

Kurzman also questioned the witness, "T", about her interviews with the Sheriff and social worker. She recalled telling the Sheriff in terms of telling her mom or a teacher, "We didn't know if it was bad enough to say something."

She also admitted that she told the Sheriff she might have said something to her speech coach . . . "Well, I wasn't sure if we really talked about it, but . . . I think we just—they just were wondering if it was really true."

Kurzman appeared confused by her last statement and inquired, "If what was really true?"

"Girl T" retorted, "What was all going on". . . . "About the muscle thing and _____ ("Girl Z")."

She admitted that there were other kids involved in the discussion with the speech teacher but didn't remember who. . . . but, "I'm not even sure" (speech team members?).

The questioning took another turn in regards to the interviews by the Sheriff and social worker:

Q: "Who was it who brought up the subject of if you had told it could probably affect what happens on the basketball court? Was that you, or was that one of the adults that was questioning you, who brought that up?"

A: "I don't know."

At this point, Kurzman had the witness refer to her written statement, Page 7.

Q: "The Sheriff says, 'And also I assume it could probably affect what happens on the basketball court,' and you agreed; right?"

A: "Yes."

Q: "And then the Sheriff said, 'Maybe he doesn't come out and say that, but does he imply that somehow?' or and you said, 'You don't get to play as much'; right?"

A: "Yes."

Q: "Now, if you hadn't told, how were you able to conclude that, if you had told, you wouldn't get to play as much?"

A: "Because if you weren't one of his favorites, you probably didn't get to play as much."

Q: "I take it you didn't consider yourself one of his favorites; is that right?"

A: "No."

As I listened to her testimony, I felt sorry for her. I knew that her parents had been great athletes. I wondered if she was going to go through life thinking that other people "got the good breaks" because of favoritism? Did she realize the value of talent? Does she truly believe we won the state championship and countless awards in the past decades because I played only my favorites? How sad.

Redirect:

As the State chose to redirect, a question was posed, "What was it that you saw in other people that made you conclude that you wouldn't get to play as much if you said something unfavorable about the defendant?" She replied, "Well, I can remember a couple girls that were pretty good, and they didn't make it to varsity, and they weren't a favorite, so I just figured. . . ."

Here again, I wish the *talented* basketball players from my varsity championship team could have heard her testimony. They would have been stunned to learn that they were chosen to play because they were my favorites . . . because they didn't say anything unfavorable. I guess the *secret* of coaching has finally been revealed by a non-varsity player: "Players who are *favorites* of the coaches will get to play varsity . . . and they will win games . . . they will win state championships.

There was a final moment during her testimony that revealed an *element* of truth. When she was asked *Why* she did not sign her transcript (prepared from the taped interviews by the Sheriff and social worker), she responded, "I didn't want to". . . . "Cuz I would rather not be here."

Me either . . . I bet the same goes for those jurors who can hardly stay awake.

13th Juror: At this point, I had hoped to stop your agony . . . do you really have to hear more? Indulge me . . . just listen to the next girl, a senior (grade 12). Let's refer to her as "Girl X".

Witness: "Girl X":

As she took the stand, I thought about her father. He was a Hancock School Board member and a devout Apostolic Christian. I wondered if he was in attendance . . . watching the proceedings. Readers, you may want to reread the chapter with regards to this girl's interviews with the Sheriff and social worker. Recall that she is the one who indicated something to the effect . . . "She was one of his (the defendant) favorites . . . but then they had a fallout." Oh boy . . . sounds like the beginning of a soap opera. Anyway, let's listen to her description of the physical contact that allegedly occured during basketball practice:

"He would be squatting as a defensive playber behind us, and we would have to push against him to get to the bucket."

Q: ". . . What part of you pushed against him?"
A: "Our back and our butt area."
Q: ". . . Can you—can you describe just as best you can the parts of his body that you would be pushing against? Just general areas is fine."
A: "Okay. Like his chest, his stomach. I don't know. There wasn't any time that I felt anything . . ."

The line of questioning continued in the realm of the above mentioned basketball drill:

Q: "And how did you feel about doing that drill where you would be—he would be testing your power?"
A: "We always thought it was kind of, I don't know, dumb" . . . "I mean, made some of us uncomfortable. I was uncomfortable.

I just thought we could probably do it against a teammate and it would be the same thing."

The questioning by the State directed the witness to descriptions of touches in the classroom. The prosecutor inquired, "Do you remember anyone in class who seemed to receive more of this kind of touch than others?" The witness referred to "Girl W". When asked if she could tell whether any other parts of my body were coming in contact with "W" during the alleged classroom touching, she responded, "His penis area, groin area. I don't know. His legs or hip area." Furthermore, this witness professed the following, ". . . It happened all the time, I mean, what I can remember . . . "Every day, unless he was in a bad mood."

Now, readers, try to follow the next line of questioning and responses:

Q: "Did it happen to you in tenth grade? Now when I say it, I didn't specify. Was there any touching of the groin to you in the classroom?"

A: "No. I mean his area, but never felt anything."

Q: "Now, you just said I never felt anything. I want to ask you not particularly whether you can feel a specific part of his anatomy. Do you know whether or not his general groin area was ever touching you?"

A: "Yes."

Q: "Did it?"

A: "Yeah, it was his leg area and groin area."

What I found so amazing was her ability to *recall* so much about the alleged touching of "Girl W":

". . . I was pretty young. I don't remember a certain year that it started happening, but probably around eighth or ninth grade."

This witness continued to provide descriptions about my alleged interactions with "W": "He was sitting in class and gave ___ ("W") the eye or say, . . . 'Don't give me that eye', or whatever. I don't know.

I always thought that was kind of sick or dumb or—"... . "ridiculous." ... "It made it like there was something going on between them, and there wasn't . . ."

I don't claim to be a analyst or anything, but if you look at this witness's claim about how she felt that *she* used to be one of my favorites, etc., but had some type of fallout, etc., and then look at her overt consternation with what I supposedly said and did to "Girl W", does it appear to be the *green-eyed monster* at work again? It certainly was not my intention to offend this girl with a lack of attention.

The witness continued to explain as to why she had never really told anyone, any adult, until this . . . "Cuz it . . . it wasn't for them to know, I didn't feel. I didn't feel it was that big of a deal until I started thinking about—thinking about it, I guess."

Cross-Examination:
During cross-examination by Kurzman, the witness indicated that she was part of the group that was accompanied by Holleman at the visit to the superintendent's home. She stated that she couldn't remember how she got to his home . . . "Some people rode in a car. I don't remember if I drove or if I rode with somebody."

As I listened to her professed lack of memory, I thought to myself, this is so bizarre. She can recall instances that allegedly happened to somebody else back in eighth and ninth grade . . . but not some details about a very important meeting that had occurred a couple months ago.

Kurzman attempted to obtain insight into some of her more personal remarks with the following:

Q: "Did you feel badly that Mr. Courneya didn't seem to be as friendly with you this year as he had been in previous years?"
A: "I remember—well, see, you always wanted to please him. I don't know. I—I was scared of him, and he was treating me bad because of an incident that happened toward the end of basketball, and I always wondered what—what was wrong,

because I didn't know, and I don't know that's why he quit treating me like he did before."

Upon further questioning, the witness explained that she had complained to her mom about some problems in practice and in games . . . "During tournaments, basketball tournaments . . . I was probably the sixth person on the team, or first person on the bench . . . I felt like I had been treated like bad on the team, they— I felt I wasn't welcome . . . wasn't as good as them . . . And, I don't know, they always had their—the five of them starters, always had their little thing and never included anybody else . . ."

As a result of her perceived alienation and her complaint, yes, I did receive quite a call from her mother! Wow! Put it this way . . . it was such a negative conversation that I hung up on the woman. I can never remember doing that to anyone else, but it was a most derogatory phone call!

The witness added further descriptions of how I would . . . "in the halls, like really young kids he'd like come up . . . and talk to them and, I don't know, put his arm around them. But I never thought anything bad of it, that he was being a nice guy. You know what I mean?" Yes, I know what you mean. Thank you.

Witness: "Girl L":

"Girl L", a sixteen-year old student was the next witness to testify for the State. She indicated that she knew Mr. Courneya as one of her teachers and as her track coach, as well as a coach for "a little bit of basketball."

Q: "Did the defendant ever touch you in the classroom?"
A: "Yes." She further added upon questioning, "He would feel my muscles on my arms with his hands, and he'd come up behind me and kind fo rub my shoulders and lean against me a little."

The State's attorney asked her to be more specific. She complied by indicating, "Kind of his hip section wold probably lean against me, was leaning against me."

Q: "Did this happen at all in the 1997-98 school year, this year, your tenth grade year?"
A: "I don't know."
Q: "Did it—when do you recall it happened? Any of the touch for now."
A: "It was throughout all my years."

To address any "confusion" about her response, the attorney continued, ". . . in the 1997-98 school year, do you remember any touching happening in the classroom between the defendant and you?"
A: "Yes."

She complied with his request to demonstrate the "touching" on the court mannequin. Following her demonstration in which she squeezed the right arm of the mannequin, she responded that in the course of that happening, no other part of her was touched.

Q: ". . . Now, as long as we've got you standing up, you also testified to something with the shoulders." (Response, "Yes.") "Would you be able to demonstrate how it would be that the defendant would come up and touch you in that manner?"
A: "And he would be rubbing against me."
State: "Can the record reflect that she took her—she came up to the mannequin, kneaded the shoulders . . . and pressed her groin area up against the upper back area of the neck?"

The attorney proceeded to derive information as to when or how often this contact occurred. She replied, "I don't remember."

Q: "Can you estimate for the frequency that the kind of touching you last demonstrated happened to you in your ninth grade year?"
A: "It was probably about once a month at least."

The witness, upon direct questioning, was able to *recall* that she was touched in that manner in her eighth grade year, as well.

As if to clarify, the attorney questioned her further, "How about again the coming up behind, kneading shoulders and groin touch that you just demonstrated?"

A: "I think so, too, uh-huh."

"Girl L" continued her testimony by describing how she had heard the defendant say things to other girls and that she had observed the defendant having physical contact with the athletes during sports practices. . . . "He was demonstrating some defense or some kind of basketball stuff."

Q: "What part of the defendant's body would touch the girl (referring to the basketball- related contact)?"

A: "A lot of it, anywhere from the—I know the behind of the girl was pretty much against him and her lower back was—probably his legs were touching her."

Cross-Examination:

Mr. Kurzman wanted her to clarify her statements about how the defendant would rub again her back while she was sitting in the classroom:

Q: "Now, then the Sheriff was asking you to describe how he—this is Page 2—how he rubbed against you. The Sheriff said, 'His crotch was on your shoulder, on your back?'

And you say, 'My back.' And then the Sheriff says, 'Kind of in the center of your back and you are sitting in the classroom school desk, is that how it went?' You said, 'Yeah.' Do you remember that?"

After she responded, "Yeah", Kurzman requested that she indicate where on her back the alleged contact took place. Following her indication of location, Mr. Kurzman stated, "Can the record indicate the witness indicated an area approximately two to

three inches down from the shoulderline or toward the center
of her back?"

The State: "I thought it was lower. I would describe it as if between her shoulder blades, I guess."

Kurzman: "Okay. I'll take lower."

The questions for this girl became more detailed: "Is that how you
remember it, that he would sort of walk up one step or so and
do the massage?"

A: "No, he would come in between the desks."

In listening to her testimony, I was certain that the State would
want to redirect. It just appeared to us that she was adding more and
more information as the questions went along. I wondered what she
would say next . . . The State's attorney only asked a few more questions, mainly focusing on her height. Interesting, don't you think?

Witness: "Girl O":

The testimony of the next girl, "O", was quite brief. It centered
around her "observations" of what had allegedly happened to some of
the other girls or how they confided in her. Kurzman, upon cross-
examination, asked her what adults (persons) other than school mates
of hers had she talked about stories involving Dennis Courneya.

She replied, "Charlie (referring to the County Attorney) and
Teresa (referring to the investigator for the school), and that's all,
and my parents."

She also indicated that she had gone over to the University
(University of MN, Morris) to meet with Jody Holleman.

In reference to the copy of her interview with the Sheriff and
social worker, Kurzman inquired, "Do you remember the Sheriff
was asking you about things that you had seen or witnessed . . .
And you saying to the Sheirff, 'Well, he just like—well, it wasn't
sexual contact, but I mean he—well, some of the things were, but
he like did a lot of verbal abuse, like he was always yelling down
there." Do you remember that?"

She responded, "Yeah."

Kurzman furthered, "Okay. All right. Do you remember the Sheriff asked you if you ever saw any physical contact with other players during practice which appeared to be inappropriate?"

She answered,"Yeah."

The follow-up request from Kurzman stated, "You told the Sheriff, 'No.' Do you remember that?"

She replied, "Uh-huh, because I wasn't there. I was on the B squad."

Kurzman proceeded, ". . . And do you remember—I guess it was the lady (social worker), she said to you, Page 3, 'Have you ever seen him move real close to anyone with his groin area?' Do you remember her asking you that?"

The girl replied, "Uh-huh."

Q: "And what did you tell her?"

A: "No."

Q: "And is it correct that _____ ("Girl Z") is one of your best friends?"

A: "Uh-huh, yes."

Neither the defense nor the State had further questions for the witness. She was excused.

13th Juror: You, too, are dismissed . . . momentarily. You are perhaps wondering how in the world this trial could possibly continue . . . My notations of the testimony for the State will culminate with the next chapter. It has not been my intention to provide you with a step-by-step account of the trial. If I had, you, too, would have fallen asleep two chapters back . . . or joined some of the jurors in slumber. However, if you feel that my account of the trial has been deceiving, I encourage you to try and attain the official transcripts of the trial. That is what I did . . . and I only had to pay $7000.00 for them. Oh, what is money anyway?

I took one draught of life, I'll tell you what I paid, Precisely an existence - *The market-price, they said* (Emily Dickinson).

CHAPTER FIFTEEN

Trust on, and think tomorrow will repay;
Tomorrow's falser than the former day.
                                        -Dryden, *Aureng-Zebe, IV, I*

Perhaps, the most critical phase of the trial took place in the judge's chambers. The State desired to discuss Spreigl evidence. In other words, the prosecution wanted to introduce testimony from individuals who were not filing charges, but could contribute to the State's case against Dennis Courneya. The crucial element of the State's case was to prove intent and absence of mistake or accident (Court File No. K7-97-155, Volume VII, pages 1274-1292) on the part of the defendant. Therefore, the prosecution proposed that through the use of additional (Spreigl) testimony, it would evidence sexual and/or aggressive intent.

Kurzman objected to the Spreigl on the terms of the prejudicial effect and in terms of clear and convincing evidence. He contended that the "12, 13, or 14 (witnesses for the State) that have testified should be suffcient to allow the State to make the argument he indicates they want to make."

The Court's response was as follows (pgs. 1279-1280): "The Court would find that the State's case with respect to the question of intent of the defendant's sexual or aggressive purposes is weak and that the Court at least with respect to that element of determining the admissibility of Spreigl would so find." Therefore, the ruling indicated that testimony would be taken from the Spreigl witnesses outside the hearing of the jury.

I could not fathom the basis for this ruling. First: The Court virtually admitted that the State's case regarding intent was "weak";

Second: Therefore, additional testimony would be taken from girls (who were not filing charges . . . but had information) that would somehow "strengthen" the State's case. From my point of view, it was like saying, "OK, your case against the defendant isn't great when it comes to proving intent; therefore, we'll give you another shot at it!

Four girls testified in chambers. It was determined that three of them would be allowed to testify in open court. Kurzman was quite infuriated and indicated, "I really don't care. I think it is so violative of law that this is going to be reversible if he's convicted." He continued his objection by citing *State v. Kennedy*: ". . . which I read it could not be clearer, evidence consisting solely of a victim's bolstering testimony without corroborating evidence cannot be said to be clear and convincing has to be viewed against what evidence has been given . . . and the evidence given is physically impossible." His objection was to no avail.

The following proceedings took place in open court:

The Court: "Members of the jury, the evidence which you are about to hear from the testimony of the next witnesses to be called by the State cannot be used by you to determine whether or not Mr. Courneya did the acts alleged in the complaint. The evidence that you are about to hear may be used by you for the limited purpose of determining the defendant's intent if you find that the acts charged in the complaint occurred. . . ."

"Girl Z": Spreigl

Guess who the first witness was . . . ? "Girl Z" again! She was asked to recall any *other* instances in which she experienced the defendant touching her. She testified about an alleged incident that had occured before the cross-country incident. She claimed that when she was in the classroom at her desk, I came up to her and squeezed her arm and placed my hand on top of her breast. She indicated that I said, "Oh, you like that?" Can you believe this? Remember, she is claiming that

I not only did the above mentioned actions/comments, but that I also did them with a classroom full of students!

Kurzman's first question upon cross-examination "hit her hard": ". . . it's correct, is it not, you didn't remember this latest story until December 12th, 1997, when you were sitting with Teresa (school investigator) preparing an affadavit?"

A: "Yes."

Kurzman wanted the Court to know something that, perhaps, was not known to all . . . He asked the witness, "When you spoke with the Sheriff—did you know the Sheriff, by the way . . . ?" She professed that she "knew of him because he works in the same building as my mom."

Kurzman: "Your mom is the deputy court administrator here in this county; right?"

Response: "Yes."

Q: "This last recollection that you shared with the jury, are you as sure about that as you are about the first two stories you told?"

A: "Yes."

In reference to her recollection of the above mentioned incident, Kurzman quizzed:

Q: "Did you take that as an act of sexual aggression?"

A: "No."

Q: "Did you take it as an act of sexual contact?"

A: "No."

Q: "How about as you are sitting here now, do you take it as an act of sexual contact?"

A: "Yes."

With regards to the December 12th meeting with the school investigator, Kurzman inquired, "So what did she say that helped you remember this overt act of sexual aggression?"

A: "She just asked me if there was anything else he had done to me, and I—it just came to me."

Q: "Why do you suppose you had forgotten it since it happened through the questioning by the Sheriff and _____(social worker), through all the conversations with your girlfriends, through—"

A: "I didn't really forget it. For those other things, I was just—I thought it was just basically talking about the one incident, and so I was just concerned, or I was just talking about that one incident, so I wasn't . . ."

* Did you follow that response? I thought she answered the question very *clearly*.

Q: "You saw Ms. Holleman before you got the recollection on December 12th of this full breast grab; didn't you?"

A: "I don't know if I saw her before . . . I'm not sure."

Let's see . . . we have the alleged incident that started the case occurring on Monday, October 6. We have this witness ("Z") telling about it on October 8th. Her statement is taken on October 13th. Then, we have a two-month gap until, with the school investigator, this witness *remembers* the alleged breast grab (in a full classroom!).

Question by Kurzman: "Between the time you claim to have been the victim . . . on the playing field (October 6) . . . and the time you gave your statement on the 13th, you had met with Jody Holleman; hadn't you?"

A: "Yes."

Kurzman then reminded "Girl Z" of her affidavit (based upon her interview with the school investigator, Theresa):

Q: "Well, do you remember that the story of grabbing your entire right breast didn't come up until the sixth paragraph in the affidavit?"

A: "I don't know."

Q: "Do you remember that it didn't come up during the third paragraph when you were talking about the touching that would happen in class with the tips of the fingers?"

A: "I don't know. I'm just . . . I don't . . ."

* Kurzman corrects himself: "It was the fifth paragraph in the affidavit. Do you recall that?"

A: (no response)

Q: "Well, never mind. What did she say, if you remember, right before you said 'I remember something else. He squeezed my entire right breast with his right hand, I gasped in shock. . . .'"?

A: "I don't really remember what she asked me before that."

Q: "Do you know how memory works?"

* The State voiced an "Objection"; Sustained.

Q: "How do you know this story of grabbing the breast, if you actually recalled it in December, isn't just a dream as opposed to something that really had allegedly happened before the field stretching incident?"

A: "I just know. I remember it clearly and . . . I just know."

The witness was excused . . . from further testimony. However, I encourage this witness to look up the definition of *memory: The act, process, or faculty of representing in consciousness an act, experience or impression . . . the experience of the mind . . . and the **accuracy and ease** with which a person can call forth single experiences from it.*

"Girl N": Spreigl

The witness, "Girl N", testified about an alleged incident that occurred during a track practice. She professed that she was watching another girl throw the shot put in the gym, and "he came in from working with another student outside, and apparently it was cold outside, and he walked up to me and he said, 'Isn't my hand cold?' and he slipped his hand under my shirt on my stomach."

Cross-Examination:

Upon cross-examination, Kurzman questioned her regarding the transcript of her statement given to the Sheriff. There seemed to be some confusion regarding her initial statements regarding the "cold hand(s)" incident. To heed clarification, Kurzman directed her to pages 2 and 3 of the transcript:

Q: "And then the Sheriff, after you told him this on Page 2, at the top of Page 3 says, 'Okay. So, in other words, he put both hands or just one hand on your stomach area?' And then you responded, 'Just one hand.' Is that a change?"

A: "Yes."

Q: "I guess you said, 'Just one hand, yeah.' And then you crossed some things off about him using his other hand to lift it up. Why did you cross that off? Is it because you didn't say it or you didn't remember it that way, or what?"

A: "It didn't happen like that. That's why I crossed it off."

Q: "Okay. When the Sheriff asked you initially and you explained it in a particular way, but then when you came back to sign it on November 5th, 1997, you—you took that out; so what was there between October 15th and November 5th that helped you remember that it didn't occur the way you had first said it?"

A: "What helped me remember that?"

Q: "Yeah."

A: "I don't—my mind, I—I—I said I must have made a mistake."

Kurzman directed her attention to other changes she had made in the written document

Q: "So, in responding to the question 'How would he rub against you?' what you took out of the answer was that 'He pressed or kind of leaned against you.' Is that correct, those words?"

A: "Yes, I took those out."

There were additional examples that were brought to the Court's attention in which the witness had decided to "change" or "correct" the words that were documented in her written statements to the Sheriff. In my opinion, it was like listening to a broken record.

However, Kurzman had a final question for this Spreigl witness:

Q: "How well do you know ___ ("Girl Z")?"
A: "I know her well."
Q: "Would you consider her one of your very close friends?"
A: "Yes."

Ahhh, one cannot underestimate the value of friendship. *As old wood is best to burn, old horse to ride, old books to read, and old wine to drink, so are old friends always most trusty to use* (Leonard Wright, *Display of Dutie, 1589).*

"Girl M": Spreigl

The final Spreigl witness, "M", began her testimony describing how the defendant would "intentionally touch my breast." She claimed that the alleged touching would occur in the classroom and in track practice. She also added, upon questioning, "He would often wink and look at me in—"

Additionally, she stated that the defendant would make comments about their age difference. However, it was the next line of questioning by the State that produced testimony of which few will ever forget:

Q: "Was there ever a time you assisted the defendant doing some measuring on the practice field or the running field?"
A: She answered, "Yes", and upon further questioning made the following comments:

"We were measuring the distance between two hurdles one day at practice" . . .

"Yes, I was a hurdler. And he had the tape measure in his hand, and I don't remember the correct distance we were measuring, but he came out with a question, 'I bet you have never seen a ten meter one before'. No, I haven't."

Q: "Did you take it that he was talking about hurdles when he said that?"

A: "Ten meter? He wasn't referring to the hurdles, no. He was referring in a sexual way."

This Spreigl witness, "M", also testified about another alleged incident during a track practice. She described that she was preparing to take a sprint and that I asked her if she was loosened up and ready. ". . . and I was like, 'Yes, I'm fine. I'm ready to go.' He said, 'Because, if you are tight, I can loosen you up.' And it meant definitely sexual."

(It would be impossible for me to count the number of times I helped athletes loosen-up—by providing stability as they stretched or by making them run!).

She continued by describing that I would touch her inner thigh, indicating where the hurdle should scrape, when coaching her how to go over a hurdle . . . She added a final comment for the Court to hear: "In fairness, I think you should know and Mr. Courneya that I am here because I was subpoenaed. And he is a good teacher. He was a good coach. And I'm not here because I am for or against, and I just want you to know that. I am here because it's for a good reason and for the other girls and myself."

Cross-Examination by Mr. Kurzman:

Q: "So what do you think you are accomplishing for the other girls?"

A: "For the other girls, I don't know if I'm accomplishing anything. But for myself—

Q: "Yeah."

A: "—comfort, relief."

Q: "So you want to amend your answer you are not here for the other girls and just say you are here for yourself for comfort and relief?"

A: "I am here for myself."

Kurzman referred the witness to the affidavit of her interview with the school investigator, Theresa:

Q: "Okay. Now, in the affidavit, it says that you always felt that he touched your breast intentionally; right?"

A: "At the time he did touch my breast, yes, I always felt that it was intentional."

Q: "Did he make sexual advances on you when you were alone in the room?"

A: "Could have. I don't remember exact times when we were alone if he made sexual advances or didn't."

The girl continued to explain that she felt I had made sexual advances to her during track.

Q: "Who else was around? Anybody?"

A: "Yes." . . . "Track people."

During further questioning by Kurzman as to how she reacted to the perceived sexual advances, the witness admitted the following:

"I didn't express my discomfort, because if I had, I either would have been ignored for the next two, three weeks, or my grades maybe would have been lowered, or whatever else."

She expanded upon these statements with more testimony: "I had him as a teacher for seven years. I can't remember all the times when he has ignored me for things that I have . . ."

When Kurzman inquired as to why she didn't express her discomfort over his alleged behaviors, she replied, "Well, he is my elder, he is my teacher and he is my coach, and I respect that."

Kurzman directed the witness, again, to her affidavit that was developed by the school investigator (Paragraph 3) in which she had stated, "When he touched me in this way, it made me feel violated and frustrated." Kurzman wanted to inquire exactly how violated and frustrated she claimed to be:

Q: "Difficulty sleeping?"
A: ". . . No."
Q: "How about academically, did you start performing poorly in school?"
A: "No."
Q: "How about socially, did you become introverted and stop interacting with other friends?"
A: "No."
Q: "How about emotionally, did you find yourself crying . . . ?"
A: "No."

Eventually, Kurzman got to the part of the testimony that I was most anxious to hear this girl's explanation: The "ten-meter" track issue. He referred her again to her sworn affidavit:

Q: "You are talking about being at track practice, measuring distance between hurdles, 'He had the tape measure in his hand when he said to me in a lewd manner—'
First of all, what's a lewd manner? What is that?"
A: "In a disgusting, seductive. I take it in that manner. I was disgusted."
Q: "But you didn't say you took it; you said he said it to you in a lewd manner?"
A: "He says it in a sexual way."
Q: "I see. How? Was his eyebrow up?"

A: "Yes, both of them were up."

Q: "Okay. And what was the sexual, suggestive way?"

A: "The way he said it."

Q: "Reproduce it for the jury. Say the words, 'I bet you have never seen a ten meter before' in a lewd manner?"

A: "I'll bet you've never seen a ten meter before, ha, ha, ha."

Q: "Okay. And at the time he was holding a tape measure in his hand; right?"

A: "Yes, he was."

Q: "Was that a tape that measure yards or meters . . . ?"

A: "Probably both. I don't know."

Q: "Probably both. You don't know. _____ (her name), tell the jury when you have seen a retractable ruling device that measures in meters."

A: "It was meters, hurdles were measured in meters and—"

I took a chance to glance towards the juror's box. Not a one was sleeping through this testimony! Just listen!

In regards to her testimony that I was standing there holding a tape measure and measuring meters in order to line up hurdles and had said "I bet you haven't seen a ten meter one before":

Q: "Tell the jury what you thought he was referring to if it wasn't the way of measuring meters?"

A: "His penis."

Q: "So you thought he was sort of trying to brag to you that he had a 38-foot long penis?"

A: "Yes."

Q: "So I guess you took that seriously, looked to see if there was— well, did you take that seriously?"

The State voiced an "Objection"; Sustained.

How could this girl expect her testimony to be taken seriously? There were giggles and camouflaged "coughing" from the spectators.

In my opinion, her descriptive "recollections" belonged in the *National Enquirer*. They were disgraceful.

Her testimony continued . . . and of the same inclination: *sexual . . . sexual . . . sexual.*

Oh, in case I forget to mention it, this witness did testify that her mother was a member of the Apostolic Christian Church.

Q: (In reference to her affadavit): "Oh. Your final paragraph is that Mr. Courneya touched you, said something to you or looked at you in a seductive and sexually suggestive manner most every day of your high school years; right?"

A: "Yes, when he wasn't ignoring me."

As I listened, an incident came to my mind that I wish I had ignored. It centered around this girl's behavior the day of our Conference Track Meet. I can explicitly recall that the hurdlers were lining up preparing for the competition. But guess what? Our hurdler, (girl "M"), was no where to be found. I asked another athlete where she was. The girl nodded her head towards a hillside that had some tall grass . . . beyond the scope of track-related events. Sure enough, she came running down the hillside, jumped over the fence, and lined up for her event. I hoped she wasn't exhausted. I can remember shaking my head in disgust and saying, "Once a cheerleader, always a cheerleader." She could have been an exceptional hurdler, but she lacked commitment and the *drive* to be more than average. I had told my athletes, not just her, that if you want to be a supreme athlete, it will require you to think and act like an athlete 365 days a year. If you were not committed to practicing every day of the year, then try cheerleading. Do something.

The Court was also witness to her lack of respect for authority. When she was returning to the witness stand after a requested demonstration on the mannequin, she mimicked Kurzman behind his back. Her little group of friends sitting in the back of the courtroom giggled. I was so ashamed of her.

However, I shall not say anything more about this young girl. I leave it to *Isaiah,* (Old Testament, *V, 18*), *Woe unto them that draw iniquity with cords of vanity, and sin as it were with a cart rope.* Yes, woe unto them.

The State rests its case.

CHAPTER SIXTEEN

How happy is he born and taught,
That serveth not another's will;
Whose armour is his honest thought,
And simple truth his utmost skill.

-Sir Henry Wotton

We journeyed to that courthouse in Morris each day—Mom, Dad, and I. It was a two-hour trip. I travelled alone in my pickup—a time to gather my thoughts. My parents were often accompanied by my brother, Tim, or my Uncle Don and Aunt Marie. Additionally, my son, Jerid, as well as my sister, Judy, her husband, David, and my sister, Julie, strengthened my resolve with their attendance at the trial. I vowed that someday, I would repay them all for their heartfelt support. Their love was my strength. At the end of each day, my parents and I would discuss the events of the day—the testimony—while eating a dish of ice cream (some things never change!). Our discussions were quite optimistic. We truly believed that the jury would "see through" the contradictions . . . would deduce that the descriptions of the alleged incidents were physically impossible . . . would see the truth. We awoke each morning with renewed hope.

Marc Kurzman, my attorney, would greet us optimistically each day as we arrived at the Stevens County Court House. He professed, however, that in all his years of legal service and all the many cases of this type that he had been involved with, he could not believe that it had come this far . . . that this trial was even continuing. Therefore, at the conclusion of the State's case, he made a motion for directed verdict of *not guilty* on all counts. He argued that the evidence on its face was inherently incredible and insufficient. He also condemned the Spreigl evidence which was allowed in the Court.

Furthermore, he expressed his concern with the possibility of the girls' memories as having been influenced: ". . . They spoke with Sheriff Sayre or they spoke with Ms. Holleman or they spoke with Mr. Larson or various adults, that their memories or facts were contaminated and twisted into a perception of evil motivation and sexual gratification." He indicated that the only girl, he recalled, as suggesting that she perceived things as being for sexual purposes was the last Spreigl witness, ("Girl M"), "Who, with all due respect saw sexual motivation behind everything that went on around her . . ."

In conclusion to his motion for directed verdict of not guilty, he professed,

"Quite frankly, I have never had a case like this, and I have had quite a few involving allegations of sexual impropriety, but I have never had one where the acts are, if you will, almost like selecting apples from an orchard—one from this tree, one from that tree, one from another tree, the orchard has been growing in the community for 22 years, and then somebody says 'these apples are rotten', and so everybody reconstructs the past and starts seeing everything as a rotten apple." Other than a dismissal of Counts XXV and XXVI relating to girl "S", the defendent's motions were denied. The defense was prepared to begin its case in the State of Minnesota vs. Dennis Edward Courneya.

Don Bolluyt:

Our first witness was my fellow coach and friend, Don Bolluyt. In response to the direct examination by Kurzman, Don testified that he knew me as a teacher, a coach, and as a friend. He indicated that about five years ago, he had asked me about a coaching position. During the summer of '96, he had coached the varsity girls, and then that fall had started coaching seventh and eighth grade girls basketball. He testified that at one time he questioned my

coaching abilities because he didn't feel that his daughter was getting enough opportunity to play. However, he stated that his view
of my coaching style or ability changed when he started attending
practices and observing me coach: "Well, you realize what moti-
vates what he does . . . if you watch enough practices, you see the
kids that are actually putting everything into it and the ones that
are kinda dogging it." Don also told the Court that he had noticed
a change in my agility, etc., the past years: "Well, he's much slower
and very limited flexibility."

The witness continued to explain that I had a limited amount
of involvement with the kids during practices. However, he described the drill in which I was directly involved. The drill he was
referring to was the one that required them to "power up"—to stay
focused on trying to get the ball into the hoop during a layup
while being fouled in the process. It meant the difference between
a possible two-point play vs. a possible three-point play. It was a
play that reaped great benefits for our team. Many times, proper
execution of this "play of strength" meant a win for our team.

Kurzman furthered his questioning by asking, "In your experience in working with girl athletes in basketball, is it sufficient to
verbalize to them what you want them to do by way of learning
plays, just tell them in your—in words?"

The witness responded, "No, it is not."

Kurzman continued, "Is it sufficient in your experience to say,
'You two get out there and go through an offense/defense thing' as
a learning tool?"

Don replied, "No."

Numerous times, Kurzman tried to propose questions to the
witness asking him to give an opinion as to "what Mr. Courneya's
intent was in feeling kid's muscles and or making statements like
'chicken muscles' ". . . or "do you have an opinion whether or not
Mr. Courneya would ever intentionally touch a girl. . . . to satisfy
sexual or aggressive tendencies . . . ?" However, "Objections" by
the State prohibited his response.

I was wondering why witnesses for the State could express a

view on "intent", but this witness was denied the opportunity. Don testified that I had a reputation in the community for truthfulness . . . "They think he's an honest man."

Finally, the defense was allowed a critical question, "You heard their testimony at the trial (referring to some of the girls who testified for the State). Were you able to form an opinion, as to whether or not the acts they described were done for sexual gratification of Mr. Courneya?"

Don replied, "Yes", and emphatically added, "He could not and did not do it."

Cross-Examination by the State:

The State centered its line of questioning around the type of basketball drills that Don had witnessed during my basketball practices:

Q: "And was it sort of accurate what the girls said, that he would sort of have to—he would squat and you would sort of sit on his knee, that your butt would be up against his groin?"
A: "No."
Q: "They weren't correct about that?"
A: "No."

The prosecuting attorney proceeded with questions as to why the defendent needed to demonstrate the drills:

Q: "Well, was it possible for the defendant to demonstrate it on you to the girls?"
A: "No."
Q: "Why?"
A: "You could demonstrate it, but you have to have the feel, you have to know where they are on your body to decide which way you are going to go."

As I listened to the questions from this attorney, I truly wondered if he had ever been involved in athletics. It sounded to me like he thought coaching could be done through the use of vicarious elements: videos, observations, drawings, etc. Any coach will tell you that athletic talent is not developed by mere observation. It requires execution of skills. Athletes are not spectators.

Redirect by Kurzman:

Q: "Were there times when Mr. Courneya would ask you to be the one who gets out there and do the drills with girls?"

A: "Yes."

Q: "Why?"

A: "Because he couldn't do it, and I can move with them."

Later during questioning regarding any physical infirmities of the defendant, the witness responded, "Well, I have walked behind him, and his—his knees are very bad."

As Don Bolluyt was excused from the stand, I was reminded of why he came to be one of my best friends: strength of character.

Julie Zieman:

We had planned to have as our next witness a former student/athlete from Hancock School; however, she was not available as of yet. Therefore, as a surprise to many, especially the next witness, we called my sister, Julie Zieman to the stand. Julie is a teacher who serves four school districts teaching/coordinating programs for gifted-talented students. At the present time, she not only was in her second year as president of her local teacher's union, but she had also served five additional years in a variety of elected offices for her union. On this particular day, she had been at a nearby school and had stopped by the courthouse at the conclusion of the school day. To her surprise, she became the next witness for the defense.

Q: "Do you know whether or not Dennis's career as a teacher was important to him?"

A: "Those of you that aren't teachers, you certainly don't do it for the money. You do it for the love of it . . . altruistic, because we hopefully are preparing people to become citizens, the type of citizens we want to take the lead in society, so we not only teach them context, we hopefully teach them character, respect, self-discipline, and responsibility."

Q: "Have you ever seen your brother around any of his students?"

A: ". . . I observed him at the basketball games in which he was a coach, with his teams over the past years. I've been at a number of track meets, but predominantly the basketball games; definitely I was there."

Q: "In watching your brother with the students or the athletes, did you ever see anything that he did to cause you to wonder whether or not he was touching kids sexually or aggressively?"

A: "Definitely not."

The next line of questioning dealt with her role as a teacher:

Q: "Have you ever known kids in that age group (grades 7-9) to make up a story to back a friend who they think otherwise might get in some trouble?"

A: "Yes."

With regards to the testimony given by the prior witnesses, Kurzman asked Julie, "As a result of what you learned and what you observed, have you changed—do you have an opinion whether or not your brother touched these girls for sexual or aggressive purpose?"

A: "I have an opinion."

Q: "What is that opinion?"

A: "If it did happen, in my opinion it certainly was not intentional."

Q: "Why not? Why wouldn't it be for sexual purposes?"

A: "Well, a number of reasons. Number one, I know my brother, and I know how we were brought up. We were brought up with a tremendous amount of respect for each other, and that was not just for each other, it was for people in general. I can't perceive anything that he would do would intentionally be done in a sexual manner."

Q: "Have you ever known your brother to be aggressive toward any women or girls?"

A: "No."

Cross-Examination by the State:

It was quite apparent that the State wanted to delve into the *aggressive* issue with Julie.

All I can say is that she met the challenge.

Q: "Would you say that the defendant can be an aggessive person?"

A: "He's very motivated, yes. Aggressive?"

Q: "And would it be fair to say he is a coach of aggressive teams, that style of play?"

A: "Definitely, yes."

Q: "And they are aggressive teams because he teaches them to be?"

Q: "They learned well."

The prosecutor attempted to gather information from Julie regarding the role of the MEA and the guidelines regarding teacher/student conduct. She informed the Court that the MEA provides guidelines, but that it was the responsibility of the school districts to develop and implement a school policy.

The State's last lines of questioning pertained to the testimony of girl "M" (the girl who described the "ten-meter" incident). However, Julie had not heard that earlier testimony; therefore, she had to have been totally perplexed as to the relevance of the next questions:

Q: "Were you here this morning?"

A: "No."

Q: ". . . if a teacher or a coach were talking, a male teacher or coach were talking to a student of the opposite sex about the size of his genitals, you wouldn't think that would be an appropriate topic; would you?"

A: "That would not be appropriate."

I felt like telling this attorney that his question was totally inappropriate . . . as were the insinuations.

Redirect by Kurzman:

Q: "Knowing your brother as you do, do you think that he would ever, whether there's an MEA policy or a Hancock policy or a law, would he ever intentionally touch the breast of any of his students?"

A: "Without question, no."

In reflection, I was so proud of Julie; she spoke with such confidence and poise. She was a true example of what our family stood for. I often wondered what the prosecution thought (as well as its advocates) as they listened to a truly remarkable young woman speak the truth. What made her testimony even more impressive and so different than those for the State was that it was totally unrehearsed. *Honesty is the noblest work of God* (Pope, *Honesty of Men, IV*).

Gwen Greiner:

The next witness was one of the finest athletes and individuals that any teacher and coach could ever hope to work with: Gwen Greiner. Gwen was presently a student at South Dakota State University and was playing basketball for the college as well. As she took the stand, I thought about her diligence and her commitment to becoming the best that she could be. Not only that, she was an extremely nice girl. She indicated under oath that she knew the defendant as a "good friend, coach and teacher." She testified that she had received a call on the telephone from the Sheriff and that he had asked her questions during that call.

Q: "Did he tell you why he was taking a voluntary statement from you?"
A: "If I remember right, I think he was going on a hunting trip of some sort."
Q: "Did he say anything about how your name came up as somebody that he might call?"
A: "A bunch of girls from school, I guess, mentioned my name."

Gwen continued to testify that she had first heard about the incidents in question while attending a football game. She added, "Oh, geez. It was about a week and a half after the incident, whenever the incident was."

Q: "When you first heard the story, did you have a reaction to it?"
A: "I was kind of—I was startled, very surprised."
Q: "Okay. Why?"
A: "Because I just—I have known him for so long that I just can't see him doing like anything in that type of way, nothing like that. . . . no, he was just . . . I never thought anything of it. Too good of a guy."

Gwen proceeded to explain that some other individuals had communicated more about what was going on: her parents, girl "W", as well as some other classmates.

Q: "When you were speaking with _____ (girl "W"), did she ask you any questions?
A: "Yeah. She just asked me if I had ever been hurt in any way by him or anything like that . . . but nope."

The witness explained that a lady came out to her house . . . "Don't know her name."

She continued, "I think she was for the school, I think. I think she was . . ."

Q: "And you recall her telling you that she was there on behalf of the school?"
A: "I think so."

Gwen explained further, ". . . She was just questioning me about things that girls that she talked to before, they mentioned my name to come and talk to me, and then she just started asking me questions about what the girls had already . . ., like things that they said, like she was asking if I had ever seen that or . . ."

Gwen responded that she did see any written reports or affidavits from that conversation. Upon questioning, she added that the lady asked her if Mr. Courneya had ever touched her anywhere, etc. Gwen indicated that she replied, "No."

Q: "Have you ever heard from her again?"
A: "No."

The next line of questioning dealt with her interview with the Sheriff:

Q: "Do you remember what your reaction was when the Sheriff asked you if you had ever heard of anything like that before, talking about the upper arm-type thing, brushing breasts? Do you remember how you reacted to it?"
A: "Well, I . . . I was kinda like, I was really astonished at the brushing the breast type thing because I have never seen that being done."
Q: "Well, wasn't that talked about all the time amongst the girls on the team, in class and stuff?"
A: "I never heard it. Ever."

I certainly hoped that the jurors were taking note of her testimony. Gosh, didn't some of the witnesses for the State testify that students would talk about my so-called *brushing of the breasts*? Here was a witness that had attended Hancock School, elementary through high school, but she had not been privy to the much noted discussions about my alleged behavior and actions. Yet, Gwen replied that she knew and/or had played on sports teams with the girls who had testified for the State.

Q: "Do you have an opinion about whether or not any of the girls might be more sensitive than others to things like how they would interpret some types of actions or behaviors?"
A: "I would have to say yes."
Q: "How often did they talk about him touching their breasts while releasing their muscles?"
A: "I never heard of touching the breasts. I have not heard that in my time. Never."

Later, in her testimony, Gwen professed her feelings about Mr. Courneya: "As a coach? I don't know. I just kinda gave him all the credit for how good of a basketball player I became. I have known him for a long time. Long, long time. So I just kinda give him all my, you know, success and everything in life. He made me who I am."

As I listened to Gwen, I was so proud of the kind of young woman she had become.

I also wanted to tell her that she was responsible for her many successes, not me. She was and still is an individual that gives 200% or more. She earned all the good things that have come her way . . . and she earned the respect of everyone fortunate enough to have worked with her.

Additional questions were asked of Gwen regarding student conversations:

Q: "Did any of the other students ever express in your presence having a problem with anything that Mr. Courneya was doing?"

A: "No, not to me."

Q: "Well, did you see Mr. Courneya put his groin against any girls? His groin."

A: "No."

Q: "How many classes have you had him as a teacher, approximately?"

A: "Five years, I think, seventh through eleventh."

Q: "Did you ever hear him talking with kids about their muscles?"

A: "Yes."

Q: "What kinds of discussions did you hear in that regard?"

A: "Well, I guess he'd just come up and say stuff like, you know, 'How are my little chicken muscles?' He always laughed at it . . . because we both kinda laughed about it. Everybody else I saw him do that to kinda chuckled too. The girls chuckled, too."

Kurzman proceeded to question Gwen with regards to Mr. Courneya's physical contact during basketball practices. Gwen described how the defendant would use a football pad during one of the drills: "He would just be holding it (football pad) and he'd push it on our back so then when you shot the basket it would just make it more challenging than to lollydoll it up there. It's more of a challenge when he sits there and pushes it."

Q: "Do you feel you would have gotten the same benefit in learning how to handle yourself under the basket had he instead had one of the other players assume the role that he ws assuming?"

A: "I have to say no, because it's like the girl thing not to like, you know, push and shove and, you know, do that type of thing. So I would not have benefited from that, no."

Q: "Where there ever times that you would be at your locker and you would have some sort of physical contact with Mr. Courneya?" . . . "What would happen?"

A: "Oh, just chit-chating, see how the day is going . . ."

Q: "Did he ever put his arm around you in any fashion?"

A: "Yeah."

Q: "While doing so, did he ever brush against your breast?"

A: "No, no."

Kurzman redirected Gwen to the statements she had given the Sheriff and the affidavit in hand:

Q: "And then a little bit further down in the page the Sheriff says, 'And some of the girls have indicated, well, why don't you talk to Gwen Greiner because she probably knows a lot more.' And what did you say in response to that?"

A: (Reading her affidavit): "See, that's what everybody has been saying, talk to me, talk to me. But I only have all good things to say. I'm, you know, because he's never did anything to hurt me in any way, so he's always been a clean guy. He's always been clean."

Cross-Examination by the State:

The prosecutor asked Gwen a number of questions in regards to the relationship the defendant had with her parents as well as herself:

Q: "Would you characterize the friendship with your parents or your whole family as an extremely close one that the defendant had?"

A: "Yeah, it was a close relationship. Yeah."

Q: And you attributed your success—well, I'm sure that you have a lot of natural ability, but you attribute your success, in large measure, to the help that you got from the defendant; didn't you?"

A: "Yes."

Q: "And would it be fair to say that it was alarming to you when you heard that people were accusing him of doing wrong?"

A: "Yes."

Q: "And you certainly felt badly for him?"

A: "Yes."

It was quite apparent to me why the prosecutor was asking these type of questions.

However, what he perhaps did not know was that Gwen's testimony was based upon fact.

She would not allow *emotion* to impede the truth. Yes, she spoke from the heart, but she also spoke from good conscience.

The attorney continued with questions pertaining to the Hancock basketball team.

Q: "Okay. The Hancock girls team, the one coached by the defendant, had an aggressive style of play?"

A: "Yes."

Q: "Physical style of play?"

A: "Yes."

Q: "Is the defendant an aggressive coach?"

A: "He's tough. He's tough, yeah. Yes."

Q: "Would it be fair to apply the term aggressive to the defendant's style . . . as a coach?"

A: "As a coach, yeah."

Q: "Did he act aggressive in practice?"

A: "Aggressive? I don't know. He was just—yeah, in practice, yeah. That's the way we got going."

As I listened to the questions posed to the witness by the prosecutor, I only wished he could have watched the Hancock girls play in basketball. He would have noted their motivation, their style, their command of the court and the game. Were they aggressive?

They were winners. Better yet, why not ask any of the teams we competed against. They would most certainly contend that the Hancock girls' basketball teams were not only aggressive . . . they were *terrors* on the court! That is not a crime. That is talent. Read the headlines.

Perhaps an appreciation for the Hancock girls' style of play and rewards from winning is better exemplified by a quote published in the *Memories of 1997 State Championships* booklet: "*It's so weird that a*

little town like Hancock can get a state c
team deserved these awards. The girls have
to make it to the state tournaments. The te
was such a great experience being on the te
William's Arena and also being in the Gop
given us younger kids more motivation to do
to everyone for all the support they gave us . .

To you, the *13th Juror*: Who do you
ute? What would you say if I told you ⁔⁔⁔ ⁔⁔⁔ the State's
witness: "Girl Z"? If you haven't thought about it yet, perhaps
now is a good time to ponder *reasonable doubt*.

CHAPTER SEVENTEEN

The heart of the fool is in his mouth,
but the mouth of a wise man is in his heart.
-Franklin, *Poor Richard's Almanac*

Each day as I entered the courtroom, I looked to see who was in attendance. Of course, I saw my family members. There were also some students from Hancock School as well as some parents of Hancock students and athletes observing the proceedings. I was grateful for the support of the Bolluyts, the Solvies, the Hansons, the Pichts, the Greiners, the Huntleys, the Byes, and the Rohloffs. However, I was disappointed in the lack of support from the Hancock School faculty members. Yes, I had received many letters of support from my fellow colleagues; however, not one teacher attended the trial. I often wondered why. I also questioned if their jobs would have been jeopardized if they had demonstrated support . . . they, perhaps, were wondering that as well. Nevertheless, the trial proceeded.

Tammy Larson:

The daughter of the superintendent of the Hancock School was the next witness for the defense. She was presently attending college at the University of North Dakota. She testified that I had been her high school history teacher, basketball coach and track coach. She also indicated that she had heard about the accusations "through the grapevine . . . Some people maybe emailed me about it. I know like people saw things in the paper in the Twin Cities about it."

Q: "How would you describe your interactions with Coach Courneya?"

A: "We had a coach-athlete/student-teacher type relationship. We were just good friends and he was somebody you could go talk to and feel comfortable with like rather than just a regular teacher. . . ."

Q: "Did he ever get sexually involved with you?"

A: "Never."

Q: "Did you ever notice him touching any students in a way that you perceived to be sexual?"

A: "I never perceived to be sexual, but maybe other people might have."

Kurzman proceeded to question Tammy about the type of contact that may have occurred during basketball practices. She described the type of touching that occurred during post drills in practice: "There's no other way—if his midsection touches you, that's because he was playing the defender. He never like tried rubbing himself against you. If—you know, that happens with a girl and a girl, too . . ."

The questioning continued in reference to the testimony given by "Girl N" (Spreigl). Tammy professed that she was "pretty close friends" with "Girl N".

Q: "Did you ever see Mr. Courneya put his hand on _____ ("Girl N's") bare stomach?"

A: "No."

Q: "Did anyone ever tell you that this was supposed to have happened, that Mr. Courneya put his hands on the bare stomach of ____ ("Girl N")?"

A: "Nope."

I was so thankful for this girl's honesty. In case you haven't figured this out already, Tammy was the girl who was practicing the shot put during which I was reported to have allegedly placed my cold hands on "Girl N's" stomach (as testified by Spreigl witness: "Girl N"). Tammy also testified that, contrary to the prior testimony of a State witness, that Coach Courneya had not asked her to straddle his knee during practices.

Cross-Examination by the State:
The attorney for the State attempted to get clarification of the basketball post drills:

Q: "And was this a frequent drill that you would do at practice?"
A: "No. We didn't practice post moves every day, and when we did, we had an assistant coach from Morris who a lot of times showed us, or even Don Bolluyt or Mr. Courneya or, you know, maybe five or six times out of the wole year he did that."

The questions continued in the area of whether different treatment was given to athletes as far as grades or testing:

Q: "Would it be fair to say that he gave his athletes maybe a little bit of extra help just to make sure they did well in class?"
A: "I wouldn't say that."

Again, I am sure when he was asking that question, she recalled how the Hancock girls' basketball team lost the state academic award because of my lack of preferential treatment. For example, if any student, athlete or non-athlete, had an academic grade that bordered between A-minus and B-plus, I gave them a B-plus.

Keith Hanson:

Keith Hanson was a 1984 graduate of Hancock School. He testified that he knew Mr. Courneya as his teacher, his football and track coach, and that he had been employed as a painter/helper during the summers by the defendant. He told the Court that he was presently a teacher/coach in St. Peter, MN.

Q: "Do you see Mr. Courneya as somebody who has had a significant role in your life in any way?" (A: "Yes.") "How?"

A: "I think I'm where I'm at today because of that man. Like I said, I went to the University of Minnesota, Morris for two and-a-half years, and then basically I ran out of money and I quit and went and worked at a turkey plant . . . for a couple years. I'd come back and talk to Dennis, and I coached football with him . . . and he just asked me if I was happy working in the turkey plant; not saying it's bad work, but you know, he says, he told me I kinda should get my butt going and maybe get back to school, and that's what I did."

Q: "Did you ever observe Mr. Courneya having any physical contact with students or athletes when you were in school?"

A: "Sure. I was one of them."

Q: "What did you experience?"

A: "Grabbing your muscles, calling you 'chicken muscles.' He always made fun of me because I was a wrestler and losing weight. I mean, it was good-humored fun."

Keith continued his testimony by informing the Court that he had gone duck hunting with me the weekend before the alleged "stretching-out" incident ("Girl Z"). When asked if he observed anything about how Dennis Courneya was handling himself that weekend, the witness replied, "Uh-huh, sure. I was giving him a hard time about getting old because he was having a hard time getting out into the slough, into the duck blind . . . stuff like that."

During further questioning, Keith was asked if he had an opinion with regards to the reputation of Mr. Courneya for truthfulness. He replied, "I feel he's very truthful."

Cross-Examination by the State:

The State did not have many questions for the witness, Keith. The initial questions, however, pertained to his role as a coach and the appropriate conduct between girls and coaches. How would you expect anyone to answer the following type of question proposed by the State. Do you, too, find it misleading?

Q: "Would you ever joke around with your girl athletes implying that you had just been off somewhere alone with one of them?"

A: "Fill me in. I'm . . . it's a very general question. Are we looking for humor or . . . I don't know what we are—what you are asking."

Q: "Would it be a fair statement to say that in some ways the defendant, you are almost as close to the defendant as you would be to a father?"

A: "Sure. That's fair to say. I think I said he was one of my best friends."

As Keith stepped down from the stand, I marvelled at what a fine young man he had become. He worked hard for his success, and any student fortunate enough to have him as a teacher and coach will, undoubtedly, be enriched.

Kim Erdahl:

Our witness, Kim (Picht) Erdahl, was a 1988 Hancock School graduate, and presently an elementary teacher at Cyrus School. Upon questioning, she replied that she had had Dennis Courneya as a teacher and coach. As Kim testified, I was reminded of her positive contributions to the school . She was an integral part of the great "turn-around" in girls' athletics at Hancock. She and her sister were members of a team that not only were aggressive on the court, they were "tyrants". Their ball-handling skills, their talent, and their *drive to win*, made her and her fellow-teammates feared by area schools. When I thought about my years as her coach, I can only smile. They were some of the best years of my life . . . because of students and athletes like Kim.

Q: "What kind of coach was Mr. Courneya?"
A: "Demanding" . . . "He wanted you to work hard, keep your nose clean, stay out of trouble and work hard. You didn't have time—if you didn't want to work hard, then you were going to sit on the bench . . . If you were going to work, you were going to play."

Kim testified that Mrs. Courneya had made comments involving the word "love":
"Yes. The term, 'Give me some loving.' It would be more of a greeting. Or, you know, he noticed you were down one day or upset, he'd try to cheer you up and kinda grab you around the arms, sit next to you and maybe just give you a little toss or whatever and . . ."
She continued her testimony, ". . . and I know that on our graduation, I mean, he cared about us. I can remember tears in his eyes when we left." Kim furthered her testimony by stating, "I think he very much cared about us as people. I remember there were times when I would sit in his room and he would say, you know, 'Kim, you're a leader. Keep yourself out of trouble on the weekends.' And he was saying that because he cared about me, not because there was anything wrong with it."

Q: ". . . would there be any other times that you would think about Mr. Courneya?"
A: "Oh, yeah . . . Well, Mr. Courneya instilled in us hard work. If I came up against something in my life . . . he installed in us work hard and you can get what you want. So, if I ever came up against something in my life that was hard to handle, or whatever, I'd think of him and get through it."

Kim was also questioned as to whether I had ever had any physical contact with her that she would consider to be "sexual in nature", she responded, "No."

She informed the Court that she had initially been questioned by the Sheriff and the lawyer for the school, but that there were no follow-up sessions with the two noted individuals. According to Kim's testimony, the Sheriff had questioned her at her place of employment, the Cyrus School: "He—he came during the school over to Cyrus, and I went into the superintendent's, or the office with him, and he had a tablet like he was going to take notes, and he asked me how I felt, and I told him, and he didn't jot anything down, and left."

Cross-Examination by the State:
After Kim reminded the Court that Mr. Courneya had not touched her breasts or buttocks, the attorney questioned Kim about the possibility of the defendant touching her while playing basketball:

Q: "Sometimes if there's another player and you're playing close defense to them, whatever, you might touch them on the buttocks lightly; is that true?"
A: "Basketball is a contact sport."
Q: "What kind of team was the Hancock girls team that he coached when you played on it?"
A: "A running team. We'd run and exhaust the other team so we could win."

The questions from the State left "the basketball court" and delved into more personal reflections:

Q: "And when he talked to you about staying out of trouble on weekends, did he ever talk to you about whether or not you were dating somebody?"
A: "Well, it's a small town. He usually knew who I was dating. I don't remember having conservations about the guy specifically. He would just tell me more like, 'You're a role model for

the rest of the students. Think about what you are doing. Don't get yourself in trouble.'"

I wished that the witnesses for the State would have been present for her testimony.
She was and still is a role model. I am so proud of her.

Heidi Olson:

Heidi (Picht) Olson was duly sworn in as a witness for the defense. She, too, was a Hancock School graduate, 1989. I had been Heidi's teacher as well as her basketball and track coach.

Q: "When you were a student or an athlete being coached by Mr. Courneya, did he ever touch you in any ways that caused you any concern?"

A: "No."

Q: "Did Mr. Courneya get physically involved in any way with the stretching that was going on?" (In reference to stretching exercises as part of athletic endeavors)

A: "With stretching, . . . at the beginning of the practice, we'd be out stretching, he'd walk up and he'd make—he'd come up to me, grab my shoulders, kinda nudge me around a little bit, say, 'How are you doing? Are you ready to go?', you know, this and that."

Heidi testified that there were some occasions where I felt her muscles, but that there was no intentional contact with her breast.

Q: "Well, did you ever get the impression that he was intentionally trying to touch your breast?"

A: "Never."

Q: "How did you feel about Mr. Courneya as a coach?"

A: "As a coach, he was excellent. He was demanding. I don't know. He was successful."

Q: "How did you feel about him as an academic teacher?"
A: "Well, I didn't like history, so he did okay."

There were some chuckles by the audience (as well as myself) in response to Heidi's personal evaluation of "history"; however, the members of the audience were reminded (for the second time) by the Court not to make any comments about the testimony. Funny, I can't recall the audience being reminded to contain their overt responses during the testimony given by the State's witnesses.

Q: "Did you form any opinions whether or not Mr. Courneya seemed to show respect for the players?"
A: "Yes, there was definitely a mutual respect for each other."

Redirect by the State:
In response to Heidi's earlier testimony, the attorney asked her, "Is it possible that your breast might have been touched in a way that you felt at the time was just accidental?"

A: "I—I just can't recall him touching my breast."
Q: "Did the defendant ever give you any compliments about your appearance?"
A: "Yes" . . . "Oh, if it was a game day, we'd have to dress up, and he'd say, 'You look sharp today,' or something on that order."
Q: "Okay. Did he ever say you were good looking or beautiful?"
A: "I think at the birth of my daughter he came up to the hospital and he said, 'She is beautiful, just like her mother.' I know that was maybe one time."

Heidi also added that she heard me compliment boys, ". . . he said they looked sharp if they had a game and they were in a suit. You know, it's . . . he complimented people."
There were also a few last questions regarding my actions while athletes were stretching:

Q: "Well, did he ever, you know, crouch down or would he ever bend over you at all when you were stretching?"
A: "No."

There were no further questions for Heidi. However, I wished she had been asked if I had a nickname for her . . . I did. It was "Shadow". Was she offended by this nickname?

Why don't you ask her what she named her baby girl. I can only hope that little *Shadow* will grow up to be as fine a person as her mother, Heidi. I know that Heidi and Kim will continue to positively impact the lives of others . . . as they did my life.

Larry Sayre:

Are you surprised by this next witness? Yes, there were a few more questions we wanted to ask our County Sheriff. The defense was extremely interested in obtaining additional information about the investigative process utilized by the County for this case.

Q: "How many people did you you interview in connection with this investigation involving Mr. Courneya?"
A: "I'm not sure on the exact number."

Kurzman was quite perplexed at the Sheriff's inability to determine the number of people he had interviewed in regards to this case and very concerned about the process:

Q: "Well, didn't you, while questioning other girls, come upon the theory that the reason the girls that are complaining here didn't tell someone sooner is allegedly they had seen the same behaviors going on the entire time they were in school, and so by the time they got to be athletes, it looked like it was normal? Do you remember that general subject coming up?"
A: "Yes, I do."
Q: "Then why is it that interviewing athletes from prior years and

finding out that similar things didn't happen would not have a bearing on this case?"

A: "Well, my purpose or intent was to attempt to establish, well, was this happening ten years ago, was it happening eight years ago or five years ago or whatever the case maybe."

Q: "So you were looking just for the one side of the coin, then, people that may be able to tell you about it happening, and not bothering, not looking at the other side, people would say no, it didn't happen?"

A: "No. I took statements from people that said it did not happen as well."

However, Kurzman wanted to obtain clarity with regards as to why some statements were documented and why others were not: He directed the Sheriff to his interview with Kim Erdahl at her place of employment, the Cyrus School:

Q: "Okay. Do you recall bringing a notebook with you?"
A: "I carry a notebook wherever I go. I assume I had one."
Q: "Okay. Do you recall it being open when you started talking with her and closing it without writing anything in it and leaving?"
A: "I don't recall that."
Q: "So what was the purpose of talking to her the first few weeks?"
A: "I already answered that."

Later in the questioning of the Sheriff, Kurzman requested a response to the following inquiry: "Did you ask many of the students to tell you what good characteristics they thought Mr. Courneya might have had?"

A: "Did I ask many of them?"
Q: "Yeah."
A: "Not many. I did ask some."
Q: "Isn't it correct that the only statement that has been transcribed

where there is asked anything good about Mr. Courneya is the statement of Gwen Greiner?"

A: "I don't recall. I would have to look . . ."

Kurzman later posed another related question: "Do you remember on Monday . . ., last Monday when you were testifying saying that if there was information that Mr. Courneya was innocent, you would follow up on that?"

A: "Yes."

Q: "Did you come across any information that suggested to you the possibility of innocence which you followed up on?"

A: "I'm not aware of any information."

Errors, like straws, upon the surface flow; He who would search for pearls must dive below (Dryden).

Kurzman proceeded to question the Sheriff about reports and/ or meetings with some of the adults who had been mentioned by the witnesses during testimony:

Q: "What was the subject of your October 29th supplemental report?"

A: "That day I met with Mrs. Carrie Jepma."

(* Upon request, the Sheriff presented a copy of the one-page report relating to Ms. Jepma)

Q: "Did you meet with Jody Holleman?"

A: "No, I did not."

Q: "Okay. When did you come to understand her to be a person that may have information relative to this litigation?"

A: "I don't know. I believe her name was possibly brought up when I was talking to Mrs. Johnson (counselor at Hancock School). I don't know."

Q: "Did you try to talk with her at any time about the meetings she had with students during the week the first accusation arose?"

A: "I wasn't aware of any meetings, no."

Q: "Is that because you didn't ask any of the children if they had met with anyone before meeting with you and talked about this, or is it because you asked but nobody told you about the meeting with Ms. Holleman?"

A: "I was unaware of that meeting until in the courtroom here, I guess."

The Sheriff testified that he had not asked any of the kids whether they had had any discussions or meetings with anyone discussing Mr. Courneya.

Q: "Don't you agree that it could be significant information that kids were talking with each other and others about the claims before it was brought to law enforcement for investigation?"

A: "In some case I think—I think it could be significant, yes."

Q: "What cases might that be significant in?"

A: "I'm not sure. Every case is different, I think, but . . ."

Q: "Okay. Let me ask you this question then. Why in this case was it not important to ask the question whether or not others had been talking to the kids before the stories of abuse came to law enforcement?"

A: "Well, simply put, I didn't ask the question."

The Sheriff was also questioned with regards to the information given by the girls in their interviews and testimonies:

Q: "Do you recall a child who testified that they came to the realization that what Mr. Courneya was doing had been wrong as a result of a conversation with you?"

A: "I don't recall."

Q: "Do you recall whether there was any apparent change in stories that the children were telling over time, where there would be more details added or more accusations that were raised?"

A: "No, I didn't see anything, any changes occurring in the investigation or the interviews."

Q: "Isn't it correct that in _____ ("Girl N's") statement that was taken she did not say that Mr. Courneya's hands were actually on her stomach?"

A: "I'd have to refresh my memory and look at the statement again."

Q: "Do you recall that she said that he had tried to put his hand on her stomach?"

A: "I think she indicated that he had touched her bare skin."

Q: "You think she said that in the statement?"

A: "Well, I may have asked her if he did, and she said yes, or that it was one way or the other."

It was quite apparent that my attorney was greatly upset over the "questioning" techniques used by the Sheriff. He was also concerned with why some individuals were questioned and why some were not: "Did you ever talk with Heather Cappas, the lady who was at UMM and who had been working as one of the assistant coaches during the time of some of these allegations?"

A: "No, I've never heard that name before."

As I listened to his replies, I wondered why he had not interviewed Heather. She had been my assistant coach and she was also doing a research project on the Hancock athletic program and on me, as well (college project). It was difficult to believe that he had not heard of her.

Q: "Did you talk with any of the other coaches who may have been assisting Mr. Courneya during the time of any of the alleged sexual assaults?"

A: "Yes, I did . . . Mr. Ken Grunig."

Q: "Did you do a report of your communication with Mr. Grunig?"

A: "No, I did not."

I knew that we were now entering an area of questioning that could lead to a whole other area of concern . . . for my fellow coach. Yes, I knew about the conversation between my assistant coach,

Ken, and the Sheriff. Ken Grunig had already informed me of the specifics of that "off the record" discussion between he and the Sheriff. I will not breach his confidentiality, nor his friendship.

Redirect by the State:

As expected, the attorney proposed questions that would clarify the Sheriff's testimony . . . from their point of view. However, there was one question asked that I found to be quite relevant in regards to *character*:

Q: "Do you remember being asked whether you inquired of various people you interviewed about whether the defendant was a good guy or they liked him? Do you remember that question being asked?"

A: "Yes."

Q: "Would it have been relative to whether or not he was guilty of a crime if he were a good guy or people liked him?"

A: "No."

I could not believe that our County Attorney and County Sheriff were indicating that the above was not relative. Kurzman, upon redirect examination, was not going to let this slide by. He quickly asked the Sheriff the following question, "If you don't see the question of whether or not Mr. Courneya was a good guy to be relevant, why is it that you asked that question of Gwen Greiner?"

A: "I'd have to review the statement. I don't really recall asking that question directly . . ."

In order to assist the Sheriff with his "recall", Kurzman directed him to page 3 of Ms. Greiner's statement, Exhibit 13: "'Well, what are some of the good things that you would like to say about Mr. Courneya?' Do you see that?"

The Sheriff responded, "Yes, I do."

Q: "Isn't it true you didn't ask a single other child that question?"
A: "I don't know. I would have to review the statements."

Yes, both attorneys continued their questioning of the Sheriff. As I listened to his responses, I became more and more dismayed. The laws of our land, and the officials thereof, are supposed to be the embodiment of truth and honor . . . and integrity. I could only shake my head in disgust and disappointment.

Karri Hanson:

Karri was a 1989 graduate of Hancock School. She testified that I had been her teacher as well her basketball and track coach. When she was asked if there was any type of physical contact between Mr. Courneya and herself, she replied, "Different things. The checking of the muscles, you know, rough you up a little, grab, put you in a head lock, mess your hair up. Things like that." When Kurzman inquired if there was anything unusual about the touch, she responded, "No." Karri also furthered her testimony by describing circumstances that resulted in physcial contact with Mr. Courneya: "Basketball, he'd show you different techniques, how to block people out, how to rebound and stuff like that."

Q: "Did you ever have any physical contact with Mr. Courneya
    that struck you as being inappropriate in any way?"
A: "No."
Q: ". . . To your knowledge, did he ever attempt to touch you in
    sexual ways at any time?"
A: "Never."

Additional questions were asked of Karri regarding verbal statements made by the defendant:

Q: "Did Mr. Courneya ever make any observations about you as a
    person?"

A: "Me as a person, he would say I'm a mature adult. He would talk about how some day when I'm older I will make someone happy and I will have a good life."

Q: "When he would make comments like that, did you form the opinion that he was flirting with you in some way?"

A: "No."

Cross-Examination by the State:

The State asked Karri many questions about the relationship the defendant had with her family. Additionally, he inquired about Karri's gratitude:

Q: "Do you feel that the defendant has helped to make you who you are today?"

A: "Yes, I do."

Q: "And do you feel you owe him some gratitude for what he's done for you?"

A: "Yeah."

Questions pertaining to my coaching style were also asked of Karri:

Q: "Would you say that as a coach the defendant expected a lot of his players?"

A: "Yes."

Q: "Demanding of them?"

A: "No. More—not demanding. Just what a coach would expect from their players—to work hard, give it your best."

Karri knew, perhaps more than anyone, the value of working hard. She continues to be a dedicated and responsible adult. More importantly, she is appreciative, giving, and honest. Getting back to this question from the attorney, I wondered, again, if he had ever been involved in an athletic endeavor. What would happen if a coach said to his/her team, "Well, I don't expect you to work hard . . . I will not demand anything of you . . . I don't want you to give it your best . . . just show up- that's enough . . . "? Those comments might suffice in basket-weaving classes, but not in athletics . . . and not in life.

CHAPTER EIGHTEEN

God will not look you over for medals,
degrees or diplomas, but for scars.
-Elbert Hubbart, *Epigrams*

As the trial continued, I became quite concerned about the juror's state of mind. When I would glance towards the group, they appeared to be more and more disinterested.

There were two of them that, as I mentioned before, had such difficulty staying awake that I knew they had to be missing some of the testimony. I wanted them to hear it all!

Had they already made their decisions? How could they remember the details of the testimony if they were not recording the information? After each court session, my attorney would say, "I don't know how much clearer I can make it." He also added, "I only hope they are listening." I wondered if he, too, was uneasy about their apparent lack of attentiveness.

Finally, it was my day to testify. It was a day that I looked forward to. I was most anxious to state my point of view—to address the negativism that had been professed about me by the State's witnesses and the media. I took the stand with assurance and optimism.

Dennis Courneya:

April 27, 1998
Kurzman directed me to give a brief description of my family history as well as my educational experiences prior to becoming a teacher. After doing so, I was given the opportunity to inform the

Court that I had a son, Jerid, who was presently 21 years of age. Jerid had attended much of the trial. He and I have a remarkable relationship. I was fortunate to have him come to live with me when he was a freshman in high school. He was a Hancock High School graduate and presently in a management position with a national restaurant chain. He was trying to balance his commitment to his profession and his devotion to his father. An additional challenge for Jerid was that he had to commute nearly 200 miles to attend the trial. Yes, this trial was also a nightmare for my son.

He knew the school, the community, and the girls involved in this trial. He, too, could not believe what was transpiring in the Stevens County Courthouse.

Kurzman's next questions concentrated on my role as a coach and how I came to assume that responsibility. I informed the Court that, in addition to my teaching contract, I was originally hired as an assistant football coach and a head boys' track coach. Following that first year, I assumed the duty of coaching girls' basketball . . . a position I held for the next 22 years.

Q: "So, over the years, how many girls would you say you have coached in basketball?"

I responded that if one looks at the number of seasons I coached varsity as well as the elementary program I initiated, "it could conceivably be 700, 800, 900 girls I've been involved with in basketball." I also added later in the testimony that as the girls' track coach for 22 years, I had worked with 300-350 girl athletes in track.

I proceeded to explain that two years ago, I volunteered to start a cross-country program upon request from some Hancock girls : "Four young ladies, two years ago, asked me—they didn't like volleyball, for one thing . . . volleyball didn't fit into their mode, and they loved to run. So, what I told our superintendent and our athletic director, I said I would be more than willing to help those kids get started for a year, and I never charged the school one penny." My intent was to work the group in with our football program—to work out an amiable practice schedule. This "volunteer" position as cross-country coach extended into two years.

Q: "Who were the four girls?"
A: I cited the names of "Girls Z, U, and Q" as well as another.

Kurzman continued his questioning:

Q: "Do you think it's—it's ever appropriate to touch the breast of
   a student?"
A: "Never."
Q: "Do yo think it's ever appropriate to have physical contact
   between your groin and a student?"
A: "Never should be done."

I continued to respond to Kurzman's inquiry about my coaching assignments, etc. I indicated to the Court that I had been away from the Hancock area with female athletes for one or another type of tournament (track and basketball) approximately 45 days which included some overnight stays due to state tournament play and/or holiday/jamboree tournaments.

Q: "Has anyone ever made known to you dissatisfaction with how
   they have seen you or heard about you interacting with students?"
A: "Never."

Kurzman directed me to describe if/why I had made some of the comments/statements to the girls as was testified by the earlier witnesses.

I replied, "Oh, I—do not deny that I ever made statements other than that. And, you know, you read all the publications, and it says that 75 percent of our youth today, especially young females, have a poor self-esteem. And there are days when they don't really feel good about themselves. It (the comments) makes them feel good . . . with the idea of helping their positive self-esteem, just having them make sure that they feel good about themselves."

Q: "Have you ever made comments along the lines of age differences in front of parents of girls?"

A: "Many, many, many times." I continued to describe that many of the comments were said following a basketball game, for example. "Hasn't she really grown up a great deal" . . . or "If I was 25 years younger . . ." I added that the comments were stated with the child and parent present.

Kurzman continued his inquiry:

Q: ". . . Why did you make statements about people's appearance and compliment them?"

A: "Basically for a couple of reasons. It's self-esteem, if their parents can sit there and listen to them at the same time. And the other is our weight program, especially with our weight program . . . And by letting those kids know that, yes, you are getting to be a strong young lady . . . you carry yourself well, boy, when those parents heard that, too, they were—well, it's kind of a coaching technique. You say that in front of their parents, the parents are going to put a lot more pressure on them to make certain they are up in the weight room."

Kurzman turned his questioing towards the topic of the Hancock weight program. He asked me the folllowing question, "What do yo mean when you said the weight program ws everything to Hancock?"

I described that when girls athletics was in its infant stage, girls were not really physically strong. I continued, "To convince girls that by building yourself up physically you would be able to compete a lot better was hard to do. But that is something that was done in Hancock. We started a weight program about 18 years ago . . ."

With that statement, my testimony concluded for the day.

Aprill 28, 1998: An astounding occurance took place in the judge's chamber. One of the jurors was indicating that something had come up that might influence his ability to be a fair juror. It had come to this juror's attention that an informal sexual harassment complaint was being filed against him and also one of unprofessional and unethical behavior. The juror continued to explain, "I thought it would be best to bring it to you, because of the nature of this trial. I might not be able to perform my duties as a juror to the best of my ability."

Kurzman argued, "I would prefer not striking him for a number of reasons. He was high on our list of people that we wanted on the jury based on the voir dire. He is currently, the way the jury is constituted, one of three males on a 12-person jury, and if he is excused, it goes to ten women and two males. And I think that there is a lot in this case that has to do with differences in perception between males and females, and therefore, the lack of one male and the reduction of the representation, I think, can be significantly prejudicial to the defense."

The juror was asked to explain his consequences a bit further. He summarized his position as such, "I'm not—I'm not sure how this . . . is going to affect, or what comes out of the meeting I have with them tonight (referring to a meeting with his supervisors) and how—nothing that has been determined what's going to happen as of yet, and that won't be determined until this meeting tonight and—but I—but I just foresee that it could—it would be very difficult for me to remain—"

Q: "Focused?"
A: "Focused, yeah, exactly . . ."
The Court: "All right. That's all. You'll be excused as a juror."

The defense was disturbed, to say the least, over the excusal of this juror. In retrospect, we often wondered what happened to him as a result of the alleged complaints. It just appeared to us that the "timing" of this issue could not have been worse . . . for the defense, anyway. Additionally, if the criteria of "being focused" was instrumental in retaining a juror for my case, then I thought we best excuse at least 9 more jurors. As I mentioned before, it was brought to my attention by many spectators that the jurors appeared "bored, disinterested . . . and very sleepy." In fact, one spectator told me in total astonishment that one juror fell asleep . . . and her head was hanging below the arm rests of her chair!

Continuing Direct Examination:

Q: "Have you ever touched the breast of a female student or female athlete?"

A: "Never, ever intentionally, ever."

Q: "Have you ever rubbed your groin area against any part of a student or an athlete?"

A: "Never."

Q: "Have you ever touched any intimate part of a student or an athlete, such as the buttock area, for the purpose of satisfying your sexual or aggressive impulse?"

A: "No, I have not."

Kurzman continued, "You are charged with two counts of criminal sexual conduct involving _____ ("Girl Z")". He proceeded to refer to the allegations made by "Girl Z" and her testimony regarding the cross-country stretching incident:

Q: "Did that ever happen?"

A: "That did not happen."

In reference to the four counts involving "Girl Y": "Did you ever touch _____'s ("Girl Y") breast?"

A: "No."

Q: "Did you ever place your groin against ___ ("Girl Y") her neck, head, shoulders, back at all?"

A: "No."

Referring to the four counts involving "Girl X": "Did you ever
   touch her breast?"
A: "No."
Q: "Okay. Did you ever put your groin against her anywhere, rub
   your groin on her in any way?"
A: "No."
Q: "You are charged with two counts involving ___ ("Girl W"):
   "Did you ever touch her breast?"
A : "Never, ever intentionally, no."
Q: "How about rubbing your groin against her, did you ever do
   that?"
A: "No."

One-by-one, Kurzman requested a response to the allegations
made by the girls. I responded no differently than I had lived my
life; I responded in honesty. My attorney did ask for a clarification
from me by inquiring, "Now, when you say 'no', does that exclude
the possibility that there might have been accidental touching?"

A: "To say no, I would say that never, ever intentionally."

I was glad that I was finally given the opportunity to state
accurate accounts with regards to some of the allegations:

Q: "Near the end of the State's case, ___ ("Girl Z") retook the
   stand and said there was one occasion where you supposedly
   just took your hand and placed it right over her breast . . .
   Did that ever happen?"
A: "That never happened, no."
Q: "Next with regard to ___ ("Girl Y"), is it correct that she got a
   broken nose and you asked her about the broken nose as she
   testified."
A: "That's correct."

Q: "Okay. Is this the first time you have experessed an interest in a student's well being or health outside of the immediacy of the classroom or the playing field?"

When I responded, "No", Kurzman asked me to cite other examples when I might have evidenced a concern of that nature.

A: "Yes. When approximately two years ago, two individuals hurt their knees very, very badly in a subsection game, and both of them required surgery, and I called each one of them, and I went personally over to their home to see how each of them was doing."

If I had been given the opportunity and time, I could have described many instances when I called and visited students, male and female, at their homes or at the hospital when they had been involved in a mishap or had suffered an injury. How sad that some individuals interpreted the empathy as "sexual interest". That says alot for their state of mind . . . how pitiful.

Kurzman requested that I address the testimony from the girl who had testified about me using the term "nippy" while touching the fabric of her shirt. I wanted to clarify that I, perhaps, did use the word "nippy" but did not touch her shirt. I really wanted to let the Court know, again, that the girl in question was dressed so disrespectfully. The athletes were asked to dress-up on game days. This was also an away game. That particular day, it was bitterly cold with a wind chill of minus-forty degrees. I was so ashamed of her attire and her representation, as such, of our team.

In regards to "Girls X and W", I admitted to the Court that I didn't get along real well with their mothers. "Girl X's" mother and I had quite a telephone conversation—one in which she told me that my basketball team was terrible, and this opinion was stated the same night in which we had just won a big game. I only wished that her opinion had been based upon first-hand observation. However, her religious affiliation prohibited her from attending the basketball games.

Therefore, wherever she was receiving her information, and from whom, was totally invalid . . . and quite malicious. With regards to "Girl W", I indicated that "possibly her mother and I, probably never saw eye-to-eye on a number of issues. The other is ____ ("Girl W") resented being an athlete and being treated like an athlete."

Another area of testimony that Kurzman addressed, in particular, dealt with the girl who believed that she saw me in a state that exhibited sexual arousal while wearing tight shorts:

Q: "Did you ever wear shorts when you were working with kids, coaching, or . . . ?"
A: "I would say I wore sweat pants 99 percent of the time . . ."
Q: "Did you wear anything underneath the sweat pants or shorts?"
A : "To protect the male athlete or coach, you wear a cup protector."

Yes, I had learned early on in my coaching that it was definitely in my best interests to wear a physical guard of sort! Therefore, what the girl in question professed to "see" was in essence nothing more than the form of the plastic covering of the cup protector.

My attorney requested that I explain how I talked with my assistants about how they should handle themselves around girl athletes. I responded, "I have explained, for the most part, that to keep your hands off them, to explain things in as much detail as you possibly can, and the other is with the idea that they are girl athletes and you are a male athlete." I continued to explain, later, that I have given special instructions as to what is permissible and what is not. In reference to this question, I wished the witnesses had been asked about my demeanor when they were in the locker rooms . . . ask them if I ever came in while they were in a state of undress . . . ask them if I was overly cautious about even coming in the locker room at all . . . ask them the number of "warnings", and the time-span in between the "warnings" that I gave before entering the locker room . . . ask them if I had another female check the locker room before I even entered. There was no question that I respected their privacy.

Kurzman proceeded to ask me questions about the importance I placed on my job as a coach and teacher:

Q: "Is—or was, I guess, was coaching something important to you
    in your life?"
A: "Other than my family, it was a top priority. I loved it."
Q: "How about teaching, was that important to you?"
A : "Teaching and coaching go together. I loved both very, very
    much."
Q: "Did you just pay attention to a particular child or young
    person . . . ?"
A: "I—in terms of singling one or the others out, no. Good kids
    are good kids, whether they are athletes or not athletes."
Q: "How about academically, did you give any favoritism to any
    athletes?"
A: "Never."
Q: "Did you ever punish an athlete who was in your disfavor for a
    period of time by lowering their grades . . . by keeping them
    from participating in an athletic endeavor?"
A: "Never."

Cross-Examination by the State:

Expectedly, the prosecutor attempted to derive testimony that
would substantiate the State's case as exemplified by the following
types of questions:

Q: (With regards to my teaching style) "Your style wasn't simply
    to stand up at the board and read a lecture to them, without
    interacting with them?"
A: "Interaction was very important to me."
Q: "And the interaction in the classroom did sometimes involve
    touching; you would agree?"

After some clarifying questions, I was able to respond to the
initial inquiry:

A: "Yes, I would."

Q: "And I'm not trying to trick you on this; I just want to go one step at a time. Is it your testimony now that you did from time to time touch students in some way in the classroom?"

A: "Yes, in some way."

At this point, I described the types of "touching" that may have occurred: "patting on the shoulder . . . squeezing their shoulder . . . arm. To me, it was a greeting . . ."

I also proceeded to describe, upon questioning, the instances when I would lean over them while they may be taking a test, for example . . . if they had a question about the test, so as not to give the answer away to the rest of the students who happened to be listening.

Q: "You didn't want what you said to give away to other students?"

A: "I didn't want to give any answers away to anybody . . ."

Q: "And would you say that you more often did that with people who were your athletes than with people who weren't?"

A: (No, I didn't say that . . . you did.) "No, not necessarily. Anybody that raised their hand and needed help, whether they be athlete or non-athlete."

It was quite apparent to the Defense that whatever I said was going to be misconstrued.

Q: "Are you saying that Coach Courneya's signature greeting was frequently a grab on the arm kind of, your little thing?"

A: "Could be a grab on the arm, could be on the shoulder, could be up on their hair."

In relation to my checking the student's muscles and making comments, the State continued its questioning:

Q: "How would you mean it in a positive fashion if you were ridiculing the small size of a student's muscle in front of the entire class?"
A: "Well, first of all, they were never, ever ridiculed in front of the entire class."
(And who said I "ridiculed" in front of the class?)

The attorney for the State started asking questions that I thought were quite foolish, to say the least:

Q: "And it's true that you would say to girls from time to time, 'My you turned out pretty good', or, 'You are turning into a grownup, into a nice young lady . . .' things like that?"
A: "That's correct."
Q: "Did you say that to the boys, too?"
A: "Not—not in the same context, but meaning the same thing, yes."

The State continued:

Q: "Why wouldn't you say it quite the same to boys?"
A: "Well, we are two different genders in the first place, female and male, and you would not—maybe some people would, but I don't think you would say to a boy, for instance, 'My, you are getting to be a good looking young man." You might say to them, 'You are getting to be a handsome man.'"
Q: "Is it because if you said, 'You are a good looking young man,' someone might take that as a kind of almost a gay thing."

At this point, I thought the attorney was getting a little "off track". Kurzman must have thought the same . . . as did the spectators who tried valiantly to disguise their giggles. But, of course, Kurzman's "Objection" was overruled.
A: "I think the implication is that it's not right to say that."

With regards to questions, again, about the alleged touching of the breasts and/or touching girls with my groin areas, I reminded the attorney and the Court, ". . . I would say never intentionally, anything on that order."

The State's attorney continued his cross-examination by asking questions pertaining to contact that may have occurred during basketball drills:

Q: "So to the extent that the girls testified that in that drill (in reference to the boxing-out drill) they essentially had to sit with their buttocks on your knee or your thigh, that's not accurate?"

A: "That's not accurate, in this particular case dealing with a coach and athlete, but it would be an accurate statement if it would be a game situation, because that in theory is what does happen."

Q: "Was it necessary for you personally to get involved with a girl and do this demonstration rather than direct two girls to do it as a demonstration?"

A: "Definitely, it was."

There were a great number of questions posed by the State requesting my response to the girls' testimony. Cited below are just a few examples of the questions:

Q: "Do you commonly tell the kids that you had a number one, a number two like that?"

A: "Oh, I would make comments if they ran off papers for me, for instance, or someone volunteered to help me out and do something, I'd say, 'Well, Jill volunteered to do that. Looks like she's number one now. It's just a figure of speech."

Q: "When you say you have sweat pants that you would wear 99 percent of the time, would you characterize them, the pants, as tight?"

A: "No, I would not."

Q: (With regards to the shorts I sometimes wore) "Well, do they—

is there enough fabric so they can flap around and breathe, or
are they tight up against your skin?"

A: "I would say there's enough fabric so they can flap around."

Q: "So if girls testify here that you would wear some sort of tight
pants to where they could clearly see your genitals, that doesn't
match any pants that you know of?"

A: "I would say that imagination be a little different at that particular point."

In other words, I was implying that their imagination got in
the way of reality.

Q: (Regarding the ten-meter tape issue: "Girl M") "Did you ever
make a comment or a joke to her about a tape measure or a
measuring device?"

A: "Never a joke."

Q: "Do you recall anything that possibly matches the incident she
told us about?"

A: "She—she's fairly accurate in the fact that we were measuring
hurdles, just exactly the way she described it. It was a ten-
meter tape that is specially made to measure what was the 300
hurdles or the 100 hurdles . . . It is a ten-meter tape, and I
said to her, 'Have you ever seen a ten-meter tape?" I had not.
It's one that was laying over on the track at the University of
MN, Morris, and that's where we were at the time placing the
hurdles."

Q: "And you recall saying to ___ ("Girl M"), after she said she was
loose, 'I can loosen you up if you are tight.'?"

A: "I have said that to many athletes."

He should have asked other coaches the same question. The
number one injury to track-related athletes is pulled muscles. Many
athletes do not warm up properly—stretch.

This girl, in particular, by my estimation was "lazy". When I said, "I can loosen you up", she knew what it meant. It meant, "I'll have you run a lap or so . . . to loosen you up."

In fact, when I said that to any of my "lazy" athletes, they knew what I meant . . . it meant a couple laps around the track. She knew.

Q: "Do you think it's possible your groin might have inadvertently touched ___ ("Girl Z") in the classroom above the back of the chair?"
A: "Highly improbable."

(Again, I would had to have been a contortsionist and a midget)

How did I feel after testifying? I was so thankful for having been given the opportunity to testify. I, as well as my family, had to endure listening to and reading about the horrific accusations. My reputation . . . our family name was in jeopardy . . . all because of a few girls. Could I forgive them? I honestly could not answer that question at that point. I knew I would never forget what they said about me. The accusations will forever remain in the darkest vestibule of my being. Forgiveness? Ask that not of me.

Caron Goll:

Caron Goll, presently a 21-year-old college student at Moorhead State University, was our next witness. Caron had been a student and athlete of Hancock High School and testified that she had Dennis Courneya as a teacher and coach throughout high school.

Q: "Have you had any contact with Mr. Courneya since you graduated from Hancock?"
A: "He's like supported me. Like I play basketball up there, too, and stuff. He's come to my games and watched me play and stuff and been really supportive."
Q: "Did you have any experiences with Mr. Courneya that you thought were inappropriate in any way?"
A: "Never."

Q: "Did you have any physical contact during either your classes or your athletic events with Mr. Courneya?"
A: "Nothing more than a coach/player would be expected to be."

The witness continued to testify that she had been involved in the weight program, as well: ". . . weights were an important thing for me. So, of course, he like was concerned if I was lifting weights and stuff, getting stronger, and knew it was really important."

Q: "Well, how did you get the impression that he was concerned about that?"
A: "Well, he's concerned for all his athletes to develop strength and stuff, to develop their performance and stuff . . ."

Further during the testimony, Kurzman inquired about the following:

Q: "If other students claim they had seen you with Mr. Courneya where he was caressing, rubbing your legs, would that comport with your recollection?"
A: "No, I deny that."
Q: "Do you know _____ ("Girl W")?
A: "Yes."
Q: "Have you had any discussions with ___ ("Girl W") about this, about Mr. Courneya and anything involving this case?"
A: "No, I haven't."

13th Juror: We should review the documented statements given by "Girl W" during her interview with the County Sheriff and Social Worker . . . what did she say about Caron Goll . . . we better double-check. How is the *reasonable doubt* issue settling with you about now?

Cross-Examination by the State:
Q: "Did I understand you to say that the defendant might touch you on the leg from time to time if he was talking to you?"

A: "Just a pat on the leg, yes."
Q: "You wouldn't characterize that as a caress?"
A: "No."

Caron continued to answer questions regarding a type of touching that may have occurred in the classroom. She indicated that he (Mr. Courneya) "did sometimes lean over her while helping with a test problem."

Q: "Did his midsection ever come in contact with your back when he leaned over you?"
A: "No."

The State concluded with the following question:

Q: "Would it be a fair statement to say that you feel where you are today as a person and achievement and accomplishments have something to do with him (referring to the defendant)?"
A: "Yes."

As Caron was excused as a witness, I reflected, again, at her fine character. She remains one of the kindest and most sincere individuals I have ever had the opportunity to teach and coach. Her successes are a tribute to her character . . . not me.

Chad Solvie:

A former student and athlete of Hancock School now took the stand. Actually, Chad had been "more" than just a star student and athlete. He had been honored as the AAA (Art, Academics, Athletics) recipient—an honor that few can lay claim. It is an award that recognizes high achievement in all three areas. Yes, he was a gifted athlete, but he was also highly intelligent—a national award winner in academics. He had earned his college degree in three years. Presently, he was an administrator of a nursing home with the Good Samaritan Society in Iowa.

He testified that Mr. Courneya had been his teacher and his football coach. He also added that he had kept in contact with Mr. Courneya, "following him and his teams". Additionally, he informed the Court that he was presently married to a girl who had also graduated from Hancock School (A girl that I had coached for six years in two different sports).

Testimony from Chad was requested in regards to his interest in running a basketball camp:

A: ". . . And we (referring to himself and a friend) approached Mr. Courneya with the idea that, you know, he knew us, maybe he'd give us a chance to let us do that, and we did have conversations about that."

Q: "Did—what kinds of things did Mr. Courneya suggest to you if you were going to be running an athletic camp?"

A: ". . . As camp approached, he did sit us down and he wanted to make sure to be aware of how we acted and things like that. . . . he did give us directions about how to position kids and what to do and what not to do . . . always grab them by the sides of their arms with open palms and direct them, and when you do that, also keep your distance from them."

Q: "Was that with regard to any student athletes, male or female?"

A: "I guess it would be—the camp we were running was only for girls."

The questions continued:

Q: "Did you ever observe him (referring to Mr. Courneya) having any contact with any females of whatever age that appeared to be inapproprite contact? Physical contact I'm talking about."
A: "No. In fact, he was very—"

Chad was not allowed to complete his statement due to an "Objection" by the State.
"Sustained."

Cross-Examination by the State:
Chad was questioned about his observations regarding contact between me and other students. In particular the State inquired, "Do you think there's a distinction between appropriate touch of teenage girls in the hallway or on the court?"

A: "I'm not exactly sure if I know what you mean."
Q: "Well, do you think that there's kinds of touch that's all right for a teacher or a coach to do in the hallway to young girls that are not all right to do positioning them on the court?"
A: "No."
Q: "Would it be fair to say that you feel the defendant has helped you a lot in your life?"
A: "I think he worked very hard for me."
Q: "And that he has helped to make you turn out to be the kind of person that you are in some way?"
A: "I think he has helped, along with other people."

13th Juror: Have you noticed that the State's attorney always seems to end his cross-examination with questions of this sort? At first, I was saddened because I thought he was attempting to demean the respect they and I had for one another . . . to question their honesty. No, I eventually came to the conclusion that he, as well as the entire Court, was witnessing what quality of *character* the witnesses for the defense possessed. What else could he say? Did they have to *tell* the Court about all of their accomplishments? Did the defense witnesses have to profess their appreciation of others? Did the defense witnesses sully anyone's name during their testimonies? They were all the embodiment of goodness. I felt so fortunate to even have been a part of their growth.

Shannon Solvie:

The final witness for the Defense took the stand, Shannon Solvie. Shannon was currently a student studying nursing at Bethel College. She testified that she knew Mr. Courneya as her teacher and basketball and track coach while attending Hancock School.

Q: "During the time that you knew Mr. Courneya, did he have any physical contact with you?"

A: "Not sexual physical contact. It was like he would put his arm around me and say, you know, 'You need a little loving,' like a tap on the knee or tap on the shoulder or like messing with your hair."

Q: "During any of the physical contact that you described, did you—did you ever come into contact with any portions of Mr. Courneya's body that stand out in your mind?"

A: "Never."

Q: "Did Mr. Courneya come into contact with your breasts when he was having physical contact with you?"

A: "Never."

Shannon described, in response to questioning, instances where "He would feel our arms, you know, and ask like about muscles. He would bring us up to the weight room when he initiated this new weight program, showed us proper lifting . . ."

Q: "Do you consider him (referring to the defendant) a personal friend?"

A: "I wouldn't say a personal friend. Respected coach, who I respect alot."

Kurzman directed Shannon towards prior testimony from a State's witness by asking, "Do you know ___ ("Girl W")?"

A: "Yup."

Q: "If ___ ("Girl W") remembered seeing Mr. Courneya caressing your legs (stated by "Girl W" in the investigative interview with the County) comport with your memory?"

A: "What's comport mean?"

Q: "Be the same as, go along with."

A: "Oh, no, I don't recall that."

Q: "Have you ever become aware of any stories about you supposedly and Mr. Courneya, anything that anyone claimed to have seen or heard about?"

A: "I remember when Mr. Courneya came this year to one of Chad's basketball games, and we were sitting in the bleachers, and I went over to the game and I started talking to him, and the next day, the next day or a couple days later, someone asked me if Mr. Courneya was rubbing my leg, and I'm like, I said 'Never,'. . . . And that is like so irrelevant, not true at all."

Kurzman concluded his questioning of Shannon by asking her if anyone, other than those from the Defense law firm, had asked her for information relative to or regarding Mr. Courneya . . . "from the Sheriff's office?" . . . "from the school district.?"

Shannon replied, "No."

Cross-Examination by the State:

The initial questioning by the State inquired about the relationship between Shannon's parents and the defendant.

Q: "Friends but not close friends?"

A: "Uh-huh. Like parents of a player, so they know him as a coach."

Q: "Do you know if they ever socialize?"

A: "Like when he comes down to my games, he will sit by them at the games, and like he's come to our place a couple times and talked."

Later, the State proceeded to question Shannon about her testimony regarding the "tap on the leg". The attorney requested that Shannon stand up and demonstrate where she indicated when she said 'a tap on the leg'. She complied with the request.

Q: "Okay. Was that a fairly common type of thing the defendant would do to you from time to time?"

A: "Oh. He'd do it. I don't know how often."

The State: "May the record reflect that the witness took an open palm and placed it twice in rapid succession on the right side of her knee area."

13th Juror: Do I need to tell you what the final questions from the State's attorney were for Shannon Solvie? All right, for the record:

Q: "Do you feel the defendant has helped you to become the kind of person that you are today?"

A: "Yeah. He's had a lot of impact on my life with like work ethic, discipline."

Q: "And are you playing ball at Bethel?"

A: "Yup."

Shannon Solvie . . . one of the finest role models that Hancock had ever had. I remember one time in class, I asked a group of younger kids, "If you could be like anyone in our school, who would it be?" The answer: "Shannon Solvie." The reasons they gave were diverse: "Smart; Athletic; Kind; Great personality; Honest . . ." How ironic that five of the girls testifying for the State were just some of the students who had answered, "Shannon Solvie".

What can I say to people like Shannon Solvie or the rest of the witnesses for the Defense. First, I wanted to express my heartfelt gratitude for their sincerity. I wanted to tell each and everyone of them that I wished they hadn't been put in this situation . . . that their integrity and honor epitomized all that is good in this world . . . that I am so proud of who they are and what they represent . . . that I am humbled by their presence in this Court of Law. I shall, forever, be in debt to all of you.

A prophecy by John Wesley (*His Rule*) professes, much better than I, my gratitude:

Do all the good you can, By all the means you can, In all the ways you can, In all the places you can, At all the times you can, To all the people you can, As long as ever you can. You have . . . and will continue to do so . . . this I know. Thank you.

The Defense rests.

CHAPTER NINETEEN

Let justice be done,
though the heavens fall.

-Lord Mansfield

Before the closing arguments by the prosecution and defense, an *argument* of sort was taking place in the judge's chambers on a number of issues. First, Kurzman requested permission to talk about, in his closing that there were questions in the State's case that might have been answered were a witness to be called: "If the witness was not called, the questions are still outstanding and have not and cannot be resolved." Kurzman had in mind a particular person that was mentioned quite frequently by the State's witnesses during their testimony . . . an individual whom the defense contended had great *influence* upon the girls' perceptions and statements. He continued, "So it is my intent to argue that there are holes from the perspective of the defense in the State's case, which holes might or might not be filled if a witness was to be called and to talk about what the holes are."

The County Attorney argued that Kurzman should not be allowed to say, "Where was_____ (woman's name) and why didn't they bring her in?" . . . Say, "The answer lies with_____(woman's name). She's the master mind behind all this," which is different than saying, "Why didn't the State call her?" According to our interpretation, the State was requesting that Kurzman should not be allowed to say that the State should have brought her in, et cetera. The Court did not have an issue with Kurzman implying this woman's involvement in the case, however, etc.

The second request by Kurzman was in reference to the following: "Judge, I would like to make a record at this point. It's
3:10 (pm), the jury's been here all day, and we are requesting
sequestration of jurors . . . and it is our preference that we, instead, have the jury back tomorrow morning, give arguments and
the law, and then give them the whole day to deliberate." Yes, all
of us had put in a particularly "draining" day. Kurzman realized
that it was already late afternoon. By the time the prosecution
concluded its closing statements, it might very well get to be extremely late by the time the defense was allowed its closing arguments. Judging from prior observations, it would be greatly difficult
to maintain the attention and concentration of an already weary jury.

The Court responded to Kurzman's request: "We will proceed
with instructions—or with closing arguments and instructions this
afternoon . . ."

Prior to the State beginning its closing statements, the jury
was given a copy of the verdict form and a copy of the final instructions. The arguments began.

For the State:
The State's attorney reminded the jurors that the closing arguments were not to be viewed as evidence, and if the lawyers
happened to state facts that were not as they, the jurors recalled,
then they should rely on their recollection. I thought to myself,
what about those jurors who have no notations . . . few recollections? He, additionally, thanked them for their *attention*, thus far.
He reminded them that there were some counts of second degree
criminal sexual conduct which relates to the youth of the victim.
He also indicated that the counts of fourth degree dealt with victims that would be somewhat older, but still underage. He continued to instruct that the companion count of fifth degree criminal sexual conduct does not speak n terms of the age of the victim.
He continued, "What remains for you to decide with regard to
criminal sexual conduct in the second degree are two things. First,
whether the defendant intentionally touched the complainant's

intimate parts or clothing over the intimate parts by use of a position of authority, and second, whether the act was committed with
sexual or aggressive intent."

He attempted to explain the distinction of fifth degree criminal sexual conduct: "Fifth degree is interesting and slightly different from the others. With regard to fifth degree, you'll note that
the touching of the buttocks or the clothing over the area of the
buttocks is not a violation for fifth degree . . . "He attempted to
continue, "The other distinction has to do with you'll be—well,
let's see here. The other distinction doesn't apply because those
elements have been stipulated to . . ."

How are you doing with his clarifications, *13th juror?* I truly
debated whether some of the jurors could comprehend what he
was saying . . . especially at the end of a long day.

Did they care? I hope so. I did.

The State's attorney proceeded to argue the issue of *intent*. He
advised, "Here in this case, you look at the defendant's words, you
look at the defendant's acts, and the circumstances make it perfectly
clear, abundantly clear, it shouts out the answer what his intent was,
and his intent was for purposes of sexual impulses or for aggressive
impulses, or a combination of both." To prove his point, he reminded
the jurors of specific testimony from the State's witnesses. . . . one-
by-one. His implication was that the alleged contact was not accidental . . . but intentional: "What was in it for the defendant was to
demonstrate, not in front of the entire world, not with the entire
world watching, but to the individual student he had control and
authority over them and could get away with doing this."

The great shock for the defense, however, was the State's attorney re-enactment of the testimony given by "Girl Z" in regards to
the cross-country stretching incident:

"Let's get this out of the way right now. Is it physically possible
for the defendant to come up to someone sitting on the ground and
touch his groin to their back or the back of their neck?" At this point,
the attorney took the mannequin and graced the Court with a demonstration, of sort. However, what we found to be totally shocking

was when the attorney got down on his knees to validate her testimony: "The defendant could also be on his knees, come up to her like this. Physically possible? No problem." Many a mouth in the courtroom dropped open! Please, *13th juror,* review the testimony of "Girl Z". Did she ever say or even imply that I was on my knees when she felt the "alleged" rubbing of my groin on her back area? I won't even waste a breath justifying what we witnessed by that attorney. In our estimation, it was a gross misstatement of testimony. Shame.

He continued to request that the jury take into consideration the manner and appearance of the witnesses (for the State): "You should consider how they acted and looked on the witness stand and whether they seemed believable . . . That's frankness and sincerity and manner and appearance." Again, readers, perhaps you should return to their testimony . . . did it appear frank? Did any of the witnesses change their testimony? Did they appear to be clear in their recollections? Did any of them get confounded . . . have to add or delete portions of their testimony? Were there statements laced with vivid, personal interpretations . . . imaginative? You decide.

The attorney characterized the witnesses for the defense: "It's interesting. You had this group of people who are like his kids, they all felt they owed him something in his life and he had done them good. They were close, their families generally were close with him, and they said it didn't happen to us . . ."

Again, all I can say to this attorney is "shame on you." If you want to use the critieria of *frankness, sincerity, manner, and appearance* as pieces of "evidence", then please, by all means, take another look at the witnesses for the defense . . . the comparison is quite evident.

He took additional efforts to remind the jurors just *who* was on trial: "It's not the Sheriff, it's not Jody Holleman, it's not Carrie Jepma, it's not Russ Larson or Roger Clarke, Carol Johnson, or Teresa Herreid. It's the defendant. And if you find yourselves focusing too much on the actions of someone else, you are off the trial in a sense."

My question was, at that point, why did he take the time to

remind them of the role of the above mentioned individuals? Was he concerned about their testimony and/or involvement in this case, too? Yes, what did these individuals have to do with the issue?

I have many conclusions regarding their role . . . however, yes, I am the *defendant* . . . it is *Dennis Courneya* who is on trial here . . . not them.

The State concluded its summation with defining *reasonable doubt:* "Reasonable doubt, the Judge will tell you, is a doubt based on reason and common sense. It's not proof beyond all doubt or all possibility of doubt." His final statement included the following: ". . . when you think about the overwhelming evidence of guilt and of intention in this case, you'll be able to see that there is no reasonable doubt about the defendant's guilt, and you will conclude that he's been proved guilty beyond a reasonable doubt of the offense charged in the complaint."

Defense Summation: 5:00 pm

Mr. Kurzman: "I know its late in the day, it's 5:00. I'm going to try to do this in less than the hour and a half that was utilized in the closing by the State. I don't know if I'll be able to or not." I surmised that he better try . . . by the looks of one juror in particular, Kurzman better have a pocketful of "smelling salts".

Kurzman began by explaining to the jurors, "It is important to keep in mind that you are not evaluating not only the question of what was supposedly on Dennis Courneya's mind, but also the question what could account for some girls to perceive something that wasn't intended. What could account for someone to remember something that didn't happen? You will find clues to that in a person's upbringing. You'll find clues to that in the values, the perspective that the family have." He continued to remind the jurors, however, that it wasn't their responsibility to "find clues to something . . . It is not whether you think Mr. Courneya made inappropriate comments . . . It is whether he acted in the ways that are alleged in the complaint, whether the touches occurred, and if they occurred, were they intentional."

He proceeded to give the jurors a "visual" of sort: "Now, you can take two glasses, one labeled with sexual tendencies, the other labeled aggressive tendencies. The State has managed to fill each one-half way, and you just take and pour them together and say, 'Okay, you've proven the case.' Huh-uh (no)." Mr. Kurzman also brought the juror's attention back to the demonstration by the State's attorney:

"Let's talk about _____ ("Girl Z's) first story. You saw Mr. Glasrud demonstrate (referring to his demonstration during the State's summation), if one were to get down on their knees, it's possible that you could actually have penile contact with the person with the area that she demonstrated. However, what did _____ ("Girl Z") say?" He then cited the testimony as given by "Girl Z" when interviewed by the Sheriff (documented): "He put his—he comes up behind me and he put his two legs on the sides of my shoulders." When the Sheriff asked for clarification, the girl continued, "Well, he's still standing up, but he's leaning over kind of."

Kurzman explained, "If this, the first act, is physically impossible as described by the child, and not as remembered by Mr. Glasrud, not as hypothesized as a possible way that that could occur, it doesn't mean that she's lying. She might be, but she could also be confused. She could also have been reinforced in saying things, because that's how memory works. Our memory . . . is not actually an actual audio vision of the past. It is impacted by all our experiences and impacted by what gets reinforced as we go back and think about it."

Yes, I knew that the defense had been perplexed by the role of Carrie Jepma in this case. Kurzman explained it as follows: ". . . critical judgement was suspended." He recalled portions of her testimony when the defendant had tried to "buck her up" when she was feeling down. "That was deemed by her to be sexual harassment", he explained.

He also reminded the jurors, "And she didn't say to her colleague, 'Hey, I know you're trying to buck me up and stuff, but this may appear a problem . . . I am feeling offended by it.' "No, as Kurzman indicated, Ms. Jepma was "predisposed to suspect something wrong from him (Courneya)" when she hears the story told to her by "Girl Z". He also pointed to some discrepancies with regards to the "time" variable as described by Jepma:

"How about the time of interaction (regarding the conference between Ms. Jepma and "Girl Z")? Ms. Jepma recalls it now as being just a couple of minutes, nothing substantial. However, in the materials based on what she had told Ms. Herreid (investigator for the school, "Teresa"), it's a long time. A long time."

Kurzman requested that the jurors look at "Girl W's" voluntary statement taken on 10/14/97 and compare it with the product of her sessions with Teresa (investigator): "See what happens? See how things change? See how things would start out being perceived by her as accidental, but by the middle of December, after some unknown conversation or conversations, now definitely is, always has been intentional?" Kurzman explained the signficance of the contradictory statements of "Girl W", "There's an incomplete picture for you to be able to decide beyond a reasonable doubt whether Mr. Courneya committed any of the offenses."

Kurzman attempted to offer explanations as to why and how the girls came to provide the accusatory statements against Mr. Courneya and areas that the jury should contemplate while making their final decision:

Pressures: "There were peer pressures to conform, to go along, to help family members, to help friends. There were pressures from the police, expectatons of the questioner, and the proof is the leading and suggestive questions that we know about. We don't have everything recorded that was going on, people that were talking to these children."

Kurzman directed the jury to look at Page 8 of "Girl Z"'s statement to the Sheriff and how he "suggests" a statement to her: "The Sheriff, page 8. 'One of the reasons I think it's hard for you or anybody else to experience this type of thing, he is a person of authority you know, in school. Is that one of the reasons or maybe one of the bigger reasons why a lot of people haven't come forward and talked about this?' Recall, please, that "Girl Z" did not state that . . . the Sheriff did."

My attorney exemplifed the "pressure" on "Girl Z" by referring to her mother: "Remember what ___ ("Girl Z") said? 'My mother always knew he's a pervert.' If her mom knew that he was a pervert, how come nobody said anything? She's a deputy court administrator here. . . . If she thinks her mother thinks this guy is this way, then there's pressure to come up with a story that supports that."

Pupils. School District: "They pick sides real early on this, it is evident. But the fact is that they were holding sessions for the kids that were going to testify, and apparently nobody was concerned about kids that were confused and crying over the fact that Coach Courneya had been charged. Now what motivations might there be? Perhaps to try to eliminate litigation, if you please those people, hey, get rid of him . . . then you have a greater likelihood you are not going to get sued. So there's school district pressure because they are pupils."

Kurzman reminded the jurors not to forget the role of "hormones" and adolescence: "Those rushes of hormones also cause people to have different emotions, different perceptions, different fantasies." In particular, my attorney described the statements of "Girl T": ". . . she comes in, she's 12 or 13 supposedly at the time of the alleged act, and she says 'Well, actually I was the first . . . Happened to me about a week before it happened to ___ ("Girl Z"). Did the same thing' Can they have confusion? Yes. Can they have fantasies? Yes."

To Avoid Punishment: ". . . Sure, they registered a complaint with teachers; sure, more joined in on it, but from their view, they thought there was a good chance the guy may come back, and then maybe he's going to discriminate against them . . . There's a motive to hang in there in the beginning. And all of us like saving face . . . I mean, Coach Courneya was devastated when they came there on Monday (referring to the administrative visit at Courneya's home). How hard is that? His entire life dedicated to that community. His entire life, not just his work hours . . . and the students got together and gave him a criminal complaint . . . That's the reality of what happened here. That was shocking to a man whose whole life, whose self image is based on being a teacher, on being a good teacher . . ."

Practice Sessions: "I guess it didn't hurt to get together every Wednesday with some counselor. We don't know exactly what went on for an hour, four weeks in a row. We know Mr. Glasrud was one of the featured speakers. We know his associate was another feature speaker. The witnesses would have you believe that all they talked about for hours, four weeks in a row, is what the courtroom experience was going to be like? You might find that a stretch."

Point of View: "What does point of view mean? It depends upon where you are and how something looks to you." With point of view in mind, he was referring to the testimony of the girl who claimed to "see" an erection while the defendant was wearing "tight" shorts . . . "Girls don't wear jock straps, girls don't wear cups. If a girl is looking at a bulge and sees a bulge in the genital area, they are going to say 'I wonder whether that's their erect penis or I'm just seeing their cup'. . . . That's your point of view, that's your perspective."

The Persuasion: "That's moral persuasion. What is your home life like? What kind of comments do people make? Are they people making comments about 'look at all those guys with bulges', or are people not looking at the crotch of basketball players? Depends upon your upbringing. Depends upon your values."

The Circumstances: ". . . One day the coach of the year, the teacher of the year, the person to whom the yearbook has been dedicated, and is walking along, and the long arm of the law came out and says, 'You're busted.' And then an individual has to try to fight the State with all of its unlimited resources. They own the building. They have police, sheriffs, investigators, unlimited resources compared to what a citizen has. And in this case, there were the resources of the school district as well. And that's why the law requires proof beyond a reasonable doubt, because we recognize the inequity."

Other Circumstantial: Contamination: "The contamination and cross fertilization and growing nature of the stories. You saw how a change between a statement given and something that comes out two months later, after some unknown conversations with unknown numbers of people . . . then it changes again between the affidavit and the time people come and testify . . . they can be led." Kurzman particularly exemplified the "growing nature of stories" theory by referring to the "genesis of the first ___ ("Girl Z") and subsequent stories . . . Sister, cousin, friend."

My attorney chastised the suggestion from Mr. Glasrud that, well, sure, Mr. Courneya was able to get some people in, but he was friendly (friends) with them. Kurzman argued, "How come it's appropriate to comment and to, if you will, discount what people who know him have to say because they are friends with him, but you are not supposed to discount what ___ ("Girl Z's") family, friends and relatives say? I suggest to you that you have to apply the same rules to both sides here." My attorney concluded this portion of his argument by, again, referring to the statement of "Girl Z": "How did it get from the field with a story that is physically impossible, not withstanding Mr. Glasrud's efforts to show that it's posssible, but not possible the way she describes it? How does that get to a 26, now 28 count indictment? Through cross fertilization, pressure, reinforcement. The State's case, the people go further and further, and as they go further, they're stuck in the briar patch, and it's hard to get out. Do you think ___ ("Girl Z") could have announced two weeks ago, 'This is crazy. I made it up. What's with you people?'"

Timing and Substance: In regards to the initial meeting with "Girl Z" and Ms. Jepma (teacher) . . . Mrs. Johnson (school counselor) . . . Mr. Clarke (principal) . . . Mr. Larson (superintendent): "____("Girl Z") says nothing was discussed about the breast in any way, including any touching. So does Mrs. Jepma . . . So does Mrs. Johnson . . . So did Mr. Clarke. However, Mr. Larson said, well, he remembered. He remembered because he had notes and he was reviewing his notes. So he was asked to bring his notes, and No. 10 (exhibit), here they are. . . . There's different ways you can construct these notes. What happened is, without doubt, when you look at this, is that the word 'grabs', g-r-a-b-s, has been written over something else that has been erased. Now what was that something else? When was the erasure made? Was it just a question of needing to save face? I mean, he's the superintendent . . . He didn't know he was going to have to produce notes to back them up, and then he did, and here are the notes . . ." Kurzman continued, "It could also be a mistake (referring to the notes). Doesn't have to be a lie. Maybe the notes were done later, looking back. Maybe, as Mr. Larson said, at some other time he was going back and made the erasure, but he couldn't tell us when that was supposed to have happened."

Connection between the Accusers: "You heard how many of them—how many of them have families that have similar moral persuasion, how many of them are related to each other, how many of them are close friends."

The Reputation of the Accusers: "Mr. Courneya's reputation is untarnished. I didn't hear a single person, not even anybody from the State, say this guy, 'he's not honest'. No. The judge is going to tell you, in jury instructions, words something to the effect that reputation evidence is as important as any other bit of evidence that is brought in front of you . . ." He implored the jury to note the testimony, as follows: "Also girls from last year's team, the team before that, two years before that . . . and so on, 'he didn't do it., he couldn't do it, he wouldn't do it.'"

Quality of Investigation: "Were there leading and suggestive questions? I hope you saw enough examples of that. I'm suggesting that the Sheriff approached his duties with, 'Here's a complaint that's come to me. I'm going to see if I can prove it.' That's why you have no exculpatory evidence, nothing that cuts against the theories that are put into the children and they are starting to repeat and share with each other. But what happened?
      Critical judgement is suspended. . . . just building a case."

The Witnesses: Mr. Kurzman explained that there were different types of witnesses: 1) The alleged victims; 2) State's "story development" witnesses (those who stated what happened each day, how it came along, who said what to whom . . .); 3) State's corroborating witnesses (those who claimed that they saw something that could have looked like this, or she told me a story, or I heard a rumor, etc.); 4) State's intent witnesses (in reference to the Spreigl witnesses): "You got _____ ("Girl M") . . . She testified that there wasn't a day, not a day, in her entire career with Mr. Courneya that she wasn't sexually harassed, wasn't sexually touched in inappropriate ways. Not a day. Go with her recollection (regarding the ten-meter tape story) . . . He's really saying that he has a 30-foot penis or trying to imply that? You will see that the possibilities are endless with this young lady, that perhaps if she was sitting here right now, seeing me sweating, that I just—that that would be an inference that I just finished having a sexual act . . . I mean everything, everything, was viewed through this filter, no matter what it was. She couldn't even concede . . . the possibility that he was referring to this tape measure."
      Mr. Kurzman continued to recall, for the jurors, perplexing issues of the case: "We don't know who met with Ms. Holleman or how often. But through some process each one of these . . . young

ladies told you the same thing, 'Well, yeah, it's going on. I've seen it. Some stuff happened to me . I didn't think it was wrong—' Now, you can fill in the blank—until Mr. Glasrud told me, until the Sheriff told me, until Ms. Jepma told me and the counselor on the Wednesday sessions told me . . . 'Don't you understand that this was somebody taking advantage of you? . . . Don't you understand that you were being sexually abused?' . . . Eventually, apparently, some of them came to that belief."

He distinctively drew attention to the fact that the defendant was not being charged with making people feel uncomfortable: "Uncomfortable doesn't mean the same thing as being sexually abused. And, I mean, there's some element of fair play here. Twenty two years, no feedback, in front of parents, in front of audiences, in front of other teachers, in front of other kids, all the behaviors are the same. Then one day it's a crime."

Kurzman particularly took issue with a concept that was communicated to the jury by Mr. Glasrud when he inferred that the kids' statements were scrutinized by the Sheriff . . . by Teresa Herreid. He continued by stating, "You saw the example of scrutiny the Sheriff applied, and one can only guess at what Ms. Herreid was doing. Mr. Glasrud said they didn't know it was wrong until they were told by Jody Holleman. Well, obviously nothing is wrong with that, but we don't know what Jody Holleman told them.

We do know she was one of the adults listed by some of the kids and identified as the point at which they found out that everything that had been normal, everything that has occurred to me . . . to be sexual, actually was I was being taken advantage of, and I'm not going to let that happen."

In conclusion, Kurzman forewarned, "I don't think any of you have ever had a decision as difficult as this one. He begged their indulgence "for another 30 seconds" as he referred them to the State Championship booklet, once more: "Words cannot describe the feeling" (Page 26 of the booklet) subheading. Kurzman read the words that I had written to my team and community following our state basketball championship. As I listened, I recalled the joy, the triumph, the pride of that moment. I never, ever, envisioned that I would be hearing this tribute, once again, in a court of law.

The words I wrote in that booklet were read in court and relived by me: "*I never want to forget you kids. I can truly say, I love every one of you. You see, it's not good bye. You are all just turning another page in your chapter. The first book has been published. Now it's time to start another book. Your book in life!! Your foundation has been covered in stone. You will all be great successes in life, and I'll always be there for you. You're part of my family. You'll always be my daughters, I love you all so much. Thanks for the memories.*" As the words were read in court, there was distinguishable sobbing from the spectators in the Court and from one juror. It was a very difficult moment for us all. Yes, we knew that, within moments, the jury would be writing the next chapter in the life of Dennis Courneya.

Thy Will Be Done . . .

CHAPTER TWENTY

They have sown the wind,
and they shall reap the whirlwind.
-Old Testament, *Hosea, VIII, 7*

Waiting for the *judgement* was unbearable. In fact, it was the most difficult experience of my entire life. I was entrusting twelve individuals with the determination of my fate. Was I confident? Yes, I was to a certain degree. I found the witnesses for the defense to be so very credible; additionally, I knew the truth. I was counting on the *power of truth* . . . However, I found myself feeling uneasy. Was it because I felt the jurors were not always attentive during the testimony, especially in the later stages? Was it because of the unexpected removal of a male juror for (allegations of possible) sexual harassment? That, in itself, was such an odd and untimely occurance. Did I feel that a jury comprised of ten females and two males would prove to be detrimental—would this become a "gender" issue? Would they attempt to "compromise" in an effort to please both sides? I was also concerned with what I called their "University connection"—I felt that too many of the jurors were associated with the U of M, Morris . . . as were many of the accusers' parents and acquaintances. Maybe it was the "parade" of witnesses for the State and, what seemed to me, their "award winning performances". As Kurzman alluded to in his summation, the State had abundant resources available to them. Yes, this was their "home court".

I was reminded of the athletic term, *Sudden Death Overtime*. I had been in that situation as a coach many times. It is described as that phase of "extra minutes" in which only one can emerge as the victor. No matter how competent and skilled one was, the ultimate

decision rested on whom "rose to the top" in the final minutes . . .
found that inner strength . . . challenged fate. Personally, I felt like I
was at that moment. No matter how I had lived my life, the personal
dedication, the commitment, the "heart" I gave to my profession, it
was now quite irrelevant. The ultimate decision would be made in a
brief period of time . . . the clock was ticking.

The jury deliberations continued for nearly three days. I con-
templated the number of challenges facing this group of twelve
individuals: 1) Understanding the charges and ballot. Twice, that
I am aware of, they came back ("We are confused . . .") and inquired of the judge additional clarification; 2) It was nearing another weekend. Some of the jurors were quite young; they, undoubtedly, wanted to "get on" with their lives . . . have some fun.
I did not blame them; 3) Their past experiences. Can an individual truly negate their own personal experiences in making a
decision that is "too close" to reality? 4) Were they aware of the
consequences of their decision? Despite these questions, I still had
faith in the legal system . . . A system that I had studied, taught,
and believed . . . in principle.

Finally, after days of waiting, the twelve jurors came back with
their decision. As we awaited the verdict, the courtroom was cau-
tioned not to demonstrate an overt emotional response: "I would
remind members of the audience that there's to be no audible or
visible comment about the verdict."

State of Minnesota versus Dennis Edward Courneya: "We the
jury find the defendent Dennis Edward Courneya":

Counts I, II: ("Girl Z"): **GUILTY**

Counts III, IV, V, VI: ("Girl Y"): **GUILTY**

Counts VII, VIII, IX, X: ("Girl X"): **NOT GUILTY**

Counts XI, XII: ("Girl W"): **GUILTY**

Counts XIII, XIV, XV, XVI: ("Girl L"): **NOT GUILTY**

Counts XVII, XVIII, XIX, XX: ("Girl T"): **GUILTY**

Counts XXI, XXII, XXIII, XXIV: ("Girl U"): **NOT GUILTY**

Counts XXV, XXVI: ("Girl R"): **NOT GUILTY**

As the verdict was read, I took heed to the judge's instructions about reacting to the judgement of the jury. I stood tall and proud; I showed no emotion; however, the pain and anguish I felt within could not be described. Many spectators in the courtroom could not maintain their composure. I could hear sobs from individuals sitting behind me and one juror was crying uncontrollably.

The Court: "Members of the jury, you are now excused. I wish to thank you for your dedication and your service in this matter. Thank you."

I was asked by the Court to step forward and the judge proceeded to state the verdicts, one-by-one, as adjudged and decreed. Additionally, the Court ordered that there be a presentence investigation conducted by the Minnesota Department of Corrections and that we should contact a Ms. Karen White (Stevens County) to schedule an appointment for that matter. A sentencing hearing would follow in approximately 30-60 days.

The Court: "The previous conditions of release shall remain in effect until further order of the Court . . . That's all."

I shall never forget the sound of the word, *Guilty*. It was like taking a knife . . . and cutting apart one's heart . . . one's soul. *13th Juror:* Please review the statements and testimony . . . what did the jurors miss? Whatever the verdict, I already knew that my life was ruined. Even if I had been found innocent, what school district would ever hire me?

My life, as a teacher and coach, ended the day the allegations began. The verdict sealed that fate. When I walked out of the courtroom, I was met by my family and friends. I made no excuses and, more than anything, I tried to remain upbeat so that these wonderful people would not break down . . . I cared so much for them. The hurt I felt was more for them than it was for me . . . they were my *heart*.

Following the verdict, it was determined that I was to appear in Court on June 29th for sentencing—approximately two months away. I made an appointment, as instructed, to meet with the pre-sentence investigator. This meeting took place the week following the trial. I met with a young female parole officer (investigator) in Morris. For the first fifty minutes of the session, I completed a written questionnaire which asked questions about my family, addresses, job description, and criminal background. The remaining 5-10 minutes were spent with the pre-sentence investigator, Ms. White. Her opening statement upon meeting me was a bit forward, I thought. She said, "You know you're probably going to spend some time in prison . . . "My thoughts were that her presumption was quite unprofessional. I wondered how she had derived at that conclusion so quickly. The trial had concluded only about a week ago and, to my knowledge, she did not have a transcript of the trial as yet. I also could not recall seeing her at the trial. Where was her information coming from? Perhaps, someone from the area had already filled her in on the necessary details. I don't know. She proceeded to explain that a major part of her recommendation concerning the sentence would come from the so-called victims and their parents. She also explained that these conferences would be lengthy and would take her at least a month.

Her following statement definitely caught me off guard. She indicated that I was to enter a sex-offender program prior to the sentencing. I thought this remark was very bizarre and premature. Wasn't she supposed to gather all the facts and opinions and then make a recommendation? It appeared that her recommendation was preceding the fact-finding/interview phase. Strange, indeed. I placed a quick telephone call to my attorney (on the spot), and her initial recommendation was immediately put-to-rest. We were informed that a sex-offender program need not take place prior to the sentencing . . . if recommended. There would be plenty of time to address that issue. Additionally, we were already in the process of appealing the verdict.

I had formed an opinion of this agent in a relatively short period. She seemed inexperienced and not knowledgeable of legal protocol. I left her office more confused than ever. Furthermore, my opinion was even more justified when the following week, she notified me to send back the paperwork she had sent home with me. When I noted the directions on the "homework", I observed that the stipulations were it was "for office only".

I had nearly two months to wait for the sentencing. I had no job . . . no income. Prior to the trial's final phase, I was presented with another $20,000.00 bill for legal services. Additionally, I was informed that the appeals process could also prove quite costly.

Somehow, we found the funds to continue my legal representation. In order to take my mind off of my dilemma, I knew that I had to stay busy: "Work is the best remedy to cure one's mind." I spent a great deal of time helping my brother, Steve, prepare his fields for spring planting. Yet, the greatest amount of time was spent in trimming and shaping at least 10,000 evergreen trees that my dad had planted ten years ago. Many, many hours were spent at this task; the "peace of mind" it offered was just the medicine I needed.

I also found great solace in the company of my parents. We spent quality time together in the evenings. Their attitudes about life remained positive even in the face of great adversity because of the trial. They continued to be hopeful . . . something would work out.

I also spent a great deal of time with my son, Jerid. I attempted to make his life as "normal" as possible. His strength was consistent and inspiring.

R. Browning (*In a Balcony*) stated, *I count life just a stuff to try the soul's strength on.* June 29th, 1998: True to form, Dad was with me. My mom also wanted to attend the sentencing; however, we thought it best that she remain at home . . . to be there for family. Very little was said during our three-hour trip to Willmar. Finally, Dad broke the silence by saying, "We've always been proud of you and that will never change." He then went on to say that I would probably be asked in Court to make a statement prior to the sentencing. I had not thought about that until he mentioned it. It wouldn't have made any difference, anyway; I would just tell the truth—the same truth that I have told my entire life.

Proceedings:

The Court: "This is in the matter of the State of Minnesota versus Dennis Edward Courneya. This is Stevens County court file K7-97-155. The appearances of counsel should be noted. And the first matter before the Court this morning is the defendant's motion to enter judgement of not guilty on all counts, or in the alternative to grant a new trial."

Mr. Kurzman reminded the Court that it had sent the memorandum (regarding the above motions) to them approximately two months ago, and he further assumed that the Court had read and studied it. He also indicated that there had been no response from the State regarding the matter (the memorandum had been sent to the State, also two months previously).

Mr. Glasrud announced that the State opposed the motions citing a number of procedural irregularities. With regards to the new trial motion by the defense, he questioned, "So what are the grounds for that?" He denied the claims made by the defense regarding the following:

1) Evidence was wrongfully admitted (pertaining in particular to "Girl Z").
* defense claimed that "Girl Z" testified about things that she had not told the Sheriff
* defense argued the *State v. Kennedy* case and the misuse of Spreigl testimony
* defense claimed that there was a physical impossibility to what happened to "Girl Z" (recall the stretching-out incident and the State re-enactment during closing arguments)
* defense objected to the Spreigl testimony of "Girls N and M"

* defense objected to the testimony of girls who were not themselves victims or claiming that something illegal had occurred to them ("Girls O and Q") (the defense claimed that because of these witnesses, the jury credited this and they convicted on the first three people who reported)
* defense objected to the fact that they were not allowed to bring in the medical experts who had completed evaluations on the defendant (Dr. Ascano)
* defense argued that the Sheriff was allowed to testify that his techniques were appropriate
* The State brought a motion to bar testimony or argument about uncalled witnesses
* defense claims that there's an inherent incredibility to the State's case, particularly with regard to "Girl Z"
* defense argued that the Court erred in failing to change venue
* defense complained about the excusal of the juror during the final phases of the trial (the juror who indicated that a complaint may be filed against him)

The Court wasted little time in pronouncing judgement: "The defendant's motions to enter a judgement of not guilty on all counts or in the alternative to grant a new trial is denied."

13 Juror: Do you agree? Please review the testimony . . . render your judgement.

The Court: "Mr. Courneya, is there anything you would like to tell the Court prior to the time the Court considers imposing sentence in this matter?"

I stated, "Yes, your honor. I've been a public school teacher for 22 years, and in those 22 years, I've tried to preach to students about the good in life. In those 22 years, I've taught sons and daughters of superintendents, sons and daughters of principals at our school, sons and daughters of school board officials, and in those 22 years there has never, ever been a case of where supposedly I touched somebody in an inappropriate way. And I would think with their fathers being in a position such as that, that that would have been the case had there been something that was inappropriate. I have nothing more to say in terms of that, and I thank you, your Honor."

The State proceeded with its proposal. The attorney indicated that he had been thinking for some time about the appropriate sentence in this case. He further stated that he had even looked at the theories of punishment . . . He proceeded to declare the following,

". . . it appears to me that the Sentencing Guidelines are correct in requiring prison for this outrageous breach of trust, for the unapologetic abuse of power and authority over vulnerable and impressionable young people, young people who are the best that our community has to offer. So a meaningful sentence is going to be required to recognize that fact." Further on in his presentation, he continued, "So while the defendant has indeed suffered, the poor young young women have too, and not through their own fault.

The Court saw what they went through having to come here and testify . . . "He finally submitted his recommendation, "What's it worth? It's worth between 55 and 59 months in prison at a minimum. It's worth a lengthy conditional release after that. It's worth everything that the presentence investigation recommends, including the DNA testing, the sex offender registration, worth the defendant being precluded as much as is possible in this court's authority to do from having contact with the victims or their families, from having any sort of position of authority over young people again." He continued to advocate that I should have to pay substantial fines.

The Court: "What is the—what's your calculation of the mandatory minimum fine?"

Mr. Glasrud responded, "It's supposed to be 30 percent of the maximum—$10,500.00 on second degree. Okay. I'm going from Ms. White's (sentencing investigator) notes. And I guess we could look at the complaint and quickly calculate what 30 percent of them would be. I don't think she has it on the fourth degree. Well, you can easily figure out what the maximums are, though. Six thousand (dollars) on the fourth and I think $10,500 on the second."

As I listened to the State's attorney proposal, I wondered *why* was he being given the opportunity to determine my sentence? Is this customary?

Kurzman presented his argument: "Judge, I think it's significant that in commenting on the victim impact, the presentence investigator noted their views with respect to an appropriate sentence. (According to the sentencing interviews with the girls and their parents, they did not advocate a strict penalty—a long term jail sentence—for my conviction. I liked to think that perhaps their "conscience" was finally taking presence). Apparently the court administrator in Morris ("Girl Z's mother) also had an opportunity to give her opinion as well."

My attorney continued, "I think it's fair to say that all of the victims together believe that Mr. Courneya has suffered sufficiently . . . In reading the interviews with the victims, there is nothing in the interviews that talks about them having been significantly impacted. Mr. Courneya's life has been destroyed. He has no assets . . . He, upon conviction, will lose his license to teach and therefore he will never again be able to be in a position such as he had occupied . . . We respectfully request therefore that the Court depart down, that the Court sentence Mr. Courneya by either staying execution and one year at the county facility, or staying adjudication on those offenses which call for mandatory incarceration . . . while sentencing on those counts which provide for one year in the workhouse with extensive probation following."

Mr. Kurzman respectfully requested, ". . . a consideration be given to what, at least to me, seems to be a perverse jury verdict and the ambiguity of the statute, together with the victim impact as reported by the probation officer and the victims' desires, that Mr. Courneya not be committed to prison."

Within moments . . . actually seconds . . . the Court rendered its sentence. As I listened to the detailed sentence of punishment for each count and each degree, I could not keep track of the amount of time I was to be committed to the Commissioner of Corrections (prison), nor could I calculate the amount of fines. I could, however, comprehend that I was going to prison for a long time; I would have

to pay a great amount of money in fines; I was being labelled a sex
offender; I would be required to complete DNA testing; I would have
to complete a sex offender evaluation; I was mandated to register as a
sex offender, etc. As I noted the brevity with which the Court had
rendered its sentence, I thought, "Why were we even given the opportunity to state our opinions in Court? Apparently, the decision
about my punishment had already been made . . ."

In the concluding moments of the session, the State made a
reply to the request by the defense for release pending appeal. He
brought up the subject of the letter that I had written to the Thielke
family (readers: you read the copy of that letter in a preceding
chapter; review it again). He argued, "Actually he wrote to the
kids and he sent that letter to the school to the kids evidently so
the parents wouldn't see he was contacting the kids . . . Basically,
the State's position is that we have a hard time understanding why
there should be any stay of a sentence. The defendant stands here
convicted of serious offenses, and he has a right to appeal just like
anyone does. He doesn't have the right to presume that he's going
to win that appeal. And so we would oppose any—any stay. We
think he should report on the 1st of July as ordered."

The Court: "The defendant's request for a stay of sentences
pending appeal is denied. The Court will order that you report to
the Sheriff of Stevens County at 9:00 am on July 1st."

I'll never forget the words and judgement of the Court that day
in June. Nor will I ever forget the sounds of giggling (elation over the
sentence) that came from certain individuals in that courtroom. I left
that courtroom with dignity . . . however, I also left behind my faith
in the respectability of our court . . . and some of its agents. One
should not *glee* over the tragedy of another. A remark recorded in
1764 (Anonymous) shall remind me every day of the inappropriate
behavior I witnessed in that Court, June 29, 1998: *The law doth
punish man or woman that steals the goose from off the common; But lets
the greater felon loose, that steals the common from the goose.* I was not
shamed that day in June . . . the Court was.

I had one day of freedom remaining.

CHAPTER TWENTY ONE

Stone walls do not a prison make,
Nor iron bars a cage;
Minds innocent and quiet take
That for an hermitage;
If I have freedom in my love,
And in my soul am free,
Angels alone, that soar above,
Enjoy such liberty.

-Lovelace, *in prison*

The *Gates of Hell* awaited me. I entered the doors of the St. Cloud Correctional Institute as a convicted felon. I was led into the prison through a series of iron gates. Finally, the two officers who had transported me from Morris turned me over to a prison officer. I was taken to a room where there were two other prisoners. We were told to strip down and they conducted a very thorough search. We were given prison clothes and directed to another station to compete paperwork (medical histories, etc.) As the three of us were led down long hallways, I noted the many security checkpoints. We finally arrived at "E House"—the cell block for new arrivals.

We were crammed into the six-by-nine foot cell with about ten other inmates who had just arrived. The noise level of the cell block was unreal . . . it sounded like a football stadium in a state of pandemonium! We were given a sack lunch, and we remained standing for nearly one hour . . . waiting . . . for what? I noticed right away that being a white (Causasian) male categorized me as a "minority". Finally, we were released and led down to get our shots, then back to "E House" where we were assigned a cell—a cell that was to be our home for the next 48 hours—quarantined. Little did we know that this "isolation" (quarantine) would extend to 72 hours because of the weekend; there was no one available to process us out.

This was the longest 72 hours of my life. In the six-by-nine foot cell, there was a small stainless steel sink and toilet, a bed (rack) that was bolted to the wall with a piece of foam rubber for the mattress, two sheets, a blanket and a pillow. Each inmate was given a paper bag which contained a toothbrush, toothpaste, soap, shampoo and a washcloth.

The cell had concrete on three walls with iron bars covering the front. Needless to say, there was no privacy, whatsoever, as hundreds and hundreds of inmates walked past each day.

My thoughts? When am I going to get out of here??? My attorney had told me that my stay would probably last only two or three days because of our appeal in progress. Those words of *hope* helped to sustain me. However, how would Kurzman ever be able to contact me? Did he know where I had been sent? What about my family . . . how would they know where I was? I was not allowed to place a call to inform anyone as to my destination. I didn't know it at the time, but my sister, Julie, had called the Sheriff's office of Steven's County . . . and she knew. She had been informed that I was taken to St. Cloud Prison and that I would be transferred shortly to Stillwater Penitentiary. She immediately had called the St. Cloud facility and, after being transferred to a number of departments, was able to talk with my assigned case worker. It was the case worker that informed her that I was in quarantine for a number of days and that I could have no contact with the *outside.* The case worker also said that whomever at the Stevens County Sheriff's Office had stated that I was going to be sent to Stillwater Penitentiary had given her erroneous information. She proceeded to inform the rest of the family. At least, now, they knew my fate. I also found out later that Julie and her husband had driven to the St. Cloud Correctional Institute that day but were not allowed admittance. They simply sat in their car in the parking lot . . . in utter silence . . . looking at the foreboding structure . . . wondering what was happening within.

The prison sounds were deafening due to the constant clanging of iron gates and the consistent screaming of the inmates. The prisoners came in all shapes, sizes, color, and age. However, they all had one thing in common—they had a "chip" on their shoulder and they had "something to prove." It seemed like everything was to the extreme: tatoos, hair, foul language, gang affiliation, and negative attitudes. Yes, this was not a movie . . . this was my reality. To add to my turmoil, I felt quite ill . . . anxiety, stress, and yes, fearful of the unkown. As a result, my chest would pound violently, and I experienced sharp pains as well as great difficulty in breathing. Now confined in a cell, the conditions only grew worse. I did not sleep one moment for three days and nights. The only people I saw were the kitchen help who brought the meals. A nurse would stop by, on schedule, to check for reactions to the shots. I mentioned that I was not feeling well, and she told me that if it got worse . . . call someone. My question was, "Who?"

The "routine" day consisted of "count" (a tally of inmates) five times daily. You better be standing by the iron bars or "in the hole" you go. The other inmates were allowed out of their cells for three meals a day—20 minutes per meal. They were also given a 35 minute recreation time in which they could shower, make phone calls, or buy snacks. I was not allowed out of my cell. Finally, on the second day, an inmate came by and said, "You want a book?" I took it and read it three times before my remaining 30 hours expired.

On Monday, the door opened for the first time and I was allowed to go and eat with some of the other prisoners. As I walked to the eating area, every 30 to 40 feet a guard was posted as well as guard dogs. You were inspected constantly; one guard would inspect your shoes, another your midsection, the third looked at your head, etc. A tray was provided and the prisoners entered a large room to eat. The big question was, "Where does one sit?" The tension in the room was evident . . . prisoners inspecting prisoners. Unwritten prison rules indicated that you could not sit where you wanted . . . you had to be "wanted"—part of the group. It was the same routine everyday . . . twenty minutes to eat and then "get back to your cell!" I further realized my "condition in life" when on July 4th—a day of celebration—I heard the "sounds of life" beyond the prison walls . . . laughter, fireworks, happiness. It seemed a world away. This was Hell . . . no doubt about it . . . *Satan the envious said with a sigh: Chritians know more about their hell than I* (Alfred Kreymborg). He was correct.

When I was allowed out of quarantine, I was given the chance to make a telephone call. I called my parents . . . it was very emotional. I was so concerned for their well-being and the welfare of my son, Jerid. My family meant the world to me. Just being able to hear their voices lifted my spirits and my resolve . . . I was not forgotten.

My next question was "what was Kurzman doing to get me released?" Yes, he had said that I would only be here for a few days, but there were major problems with the appeals process. The judge who was to make a decision regarding my release was in Alaska and could not get back to Minnesota because of an airline strike. We greatly wanted this particular judge to review my case because he was the author of Kennedy vs. State—a Supreme Court decision that was very relevant to my case. However, we had no choice; we had to wait. Upon hearing the "bitter" news, I had to dig deep inside and try to find a silver lining. However, there is no silver in Hell. The only ray of hope I had at that time was Kurzman's confidence and the support of my family. When I received my first two letters, one from Dad and Mom and the other from my sister, Julie, I knew I could endure. Shortly afterwards, my sister, Judy, and my son, Jerid, wrote endearing letters as well. I saved those first four letters . . . they were my link to life. Jerid continued to write a letter daily. Yes, he was my son, but he was also my friend. I was so proud of him.

In the meantime, I still was concerned about my health. The chest pains and shortness of breath were definitely bothering me. All inmates were required to go to health services for physicals, etc. It was at that time that I was given a chance to make an appointment with a doctor. The scheduled appointment was supposed to be in two days;

however, I was not allowed to report for my appointment until five days later. The physician deduced that my condition was stress-related and that I was experiencing anxiety attacks because of the stress. He prescribed some medication that was to arrive in two days. I waited in the "Med Line" every day for a week expecting to receive my medication. The duty nurse was very nasty and said quite heartlessly, "Don't come back." The following day I went to "Sick Call" to try and attain some answers. I was informed that there had been a major disagreement between the doctor and the psychologist regarding the prescribed medication; thus, I was told that I had to make an appointment with the psychologist for the following week.

While I was still waiting for medical attention, the evaluations of the inmates had begun. We had to watch films about prison rules and regulations, etc., and we took tests to evaluate our intelligence. The tests were to be used for evaluation by "team members" (caseworkers). During that time period, I was also moved to the top tier of the cell block. The heat, at that level, was so unbearable that I would use the washcloth and (warm) water from the sink to try and cool down my body temperature. Additionally, there was a fan that ran for 24 hours at such a loud pitch that your ears just "rang". At least, I was no longer able to hear the constant screaming of the inmates! However, I also could not hear the sound system when our names were called, etc.; therefore, I would just sit and watch for the cell door to move. Finally, one hot night, a guard while making his rounds noticed the extreme conditions I was expected to endure and he said, "This is cruel and no man should have to suffer like this." I was moved to the bottom tier where it was cooler but also less private. Inmates walked past my cell constantly and were able to observe my every move (toilet, etc.).

After my appointment with the psychologist, I was prescribed medication that arrived one week later. I also was given the opportunity to meet with my case worker for the first time as well as a prison social worker. They were supposed to evaluate me and inform me of the next phases of my life within the correctional system. The interview took less than ten minutes. I now was ready to go to "team"—

the final group responsible for determining the fate of each inmate. Their evaluation sounded reminscent of what I had heard from the judge in my case: long term rehabilitation, sex offender classes, public risk monitoring, etc. They also indicated that they saw no reason why I should be given the opportunity to further my education while in prison. Their final question for me was, "Do you have anything to say?" I didn't bother . . . what difference would it make?

I did not see the light of day for twenty-two days. I was finally allowed a 45 minute break outside in the enclosed (stone walls/ guards/barbed wire) courtyard.

I just sat down and looked at the blue sky the entire time . . . and watched the swallows fly.

I have never envied anything as much as I did those birds . . . free. When it was time to return to our cells, guards and vicious dogs would "escort" us back to our cells. One thing was for certain, you were a "nobody", and every effort was made to remind you of that reality each minute . . . each hour . . . each day.

After three weeks or so, my father was allowed to visit me. I worried the entire night before he came . . . wondering how we would both react. I was so ashamed that he had to step foot in a place like this. There were strict rules about physical contact with the visitors, etc.; however, when he came in, we embraced for the longest time. Neither of us wanted to let go. Yes, we hurt . . . we cried. Yet, his presence gave me such strength and a will to endure. He still was my hero. My son, Jerid, was allowed to visit the following week. I can still feel his embrace. Because of the prison quota, Jerid and Dad were the only two that were allowed to visit me. However, Mom would always accompany my father. She would sit and wait in the car or in the waiting room. She was there for my dad . . . and for me.

I learned *valuable information* those weeks at the St. Cloud Correctional Facility. I learned not to make eye contact with other prisoners . . . it was deemed a "challenge". The criminals were here because of all types of convictions: murder, rape, grand larceny, physical abuse, extortion, kidnapping . . . you name it. I realized that most of the prisoners aligned with gangs, according to race, but also for protection. I came to discover that most prisoners were able to get their hands on money (from the outside); no price was too high for cigarettes (and marijuana). Yes, a prison is a good place to learn how to be violent; you witnessed it everyday. I particularly remember the two Asians who got into a fight and one was stabbed in the neck with a pencil. However, prisoners should never intervene in any conflict . . . you just look away . . . you walk away. You close your eyes.

On August 3, 1998, some of us were given a plastic container in which to pack our belongings. After we were strip-searched, we were placed in handcuffs and ankle chains and marched out to a van. The van was taking us to our new *home*: Moose Lake Correctional Facility in northern Minnesota. I didn't know it then, but that destination was to be my *residence* for the years to come. Despite the intense heat in the van and the chafing and blood on our ankles and wrists due to the tight constraints, I still looked out the window of the van and marvelled at the beauty . . . of existence.

I closed my eyes and I was . . .

> *Walking along the sandy beach, the reeds were walzing to the*
> *cadence of the tide . . . Arms outstretched . . . embracing life.*
> *The evasive gulls were tiptoeing along the jagged shoreline*
> *as if to challenge the power of the foaming waves.*
> *The sunlight was glistening atop the mirrored water*
> *giving images of crystalline waterfalls of diamonds.*
> *I dipped my hands into the jeweled paradise and I*
> *was transformed by the warmth of its security.*
> *I was entranced by the freedom of spirit and the*
> *images of forgotten memories of youth.*
> *Gems of renewal—a walk along the water's edge,*
> *arms outstretched. . . . Embracing life.*

I would endure.

IN REFLECTION...

—by Julia Zieman

This book reflects the journey of Dennis Courneya. You, the reader, were given the opportunity to be the *13th Juror* . . . an awesome responsibility. We thank you.

Final Details: Dennis is presently serving his sentence at Moose Lake Correctional Facility. He is scheduled for release in late April of 2001. The Moose Lake facility houses over 700 inmates, most of which are transferred there from other correctional institutions. It is a prison in the truest sense of the word . . . razor wire fences, etc. The inmates come from all walks of life and have criminal histories that encompass every imaginable crime. Dennis has been housed with murderers, drug dealers, rapists . . . you name it. The inmates with whom Dennis has had to share his room represent an unforgettable group: one was serving time for beating a person near death with a hammer . . . another was in for murder . . . and another had a nickname of "Hit Man" (and with good reason). Shortly after Dennis arrived at Moose lake, an inmate was stabbed in the neck with a fork; another inmate was beaten to death. We worry when there are "lock downs" because of violence within the prison. A "lock down" implies no communication with the outside world . . . family and friends just sit and wonder "what is happening?"

Despite all the adversity, Dennis has retained his integrity and character. You can ask anyone at the prison what they think about #198180, Dennis Courneya, and they will willingly share their admiration. Even when we visit Dennis, the prison guards will often sit down and partake in the conversation. He, again, has earned the respect of most.

What I find even more impressive is that Dennis is still a *teacher*. He has helped other inmates with their studies and is often sought after for advice. He continues to have a sincere interest in the well-being of others—from family to community to national events.

Interestingly, he is also a *student* at the facility. He has taken college credit courses in computer studies and is also an avid reader of the books found in the prison library.

Undoubtedly, many challenges face my brother. The sentence upon conviction has given him a *label* that will be most difficult to overcome. He has lost all of his financial securities and his future livelihood. However, he has a wealth of friends and family that will welcome him back to our world. He has given us so much . . . it is time we give back.

I thought it important to note some of the "details" regarding this case that have been omitted from the preceding chapters. Read into them what you may . . .

* The cost of legal representation for Dennis has amounted to nearly $130,000.00
* The results of the appeals process have been in vain, thus far; however, it is still ongoing
* Dennis has received a letter from one State's witness (one of the students) asking for his forgiveness
* Dennis was given a copy of an email letter (by the recipient) that was written by one of the State's witnesses in which she professed that she was "pressured" into saying what she did:

"I truly think about him (Dennis Courneya) every day. I feel really bad for where he is today. I never wanted this or expected this to happen. I only went up on that stand to tell the incidents that he had done. I never thought that there was sexual intent on the things he did to me . . . *they* blew it out of proportion . . . *they* are the ones that told me D.C.'s touching was sexual harrassment." (Dennis was convicted on the counts involving this girl)

* The family of Dennis Courneya received a copy of a letter written by a State witness in which she professed that the sentence given to Dennis Courneya is way too harsh:

"This man was a good teacher and a terrific coach and I feel that putting his life on hold for five years is a waste. I'm sure that the point is across that he made us/me feel uncomfortable sometimes—but does he really deserve to spend this much time in prison—no. . . . and I don't think he ever did any of this for sexual pleasure or intent." (Dennis was convicted on the counts involving this girl.)

* Dennis received a letter (March 2000) from a State's witness requesting the following:

"If there is anyway possible, I want to ask you to forgive me. I know that sorry is not enough, but I am sorry for all the trouble and grief that I may have caused you. If there was a way to go back in time, I would, but wouldn't we all? I guess we all make mistakes . . . Please, please forgive me." (Dennis was convicted on the counts involving this girl)

* Dennis's teaching license was taken away in 1999. He will never teach again.
* It wasn't until October 13, 1998 that Dennis received an official declaration of his sentence: ". . . for the offense dated October 1 of 1997,. . . ., should be amended such that Defendant is committed to the custody of the Commissioner of Corrections for a period of 51 months, plus a term of conditional release of five years, and that the Defendent shall serve at least two-thirds of the 51 months, or 34 months in prison and 17 months on supervised release; The Court in its sentencing order also set fines of $10,000.00."
* Minnesota has one of the highest rates in the nation for conviction of sexual assault

* Dennis has received close to 1000 letters and cards while he has been in prison from former students, teachers, coaches, parents, family, and community members
* Of particular interest to Dennis, he has received many letters from members of the Apostolic Christian Church (exerpt from one: "I realize that someone from our church got you where you are now but I hope that won't affect how you look at the rest of us. I think that you really got ripped off with the sentence that they gave you . . . I hope you have a good day . . .")
* A partner in the law firm for the defense did some follow-up work regarding a student that had some important information to share regarding the case (5-28-98).

Following is a documentation of the conversation with the male Hancock student: "_____ (student) also heard _____ (two witnesses for the State) at the grandmother's home in which they were bragging and boasting about how they were getting paid to go to Court, that they went to "practice" and got out of school to testify against Dennis." (5-28-98)

* In February, 2000, Dennis (in handcuffs and shackles) was taken by prison officials to a physician in Duluth. After an extensive examination, it was determined that Dennis's knee is in such a detrimental state (no support system whatsoever) that he requires knee replacement surgery
* Community members, teachers, coaches, and concerned citizens, take note of the following: 1) No teacher from the Hancock School attended the trial as a supporter. Yet, Dennis received countless letters of admiration and support from faculty following the verdict; 2) Perhaps teachers should reevaluate the value and purpose of union dues. Where does the NEA/AFT stand on legal issues that may arise? Are educators guaranteed legal representation? Remember, Dennis ended up with a $130,000.00 bill for legal

representation; 3) Should schools be *required* to hold a faculty meeting that states explicitly the district's policy regarding acceptable student/teacher contact? There are a multitude of meetings for everything else. 4) Perhaps meetings explaining the "Due Process" should be held at the local level of every teacher's association—mandatory attendance; 5) If Dennis Courneya, or any teacher/coach for that matter, had been "making people feel uncomfortable" for years and years . . . why did it take a trial to bring it to his attention? Why were there no warnings or reprimands from the administration? Teachers receive evaluations on their teaching performance and are "written up" for various types of infractions. What happened here? 6) Where and from whom did the media receive the information before, during, and after the trial? *(13th Juror:* Please review the news articles, especially those preceding the trial. What do you notice?) 7) Why was the change of venue denied?

Following the trial, a "Letter to the Editor" published in the Hancock newspaper reflected the feelings of many individuals:

(Excerpts from the letter): "We just finished witnessing the biggest travesty of justice! The trial, the verdict and the sentencing of Coach Dennis Courneya make one truly afraid to ever have to utilize our legal system. Dennis often stated, 'These students and their parents are my friends. I know that someone would have warned me if I was doing the things for which I am accused.' We wonder if Dennis Courneya still feels sorry for these kids? Several townspeople have suggested that, 'It does make more sense that the student witnesses were manipulated by a few adults.' Incidentally . . . one witness actually privately stated to her friends that, 'Dennis really had not personally done anything to her,' but she wanted to 'back up her friend' and therefore testified to, 'whatever was necessary to accomplish this.'

Upon leaving the courtroom, after the verdict was delivered, a television reporter stated, 'They (the jury) must have been at a different trial than I was at.' Two days prior, after hearing a witness testify, a newspaper reporter stated, 'I think they thought they were auditioning for a soap opera', while still another reporter was overheard stating, 'This is a circus; my time is worth more than this.'

Dennis willingly submitted to a lie detector test and was assessed by a psychologist. The psychologist stated the following; 'There is absolutely no evidence of intent."... We wonder if the witnesses, adult and juvenile, would subject themselves to the same test scrutiny.

The biggest mystery of all is that the accusations of sexual misconduct were never witnessed by a single person, yet they were supposed to have occurred in front of the entire football squad, three other girls, and 15-20 students in a classroom setting. We realize the difficulty a small community has, with people intimately tied to one another, in business, religion and family, to stand up and be counted. The strong religious convictions of the people in the community should weigh heavily on many consciences . . .

Our hope is that there will be one parent with enough backbone to step up to the plate and admit that the accusations are nothing as was presented on the witness stand—one parent that will carry the torch . . . Never has the burden been so high! Never has the proof been so weak!

"Signed: "Concerned Citizens"

Community members, parents, and students, in support of Dennis, proceeded to sign a petition indicating the following: "We, the undersigned, believe that Dennis Courneya has been unjustly and wrongly sentenced with bias. We request that his sentence be overturned and that Dennis Courneya be set free." The petition was signed by 143 individuals. The confusion and frustration over the case continues today.

Yes, on that fateful day in April, 1998, in the case of The State of Minnesota versus Dennis Edward Courneya, the jury of twelve rendered a verdict of guilty. However, it is quite miniscule in comparison to the *ultimate verdict* that awaits us all.

Sudden Death, Overtime . . . In the game of life, your faith and ultimate fate can make the difference between eternal life or eternal death. Only those individuals who "live the truth" are granted eternal life. I will, once again, be judged someday, but this time, I feel assured of my faith . . . and my ultimate fate (Dennis Courneya).